Wireless Mobility
The Why of Wireless

NEIL P. **REID**

Mc
Graw
Hill

New York Chicago San Francisco
Lisbon London Madrid Mexico City Milan
New Delhi San Juan Seoul Singapore Sydney Toronto

The McGraw·Hill Companies

Cataloging-in-Publication Data is on file with the Library of Congress

McGraw-Hill books are available at special quantity discounts to use as premiums and sales promotions, or for use in corporate training programs. To contact a representative, please e-mail us at bulksales@mcgraw-hill.com.

Wireless Mobility: The Why of Wireless

1234567890   WFR WFR   109876543210

ISBN   978-0-07-162862-4
MHID   0-07-162862-2

Sponsoring Editor Jane K. Brownlow	**Technical Editors** Mark Tyre, Bruce Alexander	**Production Supervisor** George Anderson
Editorial Supervisor Jody McKenzie	**Copy Editor** Lisa Theobald	**Composition** Glyph International
Project Manager Harleen Chopra, Glyph International	**Proofreader** Andy Saff	**Illustration** Glyph International
Acquisitions Coordinator Joya Anthony	**Indexer** Robert Swanson	**Art Director, Cover** Jeff Weeks
		Cover Designer Jeff Weeks

To my amazing wife, Mary, who continually strives for excellence with kindness and wisdom; to my son, Martin, a young person born with a full measure of integrity and a very sharp mind. Also to my daughter, Kelly, for whom it is truly said, "When a man gets old, he'd better have a daughter." While much in life remains an illusion, the love we share is very real. What greater witness is there than joy?

About the Author

Neil Reid has been at Cisco Systems since 1999 and is the Senior Business Development Manager on its U.S. mobility channels team. He has worked in the high-technology industry for 20 years with the last 18 in unlicensed wireless technology.

Neil is an internationally invited speaker for industry and academia on mobility subjects ranging from value propositions and success metrics for executives and graduate business schools, to complex radio frequency (RF) propagation and project sequencing for engineers. He has published two previous books on wireless technology, *Broadband Fixed Wireless Networks* and *The 802.11 Networking Handbook* (McGraw-Hill), the latter becoming a best-seller.

He founded the Systems Engineering Virtual Team for mobility at Cisco in 1999 and co-wrote numerous wireless engineering certification courses for Cisco training partners. Neil initiated the current wireless written CCIE certification course for engineers in 2000 and wrote the first four course drafts, the first outline, and the RF propagation content for the CCIE and CCNA written wireless exams used today. He is the originator of Optimal Project Sequencing, which has been incorporated into some of the wireless industry's top integrator programs, and he detailed mobility sales analytics for the U.S. mobility channels team, which led to the practice of precision sales guidance for some of Cisco's top mobility partners.

His current responsibilities with major Cisco mobility partners include practice expansion through applied analytics, economic cycle resilience, smart targeting, and resolution of complex engagement issues with major mobility customers.

Contents

Foreword

In 2008 I co-authored the book *New Age of Innovation* (McGraw-Hill) with my colleague C. K. Prahalad from the University of Michigan. In our book we discussed a fundamental business transformation forged by digitization, ubiquitous connectivity, and globalization. This transformation, we argued, was about the shift in perspective of value creation in business. We claimed that customer value would be based on unique personalized experiences delivered contextually to customers in a user-friendly interface. We called this the N=1 (one customer at a time) business model. In the last two years, I've seen this trend entering into every industry ranging from entertainment and travel to healthcare and financial services. It is clear that with more than 4 billion people connected in the digital network, intelligent mobile devices such as smartphones and other handheld devices are emerging as important mediums of these personalized experiences.

Mobile devices are becoming the next stage of business competition across industries. In fact, business innovations in personal experiences on these devices are shaking assumptions behind some established and traditional industries. For example, the capacity for high-quality video and gaming on smartphones, costing $3–8, is challenging the traditional business models of television and video games. The emergence of location-based services on mobile devices is making advertising meaningful and contextual. This can also fundamentally shift the effectiveness of the advertising and media industries. In addition, the new class of handheld information devices, such as Kindle from Amazon and iPad from Apple, is likely to transform the publishing industry. However, the success of these business models will rest on the quality of experience provided by these devices. This quality subsequently depends on the appropriate private and public wireless networks enabling the experience. In summary, wireless technology is now a critical enabler of business innovation and success, and it is important for businesses to understand the user and business implications of their wireless architecture and technology choices.

In *Wireless Mobility*, Neil Reid has lucidly explained the importance of wireless in the future of business and linked the application needs of businesses to specific technology and design choices in building or buying these networks. It is evident that the author has leveraged his rich field experience in designing and implementing wireless networks for a number of Cisco customers. The book opens with a clear motivation for the critical nature of wireless in any business model today. However, the unique perspective in this book is the author's ability to link the "Why?" questions that focus on the business or user benefits from wireless to the "What?" and "How?" aspects of building a wireless network.

Neil Reid has drawn from his Cisco experience to present detailed case studies on the significance of wireless technology in several verticals including education and healthcare. These case studies are also complemented with discussion on the project implementation methodology and approaches used to mitigate risks. Unlike many other books on wireless, this book includes the financial aspects of delivering wireless solutions and provides useful insights for managing the risks involved in these technology investments. In summary, this book presents the business needs of wireless solutions with the technical aspects of wireless networks in a clear and understandable manner. I am sure both business and technical managers will find this useful.

M. S. Krishnan, Ph.D
Hallman e-Business Fellow
Area Chairman and Professor
of Business Information Technology
Co-Director Center for Global Resource Leverage: India
Ross School of Business at the University of Michigan

Acknowledgments

Having now completed my third book, I remember telling a very good friend about my first publishing contract. As a well-known television script writer, he wisely told me, "The two best days as a writer are when you sign the contract and when you finish the writing." I heard this before even beginning to write the first book, so I chuckled while making a mental note that this might be true. Turns out it's quite true, though it's also been an incredibly rewarding experience.

Writing very much challenges me in terms of what I truly believe and why I believe it. This critical process is augmented wonderfully by the team into which you must integrate to have any hope at all of completing the project. It's been my great fortune to have a team consisting of simply wonderful and profoundly capable talent. These are not only top industry professionals, but they are also really great people who inspire and help move you forward through a difficult process.

The first person on our team is my executive editor, Jane Brownlow of McGraw-Hill. We went through a fairly rough patch at one point, and through it I learned how committed she is to the publishing industry and to this project. She is as tough as she is fair, and Jane has earned my deep respect. As I may write one more book yet, I truly hope to work with her on that project as well.

Wendy Rinaldi is the editorial director at McGraw-Hill, and she arrived on the project when it was at its most difficult point for me. Her calm manner, clear mind, and steady hand got the project back on track. I don't know that we would have finished this book without her cool professionalism. This book exists in part because of you, Wendy—thank you so much.

Joya Anthony is the acquisition coordinator and is the one who chiefly kept the project on track along with Jane. She is one of the most organized people I've ever met; always quick with the right answer, she contributed and guided the project as though this book were the only thing she did each day. Nothing could be further from the truth; the best people are the busiest, and yet Joya always made her major contributions seem so effortless. Amazing.

Karen Schopp is the senior account manager responsible for the sales of this book. She has the gift of giving you the perception that you're in cahoots on something both fun and worthwhile. Her dedication to the project included a significant effort to win over various stakeholders to get the project green-lighted. Without Karen, this book would not have seen the light of day. Thank you, Karen!

The person who keeps you out of trouble on a book like this is the technical editor. If your claims and views pass muster with a well-chosen technical editor, you're in good shape. Imagine my good fortune to have not just one, but two of the best in the industry, Mark Tyre and Bruce Alexander.

Mark is not only my manager at Cisco, but he's also one of my most respected friends. He's a wireless industry pro with far more time in this industry than myself, and I'm at the two decade mark. Ever the consummate professional, he's also a constant source of wisdom and humor. He's a true southern gentleman, a patriot, and a person of impeccable integrity. Mark is one of those rare persons who makes you want to be your best.

Bruce Alexander has been my technical editor on all three of my books. A published author himself, Bruce has no superior in the wireless industry. All who know him regard him rightfully with the highest degree of respect and admiration. He's also a dear friend, fellow automotive performance enthusiast, patriot, and all-round great guy. I always walk away from our conversations with a smile.

Those outside the publishing industry probably have little idea of how much work remains after the original content is written by the author. Even fewer probably recognize how much work there is in shaping, cutting, and polishing a diamond that is very much in the rough. Lisa Theobald is the copy editor who crafted the polished version of what you'll read in this work. I owe her and the editing team a considerable debt of gratitude for making this book all it can be.

Lastly, an acknowledgment to my incredible colleagues at Cisco. A great company exists because it has great people. The talent, drive, and determination of this group are hard to overestimate, and they move with breathtaking speed. They're also a lot of fun to be around. If you're going to travel by aircraft carrier, I can't think of a better one.

Introduction

Few technologies impact our lives like wireless, because few enable the one basic human element so highly regarded above nearly all others: the freedom to move.

While many very good books have been written on the "how" of wireless, it's time for us to expand our view of mobility to the "why" of wireless mobility. The technical achievements of today's wireless networks are largely due to excellent product, deployment, and maintenance engineering. Expanding our consideration of the "why" question will largely propel most of the next phase of achievements with this same technology.

This purpose of this book is to help elevate the discussions on mobility from purely technical to include the "why" of wireless. Simply stated, my objective is to get you to consider wireless mobility in a new light. As our discussions shift from "what and how" and "cost to value," you will have a much clearer vision of the potential of this amazing technology.

As we begin to consider the "why" of wireless, the discussions change from cost-centric to value-centric. This is a major change of view, because system value has replaced technical brilliance as the primary driver for ubiquitous transport of information and services. While it is always the engineering that glues systems together, the most essential value discussions center on value proposition and success metrics. Understanding how value is derived and measured unlocks the purse strings.

The intended audience for this book begins with engineers who best deploy systems when functional requirements are distilled from business problems. From there, the audience expands to include all technology and business operational personnel who reside on the side of the link opposite of the engineers—those who ensure maximum investment returns on corporate operations.

This book is written especially for those in the system integration business. For them, Chapter 9 may be the central element of this book, because, in my view, few issues are more closely tied to corporate longevity than resilience and growth in every part of micro- and macroeconomic conditions. For them, certain elements quickly stratify the competitors such as smart targeting, operational agility, and the ability not just to respond to outside forces, but to morph into a corporate form that always capture maximum market share simply because they operate where the money flows most freely.

Chapter Overview

Chapter 1 is about how wireless and mobility changes our work and personal experience.

Chapter 2 is about why we build and how we use networks to derive maximum value from workplace operations.

Chapter 3 provides insights on the value of mobility from a chief information officer's perspective; it's an interesting chapter because one of the most interesting and relevant positions in a business is the CIO. CIOs reside at the crossroads of operational excellence and technology.

Chapter 4 focuses on the value propositions of mobility in leading specific industries: healthcare and education.

Chapter 5 concerns the value propositions and techniques for measuring value in education and healthcare, two of the industries that deploy the largest amounts of mobility technology.

Chapter 6 discusses an essential network deployment practice called network assessments. It's an important chapter because it provides context for wireless technology within the larger framework of a network. By assessing the delta between the operational aspirations of the C suite and the current capability of the network, you can best shape the evolution of the incoming technology, policies, and uses of wireless mobility.

Chapter 7 focuses on a process I developed over many years of recovering some of the most complex wireless deployments on the planet: optimal project sequencing. Discovering the root causes of projects that had gone awry was an incredibly eye-opening experience. This chapter discusses the most important elements of maximizing value and reducing deployment and maintenance costs for networks. Some of the discoveries in the chapter may surprise you.

Chapter 8 covers financing mobility technology in today's networks. The role of financing and an improved understanding of the single cash-flow stream from the end customer through the integrator and technology provider is important to understand, because it allows wireless mobility users to maximize cash flow during all phases of deployment and maintenance—not just for the end customer but also for the system integrator and the technology provider.

Chapter 9 is one of the key chapters in the book because it provides insight on ensuring not just business resilience in network system integrators, but also key practices for using mobility and business analytics to help ensure business resilience in every macroeconomic cycle phase.

Chapter 10 is one of my favorite chapters in the book and was one of the most fun chapters to write. It's about what we may expect in the next generation of technology. It also considers how wireless mobility of the future will affect every other network technology and how networks will be used in the future.

Chapter 11 highlights one of the most powerful developments in not only mobility but also for networking use in general: the advent of smart buildings. Where and how you work in the future won't be anything like what you're accustomed to today. This chapter provides insights into how that future is happening right now.

Chapter 12 was also one of the most fun to write, because it carries a look into the future forward into several key future developments in the wireless mobility industry, from a technology provider, system integrator, and end user perspective.

I hope you enjoy this book. Books are never truly finished; authors simply run out of time to complete them. For that reason, it wasn't possible for me to include all the things I've observed in the fascinating and highly essential industry of which I'm privileged to be part: mobility networking. The intent of this work isn't to provide a comprehensive look into each and every element of wireless mobility; instead, it's intended to get you thinking more about why this technology is so important and to help stimulate your imagination and creativity to use this essential technology in an ever more productive and valuable manner.

CHAPTER 1 | Why Wireless?

Much has been written about the "how" of wireless mobility. In fact, if you visit Amazon.com and enter the search phrase "wireless networks," you'll see that Amazon sells more than 17,000 books on the subject, each offering something to be learned. That's an impressive number. It's also a healthy sign for the industry that so many talented and willing people have taken a considerable amount of time to write books on wireless. I've contributed two of those books, and with thanks to my publishers at McGraw-Hill, one of them, *802.11 (Wi-Fi) Networking Handbook,* became a best-seller.

You can review the search findings for a long time and not locate book on the "why" of wireless, however. Both of my prior books, and nearly all the other books mentioned on Amazon, are deep-dive technical treatises on the "how" of wireless. It seems clear, at least statistically if not practically, that the issue of "why wireless?" has not been sufficiently studied, even though the "why" is a powerful driver of most purchases of wireless large area networks (WLANs). Surely these purchases would not be practical or worth the investment if the technology weren't reasonably sorted out by now. Much like the technical side of the equation, the "why" element of wireless is also increasing in complexity.

The wireless technological changes I've seen during the past two decades have been nothing short of breathtaking. I remember struggling with my engineering team back in the early 1990s to work out an outdoor wireless connection to remain in place after the sun went down. We spent nearly a week trying to connect a moving rental car wirelessly to the computer system inside our building.

Although the link would work well during the day, after we took a break near sundown, we'd return after dark to continue the work, and the link was invariably down. We'd retune the link and get it up and running and continue our work into the evening. But the next morning, no link. So we'd retune it again, and the link would work well all day until the sun set, at which point it would go down again. This scenario was repeated for several days.

We eventually discovered that the wireless radio attached to the car became much cooler than the radio inside the building as the sun set. This thermal difference was enough to cause the crystals in each radio to operate at slightly different frequencies, which meant that the radios simply couldn't "hear" each other. We engineered a solution to resolve this and then rapidly moved on to dozens of other technical matters.

Looking back on that experience, I still shake my head and smile. We knew so little about using radios in a business setting at that time. Today's radios are incredibly complex and highly robust, and they share no meaningful comparison in data speeds to the radios we hand-crafted in the early 1990s. Using a modern-day Ferrari as a metaphor for today's radios and the 802.11 standard (created and maintained by the Institute of Electrical and Electronics Engineers, or IEEE), we were surely plodding along in Model Ts back then.

While no meaningful comparison can be made between today's enterprise-class WLANs and the radios we built back then, two very significant aspects have changed even more dramatically: the need for wireless communications and the methods by which wireless communication systems are used today.

The need for today's wireless networks, and how those systems are used in education, healthcare, manufacturing, and other industries, is what I attempt to illuminate throughout this book. In this chapter, I discuss why wireless mobility makes things better from both architectural and application perspectives (both in nontechnical terms).

Why Mobility Makes Things Work Better

Mobility, of course, implies motion. In our normal daily routines, motion usually involves moving toward a specific goal. Little in today's society does not include an element of mobility; in turn, mobility is greatly impacted by technological usage, policy, and adoption rates.

From a business and personal perspective, wireless mobility has changed the way the world works. Although much of the actual contribution by wireless mobility vendors and integrators requires a considerable amount of "making things work," (a marketing catch phrase used by BASF) the end result is that mobility makes other things, such as unified communications, applications, businesses, and services, work better. "Work better" can mean many different things, of course, and the metrics of what is "better" are quite broad and unique.

NOTE Industry-specific success metrics are discussed in Chapter 5.

Think of the tremendous impact of mobility in your own life. Mobility is a fundamental part of a healthy culture, especially in the United States, where our First Amendment rights guarantee that we can assemble peaceably.

Paths cross even between the worlds of fashion and wireless mobility, as style is an essential element incorporated into the look and feel of smartphones and many other mobility devices such as laptops, access points, wireless routers, and other handheld devices. Even placement of wireless access points, from an aesthetic perspective, can impact us.

Mobility and Connectivity: The Doctor Is Out. And In

Mobility, of course, implies motion. It is difficult to comprehend the ability to move somewhere without an endpoint as the goal, at least as part of our normal daily routine. In other words, we move to get somewhere. Seems fundamental enough, but it's where we can make a distinction between mobility and connectivity.

Consider, for example, a doctor who relies so heavily on mobility and connectivity that they are mission-critical to the doctor, the healthcare staff, and certainly the patients. Connectivity allows activity to occur whether the doctor is in their office or in motion (mobile). And connectivity issues can be quite different when the doctor is in motion as opposed to when they are stationary.

NOTE I've read at least one account from a doctor so frustrated with a hospital's mobile connectivity problems that they threatened to remove their practice from that hospital to another, where the wireless system worked flawlessly. Doctors give sober consideration to where they practice medicine. The professional synergy between doctors and hospitals is generally handled with the greatest of care by both doctors and the hospitals and other locations in which they practice medicine.

In the case of doctors, it is well known that they require "agility" as they work—in other words, they are in a nearly constant state of motion. They need to connect to data, patients, fellow doctors, facility administrators, and other healthcare workers such as emergency medical technicians, lab technicians, and insurance companies. Doctors require connectivity both while they are in motion and when they arrive at destination points—hospitals, private clinics, their offices, their cars, and their homes.

Physicians likely use different mobile devices to communicate depending on their location. For example, at the hospital, they may use a computer on wheels (COW)— a mobile cart containing medical equipment, medicine, and communication devices such as a tablet-style computer. At home or in the office, a doctor may use a laptop or personal digital assistant (PDA) via WLANs or personal area networks (PANs) to dispense prescriptions to a local pharmacy, to look up a patient's records, to collaborate with fellow physicians, and to coordinate treatment with other medical teams in their absence. Mobile phones or radios, using wide area networks (WANs), keep them in touch with hospital staff who need to reach them if a patient is in crisis.

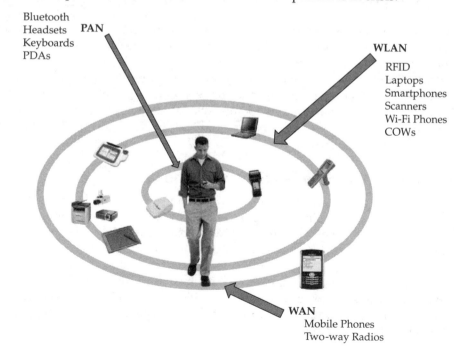

NOTE   The farther we range (move), the smaller the mobile device, and the more likely the device will use licensed mobile connectivity such as mobile wireless. Licensed Mobile devices are generally far more powerful in terms of transmission and reception capabilities than unlicensed stationary devices, and they can often be far more expensive as well. For example, handheld laser scanners such as those used in warehouses can easily run into the $10,000 per device range.

The connectivity for enterprise network purposes in a small doctor's office usually involves a few access points and handheld devices. The connectivity medium is typically unlicensed and is usually based on the 802.11 protocol. The connectivity used in a private clinic of less than 10,000 square feet typically uses the same basic network architecture, devices, and applications used in a small office, with the addition of security cameras and wireless equipment location applications. A full-sized hospital often requires all of the above, but also includes extensive amounts of location equipment, wireless video, voice, COW connectivity, and many other specialized applications for hospital administrators (from human resources, to physical security, to inventory tracking and ordering). A hospital may also use wireless control devices for the building, parking areas, and campus grounds to manage lighting, heating, cooling, and access control.

The Exploding Number of Wireless Clients

In 1991 I wrote an article published in *Auto Rental News* about how networks were evolving from systems that crunched numbers to systems that stored and crunched numbers. I predicted that the next evolutionary step was connectivity between those systems.

While I was correct in my connectivity prediction, I and most others did not foresee the impact of small, powerful, highly useful mobility clients such as smartphones. Today they are ubiquitous, owned and used by every strata in society and across all business market segments, and they are seen at virtually every recreational and educational endeavor. These devices have changed the way we work, learn, live, and play.

But mobile cellular phones alone, be they "smart" or otherwise, are only part of the picture. The networking world of mobility has moved from infrastructure-centric (access points) to client-centric because of the exploding number of client devices, from laser scanners to location sensing devices.

While the Internet is probably approaching its user saturation point, the types and numbers of mobile clients being added to home and office networks are still in the early years—we're just now "crossing the chasm," to use a common term re-coined by Geoffrey Moore in his book *Crossing the Chasm: Marketing and Selling High-Tech Products to Mainstream Customers* (HarperBusiness, 1999). In other words, mainstream wireless mobile adoption is greatly accelerating. Wirthlin Worldwide reported a study of the

Fortune 1000 executives that revealed a forecast of 200 percent growth of handheld devices by 2010.

The Incoming Mobility Wave (In Millions)

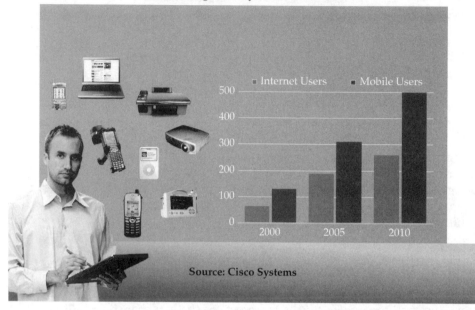

Source: Cisco Systems

The wireless client world is vastly larger than that of mobile cell phones even though esato.com reports more than 500 models from which to choose as of January 2010. Hundreds more specialized mobility clients exist, from handheld laser scanners, to location sensing devices, temperature and shock sensors, and a multitude of other devices. The demand from industries in which operational information is stored in a central location, such as manufacturing companies, oil and gas companies, telecommunications companies, banking and other financial institutions, retail establishments, and transportation companies, is rapidly increasing, and many types of mobile devices are used within each industry. Any loss of connectivity experienced by these devices can have immediate negative cash and profit implications.

Smart buildings will add a tremendous number of networking clients. The information on the left side of the following illustration indicates only a few examples of the types of data sourced from IT-based client devices, such as time, location, temperature, and so on. The information in the right column represents the end user experiences gained from the use of these devices in traditional building systems. Smart buildings combine both of these major systems. (Note that this illustration shows only a small sampling of the types of data and user experiences and is intended to help you consider the power and implications of handheld wireless devices in their respective industry.)

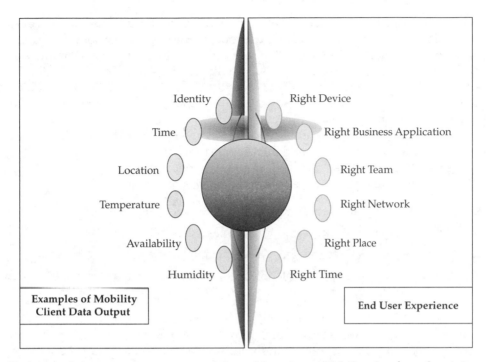

Today, mobility means we can, and do, achieve incredible levels of productivity, because we can stay productive while we're in motion. Connectivity has also improved our productivity and quality of life. Most of us would surely agree on that.

Richard Thomas Gerber, CEO of Intelegen, a Troy, Michigan, proof-of-concept company, provides a profound way of looking at connectivity: "We should consider the transition of the Internet from a communications network to an extremely powerful computational grid." And this view takes us to the next talking point—unified communications, a "game changer" for mobility.

Unified Communications

The considerations with respect to clients and connectivity are part of a much larger mosaic that seamlessly connects the network and the end user. That concept is commonly referred to as *unified communications (UC)*.

UC is described by Wikipedia (http://en.wikipedia.org/wiki/Unified_communications) as "a trend…to simplify and integrate all forms of communications in view to optimize business processes and reduce the response time, manage flows and eliminate device and media dependencies…. UC allows an individual to send a message on one medium and receive on another." UC lets us communicate freely using different types of devices—be they laptops, PDAs, smartphones, handheld laser scanners, or others.

Originally, *unified communications* referred to the ability for us to use routers and switches near the center of a network—"the core" of the system—to communicate. The definition of the term has changed and its use in the world has increased tremendously in value with the inclusion of mobility. UC usually involves an IT investment that's three to five times higher than the cost of mobility alone. According to some studies, in the United States, UC investment represents approximately $3 billion in annual sales, just in hardware alone.

While mobility generates significantly less revenue from hardware, software, and services to the hardware vendors and integrators, the mobility contribution to UC is indispensable, because about 75 percent of all UC applications require a mobility factor.

Four fundamental types of UC applications are in use today:

- Commercial applications, such as automated meter-reading apps
- Internally developed applications, such as sales report apps
- Software As A Service (SaaS), such as income tax management apps
- Composite applications, or blends of software, such as maps and weather and freeway traffic update apps

Because this is a book on mobility, not UC, I refrain from in-depth discussions about these application types. You should note, however, that within each of these general types of applications are hundreds of thousands of customized applications developed for specific business operations.

Hundreds of mobile devices feature thousands of different and unique software applications that are specific to the operation of the device. These apps, coupled with the software used to monitor, maintain, and manage business processes, engender an incredibly complex set of combinations of software and devices. Considering how this software enables connectivity among IT components, commonly referred to as the *Open Systems Interconnection (OSI) stack*, boggles the mind. These systems are so complex that I cannot name a single person who is an expert at all, or even much, of it in the aggregate. Neither do I believe that such an individual exists in any company—the scope of knowledge is simply too broad and deep, and it continues getting wider and deeper with each passing day.

The main idea of UC, however, is fairly straightforward, in principle. The idea is to connect various devices and associated software so that numerous types of applications, such as voice, data, e-mail, chat, texting, presence services like WebEx, and electronic faxes, transit seamlessly and in real time. It might be easy to think that applications run seamlessly between any two devices. Truth is, however, they don't; in fact, deployment of new wireless devices is a carefully choreographed and staged sequence. Thousands of hours go into planning, deploying, and verification testing prior to running these devices in a production format.

Think about this for a moment: The power of untethered UC provides every application to every endpoint across the Internet. This means the distance between the point at which data is captured and where it is read, stored, or processed is irrelevant. However, there is even more to consider. It's incredibly wonderful and useful to be able to be the recipient of UC while you're on the move, and this is the premise of many mobile devices. The ability to communicate and receive information while you're in motion is a powerful "why."

When you can send and receive information while in motion, *business velocity* is increased. Business velocity refers to the number of transactions that occur during a particular period of time. Business velocity is proportional to the rate of information received. It includes the concept of *error-free velocity*; speed without accuracy offers significantly reduced value, because making more decisions is counterproductive if they're the wrong decisions.

The Three *R*s of Information

Business velocity is proportional to the rate of information received. Information comprises three principal characteristics, which can be summed up as the "Three *R*s of Information":

- Is it *Right?*
- Is it *Recent?*
- Is it *Relevant?*

There is hardly a shortage of information today. Indeed, most of us find it increasingly essential to sort out the information we need from the torrent we receive, both at work and in our personal lives. Above all else, information needs to be correct, or *right*. Little else matters regarding the information if this fundamental element is not in place.

Mobility allows for the instant uploading and downloading of information with limited regard to where the communication endpoints reside. Information delays can downgrade information, sometimes rendering it either irrelevant or incorrect. And, for some, this can have serious consequences.

Healthcare is an excellent example of the importance of information being right and recent. Consider the many scenarios in which a person's vital health signs are transmitted and monitored remotely and in real time. Responses to dangerous changes in vital signs must be both immediate and correct. In the world of medical care, there is often little time to plan, yet the team or healthcare professional must respond quickly and correctly every time.

Simply put, the best run operations thrive on the freshness of data. Getting a jump on a competitor, taking advantage of material pricing, and making an early offer to a highly valued prospective employee are other examples of how recent information can make or break operations.

Such real-time information can be both an asset and a liability, depending on your perspective. An example is the well-known case of the "Cisco Fatty." In 2009, an individual was offered a job at Cisco Systems. Immediately after the job was offered, she uploaded the following on Twitter: *"Cisco just offered me a job! Now I have to weigh the utility of a fatty paycheck against the daily commute to San Jose and hating the work"* (www.msnbc.msn.com/id/29901380/). Unfortunately, another Cisco associate noticed the posting and forwarded it to the manager who had made the offer. The offer was withdrawn, and to make matters worse, the job-seeker suffered considerable public derision. This may arguably be more a story of indiscretion than the power of information being recent, but it's worth noting that the company probably saved money by not selecting a candidate who would have been unhappy to have the position and might not have stuck with the job.

Manufacturing is another great example of where information being recent is essential. Many major companies distribute critical product manufacturing across disparate subvendors in geographically disparate locations. If a natural disaster occurs or a supply runs short and affects one manufacture, agile supply-chain management practices allow real-time information to enable production to shift quickly to alternative sources. (In fact, mission-critical elements such as supply-chain agility are now a key competitive differentiator. Businesses that best manage their supply chains have a unique advantage over competitors who don't or won't.)

The third and final *R* of information is *relevance*, and it may come as a bit of a surprise to see how mobility supports this function. Determining the relevance of information is an essential management deliverable. The ability to analyze the data quickly, determine the most relevant data points, and then assemble a contextual and fact-based decision requires experience. In rapidly changing conditions, the time allotted for individuals to build such experience can be greatly shortened. Today's concepts, timing, cadence, tools, policies, regulations, and workloads create a scenario that's all but unrecognizable from what we routinely faced 10 or 15 years ago. For this reason, relevance is increasingly becoming automated, or at least augmented.

Using the three *R*s together, highly sophisticated programs can now compile data from numerous points and provide either automated adjustments to operational procedures or manufacturing processes. One of the key advantages of automation is that data can be taken from more points in real time, or close to it. Current data points can be quickly measured against historic information to help ascertain trends and patterns, which are what the best managers look for. (This doesn't imply that major isolated events are disregarded, but most management decisions are based on the larger context of a series of events versus a single event.)

Consider the tools and devices used in financial markets, where exotic applications guide brokers and other financial professionals on profitable decision-making. Rightness, recentness, and relevance are essential tools for these professionals, and up-to-the-second guidance is made available to them in many places simultaneously via handheld devices.

On a personal level, I use a traffic monitoring system in my car that advises me in real time of upcoming traffic jams, road construction, lane closures, and accidents. It also advises me on alternative routes to help me arrive at my destination quickly.

When I arrive, I use an iPhone application called G-Park, which tells me where I can find parking spots using GPS. After I park my car and put money in the meter, I simply tap the Park Me! icon and then tap the timer to enter how much time I have left on the meter. After I've concluded my business, if I can't remember where I parked, I tap the Where Did I Park? icon and my iPhone gives me turn-by-turn directions to my car.

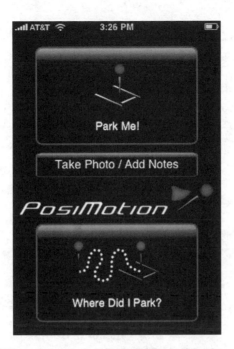

I also have access to iPhone apps that tell me not only where I might dine based on my preferences, but that also provide information on calorie, protein, carbohydrate, and fat contents of the meals available at many restaurants. It can then tell me the best dining options and locations for a healthy meal.

Mobility Changes Work from a Location to an Activity

Mobility can change work from a location to an activity, and this is one of the most profound contributions provided by mobility in the workplace.

The top industries listed here depend on wireless mobility as a technology that's indispensable to doing business. They also require agile workforces—in other words, employees spend some or most of their day in motion between floors and buildings, or with intercity, interstate, or intercontinental destinations.

Education	Healthcare
Manufacturing	Retail
Government	Professional services
Wholesale distribution	Technical services
Financial	Service provider
Transportation	Energy
Hospitality	Media/entertainment

Many of the service industries bring some or all of their deliverables to their customers instead of requiring that customers come to them. As many of these deliverables can be sent electronically over the Internet, nearly all of them can also be sent to wireless devices such as smartphones. Considering that every one of these key industries relies entirely on its own ecosystems of suppliers, partners, and customers, and the geographic diversity of these elements, the essential nature of wireless mobility is apparent.

Mobility plays a central role in expanding the concept to its fullest potential, as I demonstrate here with two personal stories.

Looking Back

I entered the full-time workforce in 1974 during my junior year in high school. At that time, I owned one of the two fastest production motorcycles on the planet, an H1 500cc Kawasaki, and I quickly combined that tool with some youthful indiscretion. Naturally, I ran up a series of rather expensive traffic violations. Without much choice in the matter, I spent a good portion of my junior year in school from 7:30 A.M. to 3:30 P.M. and at a French-fry factory from 4:00 P.M. to midnight, Monday through Friday. And I've worked full time ever since.

At the factory, we dared not be even a minute late or the foreman would place one of his size 12 boots into the back of our pants. This was back in the days when a kick in the pants (or firing) was the way many managers handled blue-collar employees who committed even minor infractions. Even making a phone call took a little ingenuity, and permission, and you'd better have a good reason for doing it. Physical presence was required.

Fast Forward to 2009

The last 10 years of my career have been very much virtual. My employer has provided me with world-class telecommuting tools, a travel expense account, and the fateful words, "You can find it online." When I interviewed with my current employer, I never even physically met with a person.

I was one of the very fortunate people to receive an employment offer. All negotiations and the "on-boarding" (except for one new employee orientation meeting) were virtual. The on-boarding process was largely wireless, as most of it took place over the cell phone my employer provided. My managers have never been concerned about my physical location, except when live meetings are required.

Mobility and Collaboration

I recently gave a mobility presentation to a roomful of law enforcement individuals in St. Louis. At this live meeting, when I asked for a show of hands to indicate how many in the room had experienced significantly increased workloads during the last 12 months, about three-fourths of the participants raised their hands. I then asked of the individuals who raised their hands how many believed their peers understood their current assignments and how much their assignments had changed over the prior 12 months. Not a single hand was raised.

While this is perhaps anecdotal information, this situation is actually more pervasive than many understand and is compounded by the fact that, as of this writing, thousands of companies are laying off employees because of economic woes.

Workers who are laid off leave behind a wake of changes at their former employers. With radical changes in personnel and corporate restructuring, many of the remaining employed personnel do not have a clear understanding of who is working where and on what. Confusion and relearning the landscape is a normal part of business life, and that takes a toll on productivity, because collaboration, like productivity, is a necessity.

On an operational basis, direct interaction between workers allows companies to move forward quickly and productively. Although employment and organizational changes are very good reasons to ensure and drive collaboration, there are obviously more, and perhaps even better, reasons for doing so. In fact, personnel who become professionally isolated are often primary candidates for layoffs or other career-limiting experiences.

Wireless mobility allows far more collaboration in a given workday, because it allows people to communicate without needing to be at a desk. Studies at Cisco Systems, for example, have shown that company productivity increased 10 percent as a direct result of using wireless technology. Although 10 percent may not sound like a huge increase, considering that Cisco is regarded as one of the highest performing companies in the world, it's an important number. Moving the performance needle that much in a high-performance company due to a single technology is significant indeed.

Collaboration also influences how company-wide decisions are made. Instead of making corporate decisions behind closed doors, today's corporate leaders seek input from stakeholders—producers who are beginning to think more like buyers and end users. The fastest path to understanding the nuts-and-bolts of a product and its consumer base is to incorporate personnel from the end user group and from intermediate groups between the deliverable's inception and end use.

Stakeholders

The concept of the stakeholder is much broader than what is widely believed. While I was working on a project at a nuclear power plant, for example, the initial group interface was very limited. It included IT personnel, some project managers, and a facility manager. After we explained what was required to complete the project, the group was expanded to include the following personnel and technologies:

- CIO
- IT directors
- IT managers
- Infrastructure IT staff (planning, deployment, maintenance, security)
- Plant security staff
- Site, facility, operations, building managers
- End users
- System integrator
- Project managers
- Applications (voice, location, custom)
- Wireless technology (design, audit, deployment, maintenance)

You'll read more about this project and the outcomes of including the appropriate stakeholders in Chapter 7.

Wireless mobility has become a mandatory technology for facilitating communication and collaboration across stakeholders. In massive facilities such as a commercial power generation plant, be it nuclear or otherwise, mobile communications greatly increases productivity because users can access important information, applications, and other personnel from almost anywhere.

And my favorite part of this amazing cosmos of interconnectivity? Mobility. It makes all of these other things operate at their fullest potential. Mobility makes things better.

CHAPTER 2 | The Business of Untethering

Billions of dollars' worth of wireless gear has been sold and installed in tens of thousands of schools, hospitals, retail stores, manufacturing plants, and a host of other facilities. My employer, Cisco Systems, alone sells more than $5 million worth of WLAN equipment *every business day of the year*. That's more than $11,000 a minute, each business day. The sales, engineering, and maintenance machine that makes this possible is staggering in scope. I know because I'm part of it, and it's an incredible experience.

It is my privilege to provide you with an insider's view of this operation. However, it's not the clockwork of this amazing machine that I'll focus on, even though it's worthy of its own story. The intent of this work is greater than that—it's to get you to look above and beyond the "what" and "how" of wireless and expand your view to include the "why" of wireless.

Moving Beyond the "What" and "How" of Wireless

In the thousands of meetings that have taken place to sell and install billions of dollars' worth of wireless gear, nearly all the discussions have focused on the "what" and "how" of wireless—that is, what wireless equipment to use and how to install it. Having participated in hundreds of meetings around the world, I can report that the most essential discussions have occurred between the engineers selling the equipment and the engineers who end up running the equipment for their employer. Some of the most common questions include these: Should we use 802.11n or 802.11g? Should we put voice on 11a only? How many access points should we use for a given area? These are all very relevant points of discussion, because you cannot assemble a reliable wireless network without resolving these issues.

To answer such questions, dozens of books have been written that focus on the "what" and "how" of wireless. Those books are necessary for this market and have helped propel an industry that is now vital to resolving critical business problems. But it's time for us to expand our view of mobility by expanding the discussions to address the "why" of wireless mobility. As of this writing, this technology has been available for nearly 14 years, with the associated standards in place for about ten years. This experience has taught us a great deal about the "what" and "how." Perhaps more important, though, is that in recent years we've learned a great deal about the "why." It's often the "why" discussions that help propel a development from its early phases to something that changes how we do things and how we think.

Changing Life from a Location to an Activity

Today, many great tools can and do bring enormous changes to how we live. Wireless mobility has changed our lives to an extent as the automobile, modern medicine, and mass media have.

Wireless mobility has changed how we work, play, and interrelate, from being location-centric to being activity-centric. Put another way, wireless mobility changes work from a location to an activity. The implications from this change are profound.

Commerce and Technology Are Tightly Linked

By focusing much more on the "why" in critical discussions on wireless technology deployment, we can innovate the sequence of major projects, the network designs, the wireless deployments, the site surveys, and how we maintain these networks. These discussions will innovate the process of commerce every bit as much as we innovate the technology itself.

Commerce and technology have long been inextricably connected. Consider, for example, that prior to the pervasive deployment of the steam engine, longshoremen had to load and unload ships by hand. It was back-breaking work—long hours, very hard, and very demanding. Loading or unloading great ships often required several weeks and sometimes up to a month. Steam engines allowed cranes to do the work of many men, and they did it much faster and often much better. Today's highly advanced systems load and unload the greatest commercial ships ever built, and they achieve this in a single 24-hour day.

Think of the impact this evolution has had on commerce and what we would lose if we were still using manual labor in this way today. Our dependence on highly complex transportation systems, which are common on a global basis, has engendered far-reaching implications. Indeed, our very standard of living in part depends on how well and how pervasively this technology and associated policies are implemented.

Consider also the profound impact the automobile has had on society (global warming discussions aside). One of Henry Ford's most famous quotes is, "If I'd asked my customers what they wanted, they'd have said a *faster horse*." Initially, that's the view many people had of the automobile. But the implications of the car, even in its relatively early years, were far greater than that.

It wasn't just about speed, ease, or even luxury. The development of the car led to the development of the truck, which eventually led to today's 60,000-pound aerodynamic behemoths that bring the goods to us so that we can shop in complete convenience.

Today's massive road machines purvey goods the final hundreds of miles following their transoceanic journeys. We are annoyed when a small item is out of stock at the local mega-mart, but it's no small miracle that grants us that expectation.

The automobile also changed how cities were laid out. Though a few Tony examples remain, gone now are the ubiquitous downtown apartments and single-family houses in which the middle class dwelled. The car allowed people to move out to the country, which eventually became the suburbs. Shopping, once the exclusive domain of the city center, became something that regularly and conveniently occurred in suburban shopping centers, which often became the great shopping malls of today.

Wireless Makes Distance Irrelevant

It is common for us to purchase items from stores we never see by shopping online using laptop and desktop computers instead of cars. The Internet has changed the very definition of a store from a bricks-and-mortar establishment only to include a warehouse the end customer never sees, and even warehouses that aren't seen by anyone because they are virtual. (Many virtual stores exist only in certain seasons, such as Christmas and Halloween.) Wireless mobility evolves the experience one generation further by untethering the shopping experience. Instead of using a desktop or even laptop computer from home or the office to make online purchases, we now can use a personal digital assistant (PDA) or smartphone from anywhere wireless connectivity is available.

Distances are being handled with improving ease over the past decades as the supply chain of commerce has increased enormously in speed and capacity. Technology is now relatively evenly interspersed along the entire supply chain. Highly granular supply chain management is now a competitive advantage in the retail trade. The impact of wireless mobility in this continuum? *Distance is now irrelevant.*

This doesn't imply that we can transmit or receive information over infinite distances. It means that the distance between the two ultimate endpoints of a link are irrelevant. For example, a wireless client can scan data in a warehouse in Beijing, and, in seconds, an inventory manager in Boston can read that data on their wireless PDA while waiting in a parking lot outside their child's school.

The Faster Horse and Then Some

Wireless mobility, in its highly evolved state, is still probably close to the "faster horse" phase. Comparing today's wireless mobility to the evolution of the automobile and its impact on society, it could be argued that wireless mobility is at about the same stage as automobiles in the middle to late 1960s. At that time, some automobile engines were very powerful, and their capacity, range, and reliability were far better than ever before. When the American "muscle car" (high-performance automobile) first came into existence, people began thinking differently about what it meant to own a car. The muscle car was arguably the first vehicle that brought true distinction to the owner on a broad cultural basis. If you owned a muscle car, you typically enjoyed an elevated social status among your peers. You could "do things" that most people couldn't.

Even though the industry has sold and installed billions of dollars' worth of wireless technology, the discussions about wireless usually remain in the "faster horse" domain versus "how do we change work, play, and relationships from a location to an activity?" Presentations today on the speed of 802.11n remind me of the discussions we had in the 1970s about how "fast" the vaunted Hemi engine was. Vendors spend considerable amounts of money demonstrating how their products are faster than their competitors' products. It's relevant and interesting, but the more meaningful discussions lie elsewhere.

As an example, discussions are now just beginning on whether or not our corporate teams, training, and customer interactions are becoming "too virtual." Some argue that the virtual pendulum has swung too far and that we are risking corporate growth in the interest of reducing expenses. Virtual engagement enables new levels of productivity, which is a key metric in the health of a business. Yet, there is also something powerful about meeting someone in person and perhaps having a meal or sharing a social occasion together.

Few businesspeople believe meeting in person is not important. The discussions now under way focus on optimal ratios of virtual and in-person interactions. The depth and breadth of those discussions are outside the scope of this writing, but they are very much the discussions we need to be having in addition to those regarding "how fast" a wireless protocol is or "how many" access points should be deployed for a given site.

The implications of commingling recreation, worship, education, and rest are now also beginning to become apparent. Wireless mobility has changed some social events; it is now more fashionable for youths to text each other at dances than to actually dance. (Indeed, it's acceptable to text others while dancing!) Discussions on the virtual element of untethered communications have begun to occur in the workplace, in the home, at school, and at church. However, they are few compared to the number of discussions spent on the engineering aspects of wireless. As wireless mobility becomes truly ubiquitous, more discussions will center on the "why" and the implications of connectivity anywhere, anytime.

The "Why" of Wireless

If the "why" of networking is part of the horizon in front of us, what issues should we be considering? Which questions are among the most important? How do these questions affect the "what" and "how" of wireless mobility?

The most important questions should include the "why" of

- Cost versus value
- Purpose and use
- Linkage between operational priorities and actual network capabilities

Why Cost vs. Value

Although I believe that discussions illuminating the purpose and use of wireless networks are the foundation of selling and purchasing wireless networking, the market nearly always begins with discussions of cost, so I'll begin there.

One of the first issues to resolve regarding deploying wireless is that of the cost versus the value of wireless mobility. Focusing on cost rather than value is one of the easiest errors to make, not only as a customer, but also as a provider of this technology. While nearly all deployments are budget based—that is, you always build to a budget—discussions that begin and conclude primarily on cost lead to the customer selecting equipment primarily on the basis of cost only.

This can be likened to installing the very cheapest tires on a car without understanding how the car will be used. While it is occasionally appropriate to install the cheapest tires because not all cars are high-performance cars, virtually all wireless networks are designed and intended to be high performance in terms of speed, range, capacity, and reliability. Very few, if any, customers direct an IT salesperson to give them the slowest, least-reliable wireless mobility in the sales brochure.

Yet far too many discussions center on how the customer can get maximum performance at the lowest possible cost. Vendors and integrators are often far too eager to race one another to the bottom on pricing. Each participant, much like the game of "chicken," contests to see who will flinch first. In the end, neither the customer, the vendor, nor the integrator is well served by this approach.

Carrying the car analogy forward, it's interesting how carefully prospective owners of a new car consider the requirements for their purchase. Long before they make the actual purchase, they decide about their needs for the car. Will the car be used to convey the family on a daily basis? If so, perhaps a minivan may be optimal. Will the vehicle be used mostly for light industrial work such as landscaping? For that purpose, a light truck may be the best machine. Will the vehicle spend part of its time off the paved road? If so, perhaps a jeep will perform the best. For high-speed recreation and to impress friends, perhaps a high-performance car would best suit the customer.

Other items are carefully factored in prior to purchase, such as maintenance, distance to the dealership in case there's a problem, reputation and viability of the manufacturer, and whether or not the customer is a long-time supporter of a particular manufacturer or local dealer. Financing is carefully evaluated because the car will be owned, in most cases, from three to five years, and occasionally longer. Research on total cost of ownership is commonly completed prior to purchase. Oil change frequency, tune-ups, tire wear, and major maintenance schedules are discussed and negotiated as part of the selling price. In other words, car selection depends on a great many elements other than price. And rightfully so.

Of course, many car owners dive headlong into the purchase. They are ill prepared and therefore very much in the hands of skilled salespersons and their management. Maximum amounts of money are extracted from these customers, who typically drive off the lot completely exhausted, annoyed, and having gone much further into debt than originally planned. Oddly, these are usually the customers for whom the new car glow dims the fastest.

While most customers do not purchase the least expensive car possible, from what I know of the U.S. auto market, discussions on lowest cost for wireless networking remain common. It is not uncommon for wireless networking sales engagements to spend as much time on cost as features. And while a wireless network is far more valuable and far more expensive than the average automobile, purchasing a wireless network commonly receives less discussion and preplanning than the purchase of a car.

The question of value for enterprise-class wireless mobility is more than appropriate to consider; it's an essential issue to illuminate. In most enterprises, there are three primary value drivers for wireless mobility:

- Reducing the operating expense of a business
- Increasing business velocity
- Enabling real-time business analytics

Reducing Operating Expense

The pursuit of operating expense (OPEX) reduction by upper management and all responsible employees may be of equal importance only to the expansion of sales. The existence of the business itself is largely based on ensuring that money is left over after expenses are paid. Increases in sales are, of course, primarily outward-facing, while the issue of OPEX reduction is largely inward-facing.

OPEX reduction is achieved when efficiencies are gained in the use of time and materials. The best-run companies constantly focus on reducing the cost of running the business. This focus is maintained in parallel with increasing product or service quality and increasing the efficiency of all operations. The stock price of a publicly traded company typically increases when the company can reduce the cost of business while maintaining or improving quality, plus provide confidence that its overall sales will increase. This, of course, assumes a reasonably rational market and macroeconomic set of conditions.

Increasing Business Velocity and Productivity

Productivity is an essential element of increasing the overall velocity of a business. Productivity is greatly enhanced by mobility because mobility changes work from a location to an activity. Having the right people participate in business operations without having to be physically next to the work eliminates time spent in transit. Conversely, having the right information reach the right people allows more time to make the right decisions and also to respond before a situation escalates due to time constraints.

Mobility takes many of the elements of distance out of the equation, making distance essentially irrelevant. The results of this are real-time responses to routine business dynamics such as inventory arrival and major order fulfillment.

Perhaps equally important, operational exceptions such as receipt of incorrect, insufficient, or damaged raw materials; equipment malfunctions; and other unexpected conditions are common to business and they draw off disproportionate management and response cycles. Bad news is best delivered early; time is quite often a critical factor when an operational exception occurs. This is another place for which wireless mobility provides tremendous value.

Mobility also expands productivity by increasing the total number of hours available for work. This comes at the expense of reducing or eliminating the partitions between recreation, personal time, education, and worship but it may be a trade well worth making because it engenders more overall freedom and job satisfaction for the worker. Job satisfaction is an important element, as workers are, and always have been, the primary asset of any business. The demand for highly skilled workers will continue to increase in the future. Job satisfaction is an important element in helping reduce worker turnover, which is expensive and has significant productivity implications.

It's now a common occurrence to respond to or make a mobile phone call during physical exercise, while waiting in a doctor's office, sitting on a plane or train, or waiting in traffic. Sometimes we find wireless communication by others a nuisance when it occurs during a movie or worship services. Without excusing inconsiderate behavior in certain public situations regarding the use of cell phones, real-time wireless mobility is vital to productivity, especially in work. For example, instead of a worker needing to return to the office to handle a problem, they can handle it over the phone quickly and without causing delay. Often, brief instructions can be afforded to manage the matter until the person can give their full attention or be physically present.

Failing to respond in real time or failing to connect a worker with a subject matter expert (SME) or important information commonly results in an opportunity lost to a competitor. A salesperson may fail to close a deal when a customer was prepared to sign an agreement. A vital piece of information may be acquired and delivered in real time, such as pricing, agreement amendments, or component sourcing.

In certain situations, such as with emergency care providers, acquiring real-time information can save lives. Real-time traffic analysis can also ensure that a person does not miss a key meeting, an important family gathering, or a social event. In military operations, updating real-time information and relaying that wirelessly enables the successful completion of missions.

Productivity affects the OPEX of a retail business by ensuring that the right number of personnel are in position to manage customers. Rather than having 30 salespersons inside a large store handling customer questions, the store might employ 25 persons wirelessly connected to databases and SMEs to handle the same number of customers.

Further, SMEs can be leveraged by the sales staffs from multiple locations, thereby even further enhancing productivity and at the same time reducing the cost of getting real-time information to customers. Consider also the productivity implications of SMEs who can roam and yet remain connected to their constituents.

Worker agility is a key element of high-performing businesses today, and it's a common phenomenon in practically every type of business today. The domain range (how far a person roams) varies enormously—from those who work in cube farms, to those who travel many miles to remote sites such as oil fields, construction sites, and farms.

The ability to remain connected now doesn't necessarily mean all physical sites must have access to applications at all times. While that concept is often the result of well-intended marketing, the reality is that today's connectivity requires various means of connecting—802.11, mobile cellular, two-way radio, and so forth. Not all are equally capable of the same capacity and reliability, and presently it is not realistic to achieve this from an architectural or expense perspective.

Enabling Real-time Business Analytics

As indicated, handling operational exceptions such as receipt of incorrect, insufficient, or damaged raw materials; equipment malfunctions; and other unexpected conditions are common to business. The early detection of these anomalies is essential in the perpetual focus on OPEX reduction through real-time business analytics. Mobility plays a special role here; although it doesn't generally comprise the actual sensors that detect these anomalies, wireless enables the data to be sent in real time to other areas of the facility, including the handheld devices of maintenance and management stakeholders.

Supply chain materials and other critical inventory and facility functions are increasingly in motion in tools such as forklifts, pallets, manufacturing robotics, and mobile workforce stations such as medical carts. The ability to retain connectivity with these essential platforms while remaining in motion or in different locations throughout a work area increases business management granularity.

There is more, however. The best of business analytics systems include the ability for the stakeholder to receive data and manage situations remotely and while in transit, while the supply chain and facility elements remain connected to the network without the disruption of a tether such as an Ethernet cable. The quality of business analytics resides partly in sensor density—that is, the more sensors, the more data, and the more data, the more analyses that can be performed. The greater the number of stakeholders that are appraised in real time, the more real time the management recognition and response time will be.

Wireless mobility therefore untethers the sensors and also the smartphones or similar devices that stakeholders can use while in meetings, at their desks, or in transit. The role for wireless mobility is not to detect or report information per se, but to ensure that data endpoints will retain connectivity while in motion, in real time.

OPEX Reduction in Healthcare

OPEX reduction in healthcare is far better understood by the healthcare industry than the wireless industry. Relatively few wireless equipment providers or system integrators understand that hospitals employ three primary types of healthcare providers: the physician, the nurse, and the administrator. Each has unique needs, metrics for success, and uses of wireless. (Obviously there are other key personnel, such as maintenance and security, but for simplicity's sake I'll focus on those three.)

Each of these healthcare providers has different responsibilities, and part of what truly separates them are their domains of operation—where and how they go about their daily tasks. Of the three types of healthcare providers, physicians are on the move the most as they transit between the hospital, their private practice clinics, and, commonly these days, a specialist practice group (sports injuries, osteopathic, outpatient surgery, and so on).

Wireless for Doctors, Nurses, and Administrators

Many, if not most, doctors spend at least half of their professional time outside the hospital and approximately 15 percent of their time in transit between facilities. While in transit, they routinely connect to a hospital, clinic, office, and home/car for patient status, their schedules, conferences, and training. The physician's primary tool for connectivity is the cell phone, which is typically a smartphone. This allows them to handle e-mail, texting, voice, and some imaging. This technology is enormously valuable to them, and it improves patient care quality, primarily by greatly reducing response time. Response time is often critical in healthcare, and it's usually related to patient pain and comfort management.

From my experience in IT work in healthcare (one of my focus industries for nearly 19 years), I know that while many nurses work outside a formal hospital setting, they tend to be the more seasoned professionals. Home healthcare typically requires exceptional clinical skills as it lacks many of the resources afforded by a formal hospital setting. For that reason, most nurses work in formal hospital settings.

Hospital nurses, compared to doctors, don't typically roam much farther than the floor on which they are assigned, and they don't typically work from an office. Nurses do travel between floors, such as to and from surgical theaters, recovery and acute care areas, and nurses' stations, but generally they are more likely to remain at a station on a single floor. Their primary communications tool is a phone, and the primary application is voice. A nurse is highly mobile and an excellent example of an *agile worker*—one who is literally in constant motion, yet constantly in connection with other nurses, doctors, and staff.

Hospital administrators, of course, use cell phones and often phones that include 802.11 type connectivity, but most of their communication is through laptops or desktop computers, with a clear trend toward laptops. Administrators typically spend approximately 20 percent of their time in hospitals on care floors, and most of the balance of their time is spent in the administrative offices where other business functions occur, such as human resources, legal, marketing, and so forth. These offices are typically near the healthcare facility but are not necessarily on one of the hospital floors.

Infrastructure

The equipment that interfaces with the client device (what the person carries) is typically referred to as *infrastructure*. These are the boxes, software, cables, power supplies, racks, and other elements that enable the clients to connect with one another, the Internet, their intranet, databases, and so forth.

The infrastructure required to support the healthcare worker's domain range is a standards-based wireless system located in their private clinic, such as 802.11 or ZigBee. Connectivity for healthcare workers who routinely travel outside the hospital requires wireless networks provided by major service providers such as AT&T. One of the key elements, of course, is that much of the infrastructure is not only standards based (for example, 802.11) but also engineered to allow workers to move ubiquitously throughout their domain ranges. The engineering task is mostly about ensuring that excellent coverage is deployed pervasively, and in the right areas.

Pervasive wireless coverage in healthcare has been the norm since around 2004 in the United States, and it's quite rare now to have serious discussions about whether or not to deploy wireless infrastructure pervasively in healthcare facilities. The discussions are much more about phasing the deployments—that is, determining what gear to install in which area at which time.

The definition of a pervasive deployment continues to evolve along with the equipment itself. Initially, pervasive deployment provided excellent radio coverage wherever a person moved inside a facility. Most early designs, and in fact most designs today, provide wall-to-wall coverage. However, to best reduce the OPEX of a healthcare facility, coverage now typically extends to the parking garage and the campus areas between healthcare buildings. The greater the physical area of increased productivity, the greater the impact on OPEX reduction. Stated another way, wireless coverage areas are an example of "more is better." The more hospital campus areas covered by wireless, the greater the gain in productivity.

If customers, vendors, and integrators simply looked at the "cost" of wireless, there would be far less infrastructure, far fewer clients, and very few of the pervasive deployments common today. In a pervasive deployment, wireless coverage is available in all places a worker may roam. In reality, it does not mean 100 percent coverage from wall to wall, because most workers don't routinely visit some places, such as wiring closets, building heating and cooling system areas, and secured areas. Interestingly enough, an increasing number of these once remote areas now also have wireless coverage.

It is my opinion and experience that healthcare was the first industry to deploy various forms of wireless pervasively in its facilities because it was the first major industry to understand the difference between the cost and value of wireless mobility. Education is widely regarded as the first industry to adopt 802.11 wireless, but I retain the view that education as an industry does not feature pervasive wireless deployments to the same extent routinely found in healthcare facilities.

It's interesting to note that pervasive deployments, both inside and outside the healthcare industry, were not driven by aggressive salespersons, manufacturers offering special pricing, or integrators attempting to expand the size of a deployment contract. Pervasive wireless deployments were initially, and remain primarily, driven by customers. This kind of deployment was ordered by customers long before today's financial modeling tools that illuminate returns on investments and assets.

Despite the lack of detailed financial modeling tools for wireless, customers pressed ahead with pervasive deployments because they understood early on that such coverage was an essential part of maximizing the value of mobility. Pervasive coverage allowed them to reduce OPEX by increasing productivity. A number of factors were considered during the push for pervasive rollouts:

- Hourly cost of employees
- Hours lost due to unproductive practices and technologies
- Cost of pervasive equipment
- Payback period
- Amortization period of the equipment

An Example: Nurse Productivity

Assume the average cost of a nurse is $60 per hour (wages plus benefits), and assume the nurse works 40 hours per week. About 30 minutes of productivity per day are lost because of the extra steps required to return many times to the nurses' station or other places where work is a location rather than an activity. Also assume that eight nurses are working per floor and in three shifts per day. That leads to a productivity loss of $720 per day. Multiplied by 365 workdays, this brings the total productivity loss to

$262,800 per year per floor. If you then multiply the number of floors by five, you can see a productivity loss of $1.3 million per year per hospital building.

Cost of nurse per hour	$60
Cost of 30 minutes of lost productivity per day, per nurse	$30
Cost of lost productivity × eight nurses per shift, per day	$240
Three nurse shifts per 24-hour day	$720
The above × five floors	$3600
The above times 365 days	$1,314,000

The preceding approximation is supported in part by a Forrester Research report from February 2006 (www.cisco.com/en/US/.../prod_white_paper0900aecd80424544.pdf) that indicates nurses lose 20–60 minutes per day in attempting to reach other staff members. Eighty-four percent of nurses stated in that same report that, more importantly, productivity loss impacts patient care. For reference also, at the 2009 Healthcare Information and Management Systems Society (HIMSS) Management Engineering symposium, it was noted that a nurse makes or receives an average of 33 calls per shift. When nurses return to the nurse call station 33 or more times per shift, considerable productivity is lost, not to mention unnecessary increased physical fatigue. You can readily understand how wireless connectivity that would allow a nurse to take a call anywhere while on shift would provide benefits, including a significant gain in productivity.

The average 802.11 deployment costs approximately $1.85 per square foot. Assume 100,000 square feet per floor, and the equipment cost (infrastructure only) is approximately $185,000 per floor. Clients and software are approximately six times that, making the total equipment cost approximately $1.3 million. Maintenance is approximately $75,000 per year, and the equipment typically remains in use for three years, with the maintenance contract renewing each year.

That brings the total equipment cost plus maintenance to $1.4 million, including 10 percent interest on the money borrowed for the equipment. The hospital will take three years to pay off the equipment, which means a yearly cost of approximately $466,000, to resolve an annual productivity loss that costs the hospital approximately three times that. You can see how that even with a quick calculation, which is effectively how the hospitals calculated this for a number of years, the solution is very cost effective.

If you add the cost of litigation for even a single patient who was injured or died from lack of nurse productivity, you can see how strong the case is for pervasive wireless in a healthcare setting.

Efforts to reduce OPEX are often focused on simply reducing labor costs. Labor cost reduction is often achieved by cutting back on hiring and compensation. It can be an effective strategy, but more often than not it weakens the business by reducing morale and personnel quality and increasing work loads. Investing in wireless connectivity to improve productivity often increases the vitality and profitability of a business by providing better tools for employees, which, in turn, increases both sales and reduces OPEX.

The value side of the cost-versus-value equation becomes highly leveraged to the advantage of the customer when the value of multiple productivity gains is considered. If we add productivity gains of the doctors and administrators to the OPEX reduction afforded by enabling pervasive connectivity, all using the same wireless infrastructure, the value discussion quickly shifts from how soon the equipment is paid off to how much mobility increases the performance and profitability of the operation.

A Wireless Inventory Solution

In addition to work productivity gains, another OPEX element benefits from wireless networks: tracking and maintaining hard assets such as wheelchairs and other expensive tools and instruments. We return to the healthcare environment to review a common OPEX reduction: wheelchair inventory and management. When you add the OPEX reduction through improved management of hard assets, the value proposition of wireless mobility increases even further.

The next time you see a wheelchair or another valuable portable business asset, check whether there's a large, stenciled sign on the chair or device. You'll commonly see these at airports as well as hospitals. The sign will say something like, "Property of the X-Ray Dept. Do Not Remove." This sign is an indication of hoarding, which is the result of lack of inventory control. In other words, departments in personnel create their own allocations of an asset to ensure that it's available when they need it. This occurs even where the total sum of assets is sufficient to serve various departments. What happens is a misallocation of assets, which end up where they contribute less or even zero to the operation.

Hoarding is an effective, if somewhat inefficient, technique used by a person or department to maintain their private allocation. On the other hand, it also has the effect of creating an underutilization of the asset. In other words, while the asset is, in effect, in storage or misplaced, other departments with a need for the device or asset do not have access to it. This can cause the departments that "have" the device to secure it even more carefully from the "have not" departments to keep it from being used by personnel outside their department. The concern or fear, of course, is that the device won't be returned. The implications for productivity, customer care, and worker satisfaction are clear in this all-too-common scenario.

When I ask hospital administrators about their wheelchair inventory, the response is nearly always prefaced by the administrator rolling their eyes, followed by a look of frustration and a frustrated tone of voice as part of the response, which is typically something like this:

> We have about 150 wheelchairs, but I'm not sure. Some are stashed in various departments, and we believe we're losing approximately one a day, typically when a patient is released from our care. It's common for a wheelchair to leave with a patient. We originally placed security personnel to help monitor the situation, but they're often asked to assist with loading the patient, and unless the security person

is trained for this, the outbound patients can be injured during the transition from the hospital to their car. This exposes the facility to litigation, so we can no longer use security personnel to assist patients checking out of the facility.

We don't have enough trained nurses, orderlies, administrative staff, or volunteers to assist in escorting patients to their cars, so we mounted cameras to monitor the exits. This would work, except either the camera is not monitored at all times or we're unable to get personnel in position in time to recover the wheelchair after it's loaded into the vehicle and driven away.

Wheelchairs typically cost about $1000 each, but specialized versions for pediatrics or those requiring attachments can readily cost more than twice that. On average, 25 to 40 percent of wheelchairs are unaccounted for in an inventory. When wheelchairs are recovered, around 30 percent of them need significant repairs.

A 500-bed hospital typically has about 150 wheelchairs. Losing one a day is an equipment loss of at least $365,000 per year. Repairs, recovery, and inventory management for 150 wheelchairs cost around $12,000 per year, bringing the total loss to $377,000 per year.

As stated previously, the 802.11 coverage model becomes highly cost effective and the value proposition becomes very clear when you add more than one service to the wireless mobility network. In this case, adding a location-based service (LBS) over the WLAN voice and data system is appropriate. This service would layer additional value onto the system outlined earlier for doctor and nurse productivity. Productivity improvements would also be gained for healthcare administrators.

Most of the 802.11 wireless coverage is in place prior to an LBS deployment, but assume for this scenario a typical 10 percent increase of coverage to manage the hospital exits. The cost of this solution would be about $140,000 on top of the existing $1.4 million pervasive wireless deployment cost. If we add $50,000 for specialized LBS equipment, plus $10,000 per year for three years for maintenance, the cost of a wheelchair LBS solution would be approximately $220,000. Even if we included the cost of an orderly, which is about $15 per hour with benefits, the total cost of the solution would be around $250,000.

Normal financial management would not include labor costs such as that of an orderly, but I'll include it in this model to demonstrate value versus cost. A sharp system integrator or wireless equipment vendor would point out that the savings for an LBS system would more than enable additional personnel to work in concert with the system for wheelchair recovery and reduction of maintenance costs.

Assuming the model outlined so far, the wheelchair LBS solution would virtually eliminate the wheelchair loss, because the system would page an orderly as a wheelchair passes a checkpoint well before the doors. One of the orderly's primary tasks is to assist patients into their vehicles, for which they are trained, and, equally important to the hospital, to recover the wheelchair and return it to its original department.

By placing the wheelchair into a holding area, or handing the wheelchair over to a volunteer or lower-paid worker, the wheelchair would be returned to its original department. This would also ensure an appropriate distribution of wheelchairs, and thus greatly mitigate, or eliminate, hoarding of inventory. This in turn would increase patient satisfaction and quality of care by ensuring that patients wouldn't have to wait too long for a wheelchair. (I speak from some personal experience on the customer satisfaction point: Following knee surgery, I had to wait nearly 30 minutes for a wheelchair. My entire family was also waiting, and the family vehicle was parked just outside the hospital doors, creating unnecessary and prolonged traffic congestion.)

The LBS solution would likely remain in place for three years. Even if the equipment maintenance expense and the orderly expense were included, the value of the solution would be far in excess of the cost. Left unchecked, the hospital would lose more than $1 million worth of wheelchairs over a three-year period. After the initial expense plus the annual maintenance and labor costs, the total cost would be $280,000. This would present a net value of approximately $720,000 to the hospital. Other softer costs are harder to evaluate, such as customer and worker satisfaction, but even on the most conservative basis, those value contributions only further enhance the necessity of wireless mobility in healthcare.

Purpose and Use of Wireless Mobility

The following content may appear overly obvious, but in my view, based on working closely with mobility integrators and many customers in this industry full time since the early 1990s, very little discussion occurs on this point in advance of the wireless mobility purchase or upgrade.

Within each enterprise-class customer are usually an array of stakeholders, including end users, technology managers, finance personnel, security staff, applications engineers, and system integrators. I've noticed that, of all the thousands of deployments that occur each year, less than 5 percent of the customers have meaningful dialogue across the stakeholder group prior to a major wireless network purchase and deployment. Even when it comes to deploying major applications over the WLAN such as voice and applications that enable the location and status of equipment, the consent, alignment, and discussion across the stakeholder base is anything but inclusive and cohesive.

I have worked with major customers who have five or more disparate WLANs operating in parallel with one another. The cost and complexity of this array are far greater than when unified under one operational umbrella. By far the greatest sources of RF problems result from devices owned by the same customer but managed by different groups who do not communicate with one another.

Broad alignment is essential because it takes many people to get a wireless mobility network to operate at peak efficiency and to achieve peak OPEX reduction. How well the network performs is a key element of quality. Quality is conformance to functional requirements that are set forth by the stakeholders through a sequence of decisions, stakeholder collaboration, design, deployment, and maintenance.

At first, the primary purpose of a wireless network is to achieve at least the following:

- Untether applications
- Enable real-time business analytics
- Reduce product/service time to market

In an IT world in which unified communications (UC) generates 20 times the cost, value, and mindshare of wireless mobility, it should be added in balance that the role of mobility is to untether many UC applications. Not all UC applications can or should be untethered, but many of the more valuable ones gain impressive value leverage when untethered.

The most common types of UC applications often include the following:

- Contact management
- Seamless information for mobile personnel
- Resource identification/problem resolution
- Collaboration acceleration
- Job-specific communication-enabled portals

All of these can be, and are, untethered and sent to various personnel via wireless clients such as smartphones, PDAs, laptop computers, and customer-specific devices such as handheld UPC code scanners with built-in WLAN connectivity, RFID readers, and so forth. It's also common, and many times essential, for the UC platform to have upstream data fed into it. Upstream data can be inventory data; personnel and physical asset tracking; environmental, building, and machine status and conditions; as well as building physical security and environmental controls such as heating and air conditioning.

One of my favorite stories about network purpose occurred at a military aircraft fabricator in the United States. Near the end of a complex design phase, as my team was beginning to pack up our RF measurement equipment, I noticed a gray wooden box about 3 feet long by 1 foot high by 2 feet wide. I was told it contained an extension device used for connecting the factory WLAN to the inside of the aircraft so that the workers could send and receive up-to-date engineering data specific to each aircraft.

After indicating that I was impressed by this customer-built WLAN extension device, the employee commented, "We're careful to always ensure we pull the WLAN equipment out of the aircraft before we complete the assembly and send the plane out onto the tarmac to be flown overseas. Tools get left in the aircraft all the time, and when the military people land in the desert at the end of the trip, they kick out anything that doesn't look like their gear into the sand and there it stays. Some of those tools are $10,000 to $25,000 each and we lose dozens of them each year." My team and I then took the time to explain the principles of how this customer could invest about $35,000 in location-based services and eliminate the loss of approximately $175,000 worth of tooling annually.

That would be a well-stated network purpose: "Install a wireless LBS system to prevent the loss of fabrication tooling." More than once did we stumble across ways to expand the usefulness of a mobility network.

A Nuclear Power Plant Experience: Increasing Business Velocity

I was called in at the last minute to help win a wireless account at a nuclear power plant that was just about to be awarded to a competitor. The purchase order was sitting on a desk for final signature before being sent back to the competitor. I asked for one final meeting before the purchase order was signed, and the customer agreed.

Upon arrival at the power plant site, I asked to see a preliminary diagram of the proposed 802.11 network. The customer showed it to me and described it in detail. I asked a single question: "What is the primary use for this network?" The response was clear and compelling, "To migrate to VoIP from two-way radios that are just about completely worn out." That's another example of a solid purpose statement by a customer.

It turns out that a nuclear power plant includes many rooms in a "power block," which is the area in which the nuclear reactors and generator deck reside. This particular power block included about 500 rooms. Safety protocol requires that the doors to these rooms be kept closed. Given the concrete walls and thick, watertight steel doors, it's no wonder that the two-way radios wouldn't work well in this environment. The only reason they did in fact work was because of some very large holes in the various ceilings, walls, and floors, through which ran a 1-meter-wide pair of high-pressure steam lines, plus an assortment of cables.

Regardless of these issues, wireless VoIP is a far better architecture than two-way radios for an environment such as this, because it can carry data and use various voice features such as one-to-many, voice messaging, texting, and video.

After the customer described the intended use of the network, I took a second quick review of the proposed architecture and determined that voice wouldn't run reliably over this network. Voice requires some very sophisticated network architectures, software packages, clients, and infrastructure, including some of the most complex access point placement designs.

Our competitor had treated the WLAN as though it were intended for data only. Further, this competitor, like many others, considered technical problems at the discrete element layer (such as an access point) only versus viewing the problem from the end-to-end network. The competitor had neglected to ask the purpose of the network, and the customer assumed our competitor already knew.

After we had detailed how different a wireless VoIP WLAN needed to be from the proposed system, the purchase order to the competitor was cancelled and the project was awarded to my employer. That system has been in place since approximately 2000 and is only now being upgraded.

The current project is an expansion from the original 750 access points to a completely state-of-the-art, centralized architecture with 802.11n and nearly three times as many access points. The original project was one of the largest 802.11 deals I'd ever completed up to that point. The refresh is also quite large compared to most enterprise-class projects. All this from asking a simple question about network purpose!

The Importance of Purpose

Understanding the purpose of the wireless network is essential before beginning to design it. And, in cases such as the nuclear power plant customer, future uses of the network should be discussed in great detail. Designing, auditing, and deploying a network for the most challenging applications that may run over the network in the years to come is nearly always more cost effective than deploying for voice today and then returning to optimize the network for voice and other latency-sensitive applications at a later date. If voice, video, or other latency-sensitive applications are going to run over the network in the future, the network deployment should be designed with that in mind from the beginning, even if only data is to run on the WLAN originally.

If insufficient budget is available to deploy voice-sensitive wireless networks across a facility, it's far better to deploy properly in fewer areas and establish a budget-driven set of phases for deploying latency-sensitive wireless networks throughout the intended areas across the business, building, or campus.

In the case of the nuclear power plant customer, we demonstrated some very interesting wireless video capabilities, suitable for physical security purposes. The system allowed any security team member to view any part of the external campus, and the critical parts of the internal areas in certain buildings, from any wireless site internal or external on the campus and indeed from anywhere in the world via a small handheld PDA.

It was impressive then, and it's more impressive in function now. We also demonstrated how we could mount wireless routers, called Mobile Access Routers, to the security vehicles so that, in addition to cameras mounted on the vehicles, the security vehicles could beam back images, sound, and other security data to any other security personnel around the world—all in a highly secure and reliable format.

Another purpose we discussed with the power plant customer was the issue of greatly reducing the time it takes for a technician to get their work approved by a manager. Power blocks are enormous in size, and it can easily take a manager or foreman 20 minutes or more to traverse from one area to another inside the power block, and much longer if the manager or foreman is outside the power block somewhere on the campus, which itself is enormous, covering about 700 acres.

To make the problem more challenging for the customer, it's been estimated that about 45 percent of all technical personnel are planning to retire from the nuclear power industry by approximately 2014. This means not only an increasing shortage of qualified nuclear maintenance engineers, but also a shortage of experienced managers and foremen who can approve technical work prior to an assembly returning to service. This development, combined with the considerable distances a manager needs to walk between job sites at the plant, typically causes considerable delays in getting project signoff and records updated.

Our system concept involved having the technicians use shoulder-mounted or handheld IP wireless cameras that had sufficient quality images to enable a remote supervisor to inspect and sign off on the work. This would save the company millions of dollars over the life of the system deployed to manage this. With dozens of technicians in motion on simultaneous projects, the increase in productivity realized from allowing managers or foremen to check and sign off work tasks remotely enables a very strong return on investment.

In addition, each nuclear power plant is required to shut down for 30 days twice per calendar year for required maintenance and inspection. These maintenance phases are highly organized and are timed to begin and end to the minute, because the power plant typically generates $1 million worth of electricity per calendar day. During shutdown, of course, zero power is being generated and sold. The aforementioned time savings for the signoff of work orders during the mandated shutdowns is an essential OPEX reduction element.

Pervasive wireless for this customer had another important purpose: wireless guest access. Given that the maintenance is so specialized and must be completed quickly and without error, and also given that the scope of mandated maintenance is enormous, only certain contractors could be brought in for a successful maintenance shutdown. Success, in this case, is having the work completed properly, under budget, and, critically, on time.

We demonstrated with wireless guest access, configured in such a manner that the customer's network itself would remain completely secure, the customer and contractors could complete the maintenance work ahead of schedule. Given that the plant shutdown was costing the customer $700 a minute, saving even a few hours was highly valuable, and we were able to demonstrate that this was readily achievable and that, in fact, wireless guest access could improve contractor productivity by 25 percent.

No longer would the contractor have to walk outside the building to make a phone call or have correct drawings sent by courier. A state-of-the-art WLAN could provide all that literally to within feet of where the work was taking place. Wireless guest access for the purpose of reducing contractor access time is a very good and well-stated purpose indeed.

Linking Operational Priorities and Network Capabilities

One of the most interesting aspects to observe when working with enterprise-class customers is the communications among the various levels within the company. Of course, it's easy to offer the view that communications flow constantly between top management and the individual contributors, and indeed many memos and much information do traverse the various strata within a company on any given day.

However, it's my observation, after meeting with enterprise-class customers for years from around the world, that probably less than 5 percent of companies are tightly aligned across the various stakeholders for major IT projects. The concepts of identifying and aligning the stakeholders and detailing a strategy for assessing the current condition and capability of the network, prior to further buildout, are vital for both customers and systems integrators.

In most enterprise-class companies, improving the operational capabilities of the company is a priority, and this is central to the performance and steering of a company. What is not so well understood broadly in the corporate world is that IT is central to every major operational effort. The companies that understand this move IT from the liability side to the asset side of the balance sheet.

The purpose of wireless mobility is to untether data, voice, video, and other applications. We want users at both ends of the links to send and receive information, and be able do so while far apart, and in motion.

Henry Ford would have loved it.

CHAPTER 3 | Mobility and the CIO

The most successful chief information officers (CIOs) operate consistently while dealing with a wide array of priorities. They excel at managing what they can control and are adept at maneuvering around what they can't control.

Most corporate operations involve enormous amounts of inefficiencies. Millions of hours of a CIO's time are spent in corporate meetings, most of which are longer than they should be, with most delivering moderate value (at best) for the time used. In addition, a considerable portion of strategies, investments, and assets fall far short of their potential. Most business experience is gained by trial and error or by applying varying degrees of guesswork. This is hardly an indictment of the talented and hard-working people in today's workforce; simply put, it's a difficult task to move a business forward.

In addition, the actual amount of time a salesperson spends closing purchase orders is a small fraction of their total week. Large amounts of time are required to prepare for, travel to, and follow up from meetings. Think of the tremendous cost and productivity gains that could be realized if an hour-long meeting were replaced by single PowerPoint slide, a text message, or a short e-mail that was distributed to the right stakeholders.

It takes a tremendous amount of work to culminate a purchase order, including finding customers interested in the salesperson's offerings. Consider the enormous advantage a business would have with a precision-guided sales program featuring smart targeting of customers and verticals that directed sales personnel to accounts with the shortest sales cycles and largest average purchase orders.

Accurate predictive modeling can prioritize investments and free up cash flow to expand and improve an operation. Reliable forecasts of when an information technology (IT) mobility investment would amortize would allow more comprehensive planning of new generations of technology. It would also enable new technology to be phased into new physical areas within the business. Replacing informed guesswork with the right information at the right time in the right place is an enormous advantage for a business. And that's precisely the purpose of information technology.

The CIO, Information Dominance, and IT

The primary CIO deliverable in today's business world is *information dominance*. Today, all CIOs have IT assets on their balance sheets, and the best of them understand that their job is about knowing what to do with the company's assets.

A corporate CIO is often mistakenly viewed as little more than a chief technology officer. While this may often be the case, and the CIO must be closely aligned with technology that sources, delivers, and analyzes information, the primary deliverable of a CIO is *information*, not technology. The CIO must certainly understand technology, but far more important, they must clearly understand how technology delivers useful information. For this reason, the CIO is rightfully at every fork in the road where a major decision exists.

While the *functions* of IT assets rightfully reside in the realm of engineers, the *purpose* of IT assets is to deliver information dominance. Consider that the vast majority of enterprise networks use their networks primarily for ease of simple communication. This approach, however, allows the IT investment to perform only its most rudimentary functions. Information dominance is about consolidating and effectively distributing information from many sources, both within and outside a business, to enable an overwhelming competitive advantage.

Competitive advantage means more than offering the lowest price. It involves a convergence of increasing market share, profitability, corporate agility, and intelligence gathering. The role of mobility in all this is to untether not just each of the communication endpoints, but to untether almost all communication endpoints. An essential element of information dominance is ensuring that information is delivered with as little regard as possible to where the communication endpoint is physically located. That a communication endpoint may be a person or an asset such as a machine or instrument requires only the briefest consideration.

All businesses compete for market share. Competitors that acquire and retain information dominance finish ahead in the marketplace because competitive information dominance, in addition to smart targeting attributes, enables producers to think more like users. Businesses with information dominance are more effective in neutralizing competition.

The only competitive technique better than closing a purchase order before the competitor arrives is to take the money off the table for future deals. This occurs when service and technology providers are embedded into the customer's operational improvement process. In competitive terms, the power of collaboration is more than a sound bite; it elevates the role of a mobility IT provider beyond that of a business advisor to that of co-developer of operational solutions for the customer. To catch a fox, you need to think like a fox, so to speak. The more a producer thinks like a customer, the less a customer has reason to look elsewhere for a supplier.

IT assets are part of every major corporate policy, program, and objective. The better the quality of available information, the less likely an operational error will be made. For that reason, IT and mobility are not about radios; neither are they about solutions, except in engineering discussions. The purpose of mobility and the IT investment is to solve business problems. CIOs who connect the resolution of business problems with specific applications of the correct technology—not too much and not too little—will not only resolve key operational problems, but will deliver the golden fleece of business—information dominance.

Analytics Change the Trend

The IT engagement trend in nearly all IT mobility discussions between system integrators and end customers today begins with the technical merits of the items being sold. The same is true farther up the supply chain: IT equipment manufacturers use the vast majority of the engagement convincing resellers that their technology is superior to that of others. That much is certain at the present.

However, I'm observing an interesting development within the ranks of the most elite mobility integrators in the United States. It's an early trend, though one I'm trying to help expand across the industry, because it will make a genuine difference in the outcome of the investments made by customers. This change will also expand revenues for the integrators and equipment suppliers as they learn to think more like customers than producers, thereby enhancing their deliverables.

The new development is the dialogue used by the IT industry to engage the customer. To be specific, discussions are beginning to focus much more on the "why" of mobility, well before deep diving the "how." As a "recovering engineer," I realize that a portion of my heart will probably always beat a little faster during technical discussions, but I know that it is becoming increasingly important to alter the sequence of the engagement between the vendors and the system integrators, and the system integrators and the customers, by placing the "why" ahead of the "how."

Measuring the "Why"

Little will be more central to the discussion of "why" than that of performance metrics, primarily in terms of *monetized* metrics. These metrics specify the returns of new IT investments on an increasingly stringent basis. Put another way, IT equipment providers and integrators will increasingly need to sell far more of their deliverables based on values supported by analytics. The likelihood of a sales engagement resulting in financial reward will be largely based on the quality of the financial modeling offered by the technology providers.

Eventually, the best of the technology vendors and integrators will optimize their deliverables based on close collaboration with customers. Customer instrumentation will drive the functional requirements, pricing, and profit margins traditionally held and controlled by the technology providers. Those who best incorporate the financial modeling of the customers into their deliverables will have an enormous advantage over competitors, as the collaboration process will be highly comprehensive, ongoing, and quite fast once engaged.

Return metrics mandated by customers will be formatted primarily in monetized terms such as amortization schedules—in other words, an estimation of when the advantages have paid off the costs. While the trend to include nonmonetized measurement criteria such as "employee satisfaction" will continue, they will be increasingly linked to monetized values. The lifeblood of businesses that exist for profit is, after all, profit.

Vendors and integrators that adopt this strategy will not only satisfy important financial models, but the quality of the deliverable will be of an operationally superior system. Design, deployment practices, and maintenance will be more closely coupled to the business problems originally posed. The CIO will then be better served by integrators and equipment suppliers on two fronts: the financial return modeling and operational superiority. There are few faster ways to lose money—from the technology provider and also the end customer—than to spend enormous cycles debugging

IT equipment at a customer site. It happens far more often than those outside the IT industry might think.

The driving force going forward for improved value propositions won't be pure customer satisfaction, though; it will be the "C suite"—CIO, CEO, and similar—mandate to meet increasingly stringent investment return criteria. The metrics required by top and midlevel executives and managers will become increasingly granular and specific. There is no greater drive in a well-run business than to improve insight into operational processes, costs, and the specific value each IT investment brings to the corporation. These insights have a major impact in profitability and other key performance metrics such as inventory turnover, asset utilization, and cash flow.

Typically these analytical tools will originate from the finance and project management departments, which use increasingly advanced tools to determine the value of IT contributions. Importantly, this data will be delivered to not just to the C suite, but across all stakeholders who are part of the IT major projects team. The primary metrics of those tools will be increases in operational efficiency and reduction of operating expenses.

A considerable portion of this analytical tooling will come from suppliers outside the company, through industry expert consultants who bundle this expertise with the technology and systems integration. This is an early trend, but the few integrators providing this service are quickly gaining visibility and investment prioritization. It doesn't take a long meeting or many PowerPoint slides to demonstrate prowess in showing customers how best to use IT assets.

The publicly acclaimed alliance between Cisco and Accenture is a textbook example of this concept. Cisco is by far the dominant supplier of IT technology worldwide, and Accenture is a leading business consulting firm with a long and successful history of maximizing the value of IT investments. Other major integrators such as IBM and some of the leading midsized integrators such as INX and Perot Systems routinely include analytics as part of their offering to customers. Cisco also provides analytical tooling directly to some of its top customers through its well-known Internet Business Solutions Group (IBSG).

Many success metrics are used, of course, and they are not only industry-specific, such as reducing response time for emergency service providers, but corporate-specific as well. Most businesses within a common industry share most of the same success criteria—they're pursuing reasonably similar objectives and have reasonably similar deliverables. The difference is the general order of the priorities, the weight given to each of the priorities, and how well the priorities are executed. In some instances, it's about priority agility in rapidly changing scenarios, such as the release of a new and large request for bid. In other instances, the changes are slower but no less important, such as the identification of advancing or retreating markets.

Some businesses emphasize reductions in employee turnover, geographic expansion, or inventory turnover rates as examples of agility. One of the key aspects of corporate priorities is that few, if any, permanently reside at a particular level of importance. Business conditions and needs are dynamic and require an adaptive set of priorities.

A few priorities remain consistently near the top of the list, such as revenue growth and profitability metrics. Top priorities such as customer satisfaction and customer focus are a result of the hard coupling between those priorities and the lifeblood of a supplier—that is, sales and profit. Very few, if any, businesses rely on the ineffectual metrics of the late 1990s, such as "stickiness" and "eyeballs." These various types of success metrics and their corresponding value propositions are detailed in Chapter 5.

Growth Drives Progression and Instrumentation

IT is rapidly evolving from a communications platform to a pervasive asset that enables precision-guided businesses success. As technology matures, it is increasingly well-monitored. This maturing process increases in measurement precision and accelerates proportionately with growth. The amount of data instrumentation now incorporated at various physical points in an enterprise class network is unprecedented, though this trend is still in its earliest phases. Endpoint devices such as temperature monitoring, weight, and time-at-station, for example, will reside on intranets used by those inside the company.

IT's evolution is driven by enormous increases in network growth. More specifically, it's driven by the enormous amount of IT assets currently in place and those planned for the future.

Intranets and the Internet

Intranets vary in size from a few boxes and some wiring and antennas in a small home office, to massive multibillion-dollar complexes that facilitate information flow in the world's largest companies. The Internet, the worldwide network that connects intranets, carries information from one distant point to another—from a mile away, to the other side of the world.

On the Internet side of the equation, regional and national IT infrastructure elements have been in place for nearly 20 years, predominantly deployed by the major service providers such as AT&T, Verizon, and other mobile cellular carriers. The growth rates in terms of new equipment sold to these major service providers is typically less than 5 percent per year over the last few years.

The following illustration shows a high-level map of a high-capacity network owned by a major Internet service provider (ISP); this affords a glimpse into the scope of one of these networks. Many such networks across the United States maintain connections to every continent, and are similarly threaded across every continent. Our planet is not only well wired, but the entire atmosphere is filled with wireless electronic information in a constant state of ebb and flow.

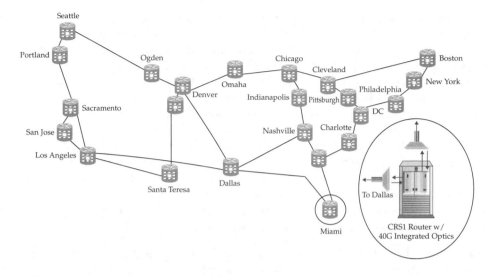

Internet Traffic Growth: Big and Really Big

Of course, the Internet will continue to grow both in capacity and speeds for the movement of information. However, the real growth of IT isn't in the huge "pipes" owned by the national players. It's the growth of the *intranet*, primarily due to enormous increases in the numbers of devices, types, and areas of coverage.

Overall network traffic estimates have been forecast by nearly every industry expert to continue to grow substantially. The following graph shows forecasted traffic increases for cable, wireless, and wired data. Notice the graph indicates the amount of data transmitted *per month*!

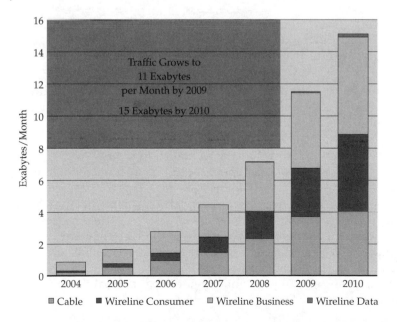

The data for this graph was compiled by Cisco Systems with information from Ovum, Gartner, Interactive Data Corp. (IDC), Merrill Lynch, Management Research Group (MRG), and Public Company Data. You'll note the data here is presented in *exabytes*. One exabyte is equal to five times the world's current printed matter. Five exabytes equals all the words ever spoken in all the worlds languages combined, according to a study by University of California, Berkeley. Although the UC Berkeley estimate has received some criticism, it remains beyond enormous and has been widely accepted.

Because Cisco equipment carries more than half of all the world's Internet and intranet traffic, the company has a vested interest in growth predictions. Much of the traffic growth at present is from social networking, video, and collaboration, the combination of which is termed *visual networking*. The Visual Networking Index (VNI) was created to forecast the growth and use of global Internet traffic. The scope of forecast is impressive and provides a general corroboration of the growth indicated in the graph (see www.cisco.com for more information on the VNI).

- Global IP traffic will increase by a factor of five from 2008 to 2013, approaching 56 exabytes per month in 2013, compared to approximately 9 exabytes per month in 2008.

- By 2013, annual global Internet traffic will reach two-thirds of a zettabyte (673 exabytes). A zettabyte is a trillion gigabytes.

- By 2013, the sum of all forms of video (TV, Video on Demand [VoD], Internet video, and peer-to-peer [P2P]) will exceed 90 percent of global consumer traffic.

- By 2013, global online video will be 60 percent of consumer Internet traffic (up from 32 percent in 2009).

- Mobile data traffic will roughly double each year from 2008 through 2013.

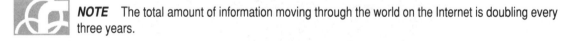

NOTE   The total amount of information moving through the world on the Internet is doubling every three years.

A highly relevant point with regard to mobility is that wireless traffic makes it onto the exabyte chart in 2009, and it increases significantly in 2010. The amazing part for those of us who've been in the wireless industry for decades is that at some relatively near date, very possibly in 2012, the amount of data sent over wireless will equal five times the total amount of printed matter in the world today.

The Cisco VNI forecast also features a second notable reference to mobility: the amount of mobile data traffic will double each year. This forecast refers primarily to mobile phone data traffic across the Internet, rather than traffic from devices such as handheld scanners and other intranet-based devices. With the aforementioned estimates by Cisco of endpoint device growth in the 1.2 billion unit range over the next several years, the amount of increased traffic inside corporations will be massive in comparison to today's network use.

My personal view as a 20-year industry participant is that the growth forecasts are conservative, because few "big picture" analysts observe ground-level developments inside corporate networks—an incoming tsunami of data generated by more than a billion devices as small as a thumbnail and as large as a handheld scanner. Individually, their traffic contributions aren't that large, though many deliver flows of information in the kilobyte and megabyte range, and some much larger.

While most of this traffic won't make it onto the Internet, the buildouts on intranets will continue to be substantial. The infrastructure buildout required to connect and support those devices in the United States alone will be in the tens of billions of dollars for hardware and two or three times that for design, deployment, and maintenance engineering services. An important perspective is that CIOs spend far more time managing intranet developments than the Internet at large.

It's appropriate to debate matters such as Internet growth, though I discount the pundits who claim Internet traffic growth is slowing. It may vary in how much growth is occurring over a given period, but the larger trend is fairly clear for most to see. Few IT industry critics have been close to where actual equipment was sold, deployed, and maintained. The industry has always moved forward in surges, and the occasional growth or even modest retraction has and will be driven by macroeconomic scenarios. But even in the worst of economic times, no business rips out its IT assets to save money.

While we can honestly debate growth rates, it's pretty hard not to see the long-term trend ahead. Once initiated, instrumentation has rarely, if ever, regressed to a simpler state, regardless of what is being measured. Instrumentation complexity parallels or exceeds macro growth trends. Connecting that instrumentation is the basis for the evolution of the network, not just as *a* platform, but *the* platform for precision-guided business management. The question that should generally settle the debate of growth or no growth is this: Are intranets in the aggregate and the Internet itself vastly larger than they were ten years ago? The answer is self-evident. The next question, whether they will both be much larger at the end of 2020, can be answered thus: Most certainly.

Intranets Are Growing Faster

Yet another vista worth considering is about how much traffic crosses long distances via the Internet. It's generally accepted by IT professionals that more information is generated and retained *inside* a corporate network than traverses *between* corporate networks and the world at large.

Most corporate information is retained inside a business for a number of reasons—confidentiality being one of them. Most information sent to or arriving outside the business intranet is information supporting existing processes, summaries of processes, or communications to sustain the business, such as payment of the electrical bill, requests for outside maintenance, and management of assets such as route maps for delivery drivers.

It follows, then, that that most of the Internet traffic growth will come from new data generation points within intranets, largely for improving business management. While microwave and other wireless devices will continue to be part of the Internet backbone for many years, and an important part of the voice-landline backbone for many decades, the intranet has been the home for enterprise-class wireless mobility solutions.

Evaluating enterprise networks reveals an interesting distribution of devices. Warehouses and retail floors have three to ten times as many wireless handheld devices as access points with which they communicate. It's been that way since around 1995. And the area of greatest growth now for data-point gathering devices is in healthcare and manufacturing.

Projected growth in the number of endpoint devices is colossal; in fact, most estimates in the IT industry place the estimated incoming new devices at 1.2 *billion* during the early years of the new decade. Virtually every business system known will expand to include sensors in places such as smart buildings, inventory management systems, and transportation platforms, from pallet jacks, to railcars, to jumbo aircraft. IT assets will mature to something completely unrecognizable from the original systems initially deployed for e-mail, then web browsing, and then the incorporation of all major business data systems.

This long-term growth, most of which will occur within corporate intranets, will drive unprecedented levels of instrumentation tools that allow businesses to evaluate IT investments provided by equipments vendors and integrators.

Impact of Device Proliferation

It doesn't take a large influx of data measurement devices to improve business analytics in a major way. Even using a wireless handheld device with voice recognition will improve productivity for a single warehouse worker by 10 percent, according to John Sweitzer, Alliances Manager at Intermec, one of the world's leading wireless handheld device companies. In a normal work shift, that adds up to about 48 minutes of additional productivity. The following graph shows that about 60 percent of businesses that incorporate speech recognition technology into their warehouse operations experience at least an 8 percent productivity increase (courtesy of the ARC Advisory Group).

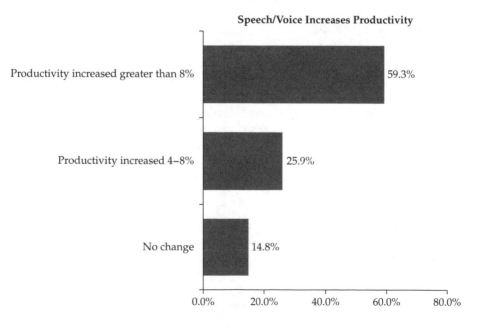

Speech/Voice Increases Productivity

Multiply that productivity gain by ten—an average number of workers in a warehouse—and it's like gaining an extra person on the crew. Additional advantages are factored in consideration of the point that this "extra person" doesn't require the expense of healthcare, vacation days, and training. Investments in devices such as handheld laser scanners also enable significant reductions in errors and rework. Handheld scanners often cost approximately $2500 each, although in some verticals such as healthcare or the auto-rental industry, they are commonly in the $7000 range. Even with their wide range of costs, the productivity enhancements they afford pay them off in 6 to 18 months of use. The percentage of devices that recover more than their cost in less than a year is shown in the following graph (courtesy of ARC and Intermec Technologies).

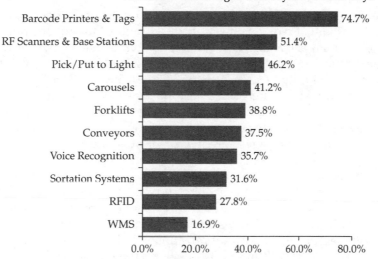

Warehouse Technologies with Payback Period <1 yr

From Data Pipes to Analytical Potential

Wireless sensor networks and unified communications will drive network evolution from *data pipes* to *computational grids*. As you learned in earlier chapters, mobility enables access to real-time information with minimal regard to an endpoint's physical location. As information continues to be accessed over time, the need for that which is accessed also evolves, from pure data to analytical and computational data. This evolution is why the CIO, IT integrators, and equipment providers will necessarily expand discussions from pure engineering to *analytical potential*.

An example of this is readily found in the evolution of the mobile cell phone. It has evolved since the 1980s from limited and expensive connectivity, to what we see in smartphones today. Using my smartphone, I can now stand anywhere in most cities and not only find a good restaurant, but exactly the kind of food that suits my mood, and I can prioritize the list of restaurants according to distance, the healthiness of the food, and even whether I have a coupon for them. Not only can I easily get driving or walking directions to the establishment of my choice, but in many cases, I can view an image of the inside and front of restaurant, as well as a 360-degree view of the environment outside the restaurant. Of course I can also make a reservation, evaluate the menu, and even place an order in advance if I'm in a hurry.

This remarkable achievement is enabled by many collaborations, including those between the manufacturer of my smartphone, the service provider, the restaurant, the company that lists the restaurant information, global positioning providers, and one of the largest search engines ever devised, Google Earth. While a meal is important and interesting, a computational grid and analytics are vital, for important data businesses need to capture and manage as much market share as possible, in the most efficient and cost-effective manner.

Smartphone search capability is an excellent example not only of a computational grid and analytics, but also of the power of collaboration. Smartphone purchases in 2009 remained a small percentage of the overall mobile phone market, at 16 percent; however, some reports predict that smartphones will capture 37 percent of the cell phone market by 2014 (http://news.cnet.com/8301-1035_3-10415577-94.html).

While not everyone will purchase a smartphone, with more than 1.5 billions cell phones in use today worldwide and with something less than 7 billion people on the planet, the marketplace is surely near a saturation point. Using a smartphone for day-to-day needs, such as for finding a restaurant, is of far more interest to users in the general market than any considerations of handheld features or aesthetics, assuming the cost of ownership is similar. For business users, the migration to smartphones is dramatic and sweeping; computational grid capability and analytics are far more valuable and compelling for that group of users than the lowest monthly fees or fancy apps.

The wireless network platform has become mission-critical for measuring data points such as inventory, for energy optimization in buildings, and for location and use of key corporate assets. It's inconceivable that a business would regress from using these devices to using clipboard, pencils, and blank forms piled high in in-boxes. In the future, it's just as inconceivable that enterprise network users would revert to simple cell phones instead of the smartphones and other intelligent, highly connected wireless handheld devices available in the marketplace today.

Cash Flow and the Demand for ROI Specifics

According to a May 2009 study completed by Discover Credit Card (www.discovercard .com/business/watch/), about half of small to medium-sized companies have endured significant cash-flow shortages—the highest recorded amount in the preceding three years. Relevant to the IT industry, this group of businesses represents the vast majority of the customer base. A large percentage of IT product development is also aimed at this market space, which means the IT industry is placing large bets there for the near future.

This situation is challenging because these companies are affected the most by the nationwide credit crunch. A shortage of cash is compounded by a general inability to borrow through short-term crunches. Cash-flow weaknesses often extend to weak balance sheets, which can be accurate predictors of a company's future. It's an irony that companies with the weakest cash flow and balance sheets would benefit the most from using the network as the platform for precision-guided business.

It can be argued that many troubled companies are compromised by a lack of information assets and knowledge of how to use them. Shrewd and steady corporate management can steer a ship away from the rocks, but regardless of how good a management team is, it needs instrumentation and business intelligence to navigate the way. The best management teams use these tools to the greatest advantage. While no company rips out its IT investments in even the worst cash-flow situations, it's quite common to see management make the wrong investments while under corporate stress. The better a management team uses its analytical assets to draw a line from where it is to where the money is, the shorter the recovery phase.

It's likely that a significant portion of small and medium-sized enterprises will continue for some time in a tight cash-flow phase. Part of this results from an excess reliance on a credit-based operation, and it's not realistic to expect the United States and the world economy to shift rapidly from credit-based operations to a cash-surplus basis. Most companies and customers will continue to rely on credit for most of their transactions, including corporate investments such as those in IT.

There is more risk now than at any time in the past few decades that any failed investment made by a business could prove the undoing of the entire business. Return on IT investments in a cash-strapped company is profoundly mission-critical. Collaborating across the entire supply chain and using mobility-enhanced IT assets to maximize the network as a precision business guidance platform are more essential than ever. When a company thrives, the effects are far-reaching, even to professional and personal lives, and the line from the existence of an automobile manufacturer to the purchase of a toaster is straighter and shorter than you might think.

When the macroeconomic cycle improves, which will free up credit, few businesses will discard practices that ensure maximum cash flow. Therefore, how the cash flows on a return basis from a technology will be important well past the short-term credit and cash-flow crunch. Technologies such as wireless that offer the largest and earliest return *and* resolve the largest operational problems will receive a priority ranking for deployment.

Hence, those system integrators (SIs) and vendors who most carefully and clearly model *exactly* how and when a wireless technology will pay off will retain a priority position in receiving revenues from their customers. Technology vendors and SIs that stumble when asked how their approach is more beneficial than that of their competitors, will finish behind those that can tightly link technology to the business problem being resolved.

A performance premium will be enjoyed by technology providers who can take the additional step of demonstrating how their deliverables provide actionable information to their customers. Technology is important, and even mobility is important. But they're only a medium through which management can acquire business guidance through impactful, real-time information made available to every stakeholder with minimal consideration to physical location.

In all but the largest competitions for IT contracts, finishing second means ending the competition with no financial reward. This is worse than simply losing a sales opportunity, as a direct cost is associated with competing for contracts and opportunities. Therefore, when a company finishes behind the contract winner, it's commonly worse for the company than if it did not compete at all. IT technology suppliers are often in about the same financial shape as the customers to whom they are selling—that is, there's not much margin for error. The ability to model accurately when and how an IT technology will work in regard to the cash flow and profitability of a customer will also benefit not just the end customer, but the suppliers themselves.

CIO Priorities

The CIO and/or CEO of a well-run company can quickly list the top three operational issues of their company. In stark contrast, very few IT equipment vendors or SIs are aware of these priorities on even an industry level, much less for a specific corporate entity. Most equipment vendors provide equipment that's "horizontal," which means it's designed for use in any industry, as opposed to a "vertical" industry that is more specific, such as manufacturing, education, or healthcare. Leading integrators are typically much more versed in certain verticals, primarily in education and healthcare.

IT vendors and SIs would do well to understand the top operational priorities of a specific business and industry. Improving business efficiency is a never-ending task, and the vendors and SIs who best resolve these issues for the customer have a significant competitive advantage over those that sell boxes versus solutions. In this case, I am referring to business solutions, not compilations of IT architecture.

Understanding a customer's top business priorities is fundamental to the quality of the network deployed, because operational problems can be neatly developed into functional requirements that the technology must provide—such as "pervasive voice quality WLAN coverage," for example. That statement alone would enable an enterprise wireless engineering team to assemble the entire deployment sequence from design and onward through audit, certification, and final delivery. Functional requirements are the launch point from managers to engineers.

Following are the top three operational priorities at most enterprise-class companies:

- Real-time and predictive business analytics
- Collaboration tools to break down group silos
- Operational efficiency improvements

Nearly every major effort to improve business operations falls under one of these three focal points for the executive management of an enterprise company. (It can be rightfully argued that the real list of concerns of a corporate executive is far broader than this, but this is the IT-centric version of the list.)

Profitability is the lifeblood of a business, for if a business spends more money than it generates, it cannot survive for long. Productivity, business velocity, and time to market are dependent on the performance of analytics, collaboration tools, and improved operational efficiency, or reduced time to market. Of the three primary operational focal points—analytics, collaboration, and operational efficiency—perhaps none of them is more critical to perform consistently well than analytics.

Real-Time Business Analytics

Analytics are generally no better than the quality and age of information. It takes an exceptional analyst to overcome poor data. Perhaps nowhere else is the value of wireless mobility more relevant in the corporate enterprise. The concept of "flow-based control" means monitoring, in real time, how inventory and assets (including the most important asset, personnel) move from receipt to shipment. This is true whether the product is information or the service is housekeeping.

The better the real-time image of a company's inventory and assets, the better the management will be able to use this information to the maximum advantage of the company. Having assets in motion is essential to a healthy and profitable operation. The fundamental concept of a business is to intake resources, alter them, and send them out to the next user. The more accurately this process is measured and managed, the more efficient (profitable) a business will be. Connecting this information with the balance of the supply chain is essential, both upstream where raw materials are sourced and downstream so the business can more accurately manage when and how much it will be paid.

Automated flow-based control means that a manager does not need to stand on the loading dock or personally count every product coming off the assembly line. No longer does a salesperson or contractor need to make the long drive back to the corporate office or library for critical information. No longer does a manager need to travel considerable distances on foot or by vehicle to approve work properly completed. Managers and staff can manage their workloads from any point at which wireless connectivity is available.

Mobility enables this by enabling sensors to rove with people, locations, or equipment. The latest generation of forklifts, as upgraded by Intermec to include a variety of wireless devices, is an excellent example of this and is shown in the following illustration (courtesy of Intermec, Inc.).

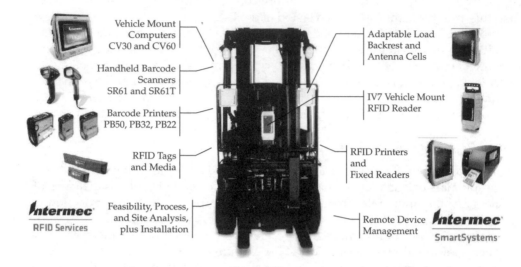

The most valuable asset in business is, of course, people. Enabling personnel to be in the right place at the right time, to perform the right operation, is an enormous competitive advantage. The concept of mobility in this light is something to which we're quite accustomed. What doctor, salesperson, or professor works without at least a mobile cell phone? Virtually all employees covering any distance beyond that of a single room rely on wireless connectivity to guide them to the right locations at the right times. The current generation of smartphones commonly include global positioning systems (GPS), calendars, and collaboration tools such as WebEx, which enables teleconferences almost regardless of the individual's location.

Placing static sensors in businesses such as manufacturing and warehousing is good business. It's even better to use dynamic sensors that can move about. This maximizes the flexibility of a facility, which drives efficiency. Very large incoming inventories may require extra room, and incoming materials requiring special handling or processes that are quickly accommodated reduce investments in infrastructure such as extra buildings and handling equipment. Mobile sensors can be embedded in industries outside manufacturing and warehousing, of course, and include healthcare, retail stores, and transportation. Many of these are small businesses, which routinely use mobile technology such as scanners and voice devices.

Bringing the network to materials and people in motion is part of a much larger connectivity trend that brings elements together in a new format. Examples include bringing education to people across the country or around the world instead of requiring that students enter a physical building on a dedicated campus; getting weather reports from your smartphone instead of waiting for the 6 o'clock news and weather report on the television; and bringing healthcare information to patients instead of requiring that patients visit clinics or doctor's offices to get information on the side-effects of prescriptions, for example. Mobility enables the IT platform to be brought to the inventory instead of processing the inventory through machinery or other portals. This is flow-based control in its most efficient variant.

Predictive Analytics

The better the *predictive* element of flow-based control, the easier it is for management to make the right decisions in the right time frame, consistently, and with error-free velocity. A good decision is a correct one made on time; a better decision is a correct one made ahead of time.

Mobility is exceptionally valuable in this regard, because it offers considerable time-savings by bringing the network to managed business elements, such as inventory, instead of the other way around. Mobility assets such as wireless sensors and handheld devices such as laser scanners and smartphones are essential in providing forward-looking estimates to managers and executives.

Following are five rationales for using predictive analytics:

- It enhances decision-making at the point of greatest relevance within the company.
- It reveals hidden information.
- It reveals advancing or retreating conditions—that is, trending.
- It increases return on IT investment and mobility assets.
- It provides inexpensive modeling for future conditions.

The primary role of predictive analytics is to make advance adjustments at the operational point of greatest relevance within the team or company. A good example of this is the purchase of jet fuel for commercial aircraft. Jet fuel is often purchased well in advance and carefully timed to take advantage of alternating market conditions. Even small savings at the gallon increment of jet fuel aggregates to one of the largest single expenditures for commercial aviation companies. Analytical guidance helps govern the timing of market conditions that alter jet fuel pricing. The computational grid element also plays a role when fast-breaking news is incorporated, such as a refinery fire, a terrorist act, or the discovery of a new, rich oil field. Purchasing agents for the airlines have the option of fine-tuning contract timing, and fast-breaking news incorporated at this stage could likely alter not only the timing of a contract but also the total size of the contract.

Hidden information is often found through predictive analytics. Not all patterns repeat themselves, because new markets enter into existence and traditional markets evolve into something of either greater or lesser value to the company.

Indeed one of the uppermost concerns of a corporate executive is that of increasing both sales and profitability. Most C suite executives push for new revenue before they worry about profitability, especially in publicly traded companies. Growth is an important element to demonstrate to the market, because it can raise the price of the company's stock. The question is, however, where's the money?

The answer is more elusive than you might think. Although most sales executives are well resourced to track how much money is coming in, comparatively few know which verticals perform the best in which point in the macroeconomic or seasonal cycles. Fewer yet know how to improve sales yield by using IT assets for precision-guided sales efforts.

A recent analysis of a mobility partner with whom I work closely showed a market vertical generating much more in bookings than broadly believed by corporate management. In fact, the bookings generated in this vertical were nearly identical to those of another vertical undergoing considerable focus. Bringing this information to my client's attention, along with predictive analytics to indicate where this market was heading, were valuable to the client and impacted the company's plans. Sales yields are now expected to increase with this previously unknown opportunity.

Sales personnel work hard, and the best performers year after year tightly integrate market, customer, and product intelligence. Those elements require collaboration tools and excellent predictive analytics.

In warehousing, an interesting trend is that of ensuring the right number of personnel at the right place at the right time. In major warehouses, this is viewed as a fundamental element in supply-chain management. In numerous verticals, specifically retail, competitive advantage is tied closely with supply-chain management. In the very largest retail companies, supply-chain management is the major contributor to competitive advantage. Systems and procedures continue to evolve rapidly at the warehousing portion of those businesses to ensure that both inbound and outbound freight loads are handled with the greatest achievable speed and accuracy.

Simple predictive analytics guide retail supply-chain managers for the busiest season of the year. More sophisticated predictive analytics guide exactly how much inventory to purchase, where to best locate it, when to order it, and when to transition through the various transportation carriers including ships, rail, and heavy and light trucks, right down to specific pallet loads. The quality of life in most modern countries is affected to a greater degree by this efficiency than may be widely understood. The computational grid incorporates information on highly fashionable items such as toys and clothing, enabling the retailers to discover hidden opportunities for additional revenue.

Most markets, except for the very hottest expendable items such as fashion and high-demand toys, tend to exist over a period of numerous years. Few, if any, major markets remain stable in their consumption and output. This is what creates opportunities for companies in the supply chain and other market adjacencies such as maintenance, utilities, and labor. The predictive ability to match market changes is important for companies, and the role of predictive analytics, in part, is to provide optimal timing for corporate decision-making.

It's important not only to capitalize in a market that's on the upswing, but to retreat from a market at just the right time. This is often termed *agility* and in its newest variant, it means that companies are shifting from one vertical to another as macro conditions alter. Vertical agility ensures maximum revenue opportunities by ensuring output to healthy markets. By shifting priority targets in an agile manner, producers can more often maximize their output. Importantly however, retreating from declining markets reduces wasted cycles and excess inventory, and allows adjustments in expensive assets such as personnel to more lucrative opportunities.

Business investments are made with the intention of gaining something beyond the purchase value of the item or service. Because IT assets are major investments at the time of purchase, such assets are rightfully being carefully scrutinized. Most IT assets are significantly more expensive to maintain than they are to purchase, and maintenance cost management is a significant element of discussion between equipment providers, IT integrators, and customers.

The evolution from data pipes to computational grids enhanced by mobility highlights the value of an IT investment. The position of my employer, and certainly my professional and personal opinion, is that the entire viability of a business hinges not just on having IT assets, but in how well those assets are used. Predictive modeling resides on the IT platform, and many financial return models are commonly used in the IT market to measure in mobility, Voice over IP (VoIP), security, applications such as inventory management, and a wide array of many other IT technologies. IT systems are repositories for large amounts of highly valuable and highly relevant data.

What is becoming much better understood by top-performing companies is the value of this treasure trove of information on customers, market cycles, and costs of specific business initiatives.

Predictive analytics combine this information in a clear way to guide decisions executed in varying stages that begin early on and continue well after the event in consideration. This knowledge is precisely what major IT entities such as Cisco, Accenture, and IBM can bring to the end customer. It's interesting to note that relatively few customers are well acquainted with the size, scope, and relevance of their existing databases; predictive analytics offer a tremendous opportunity for the customer by applying existing, and, in some cases, new IT technology, to convert databases into accounts receivable.

Another virtue of modeling is that it's highly cost-effective, because it allows experimentation without the dedication of real assets. Numerous iterations can be assembled and analyzed with minimal expense and virtually no risk to the company. It's akin to betting with play money, except it involves an enormous number of players and rules that change with varying degrees of reliability, and it can be played in many different geographies that simultaneously interact at high speeds.

Velocity is an important element in both science and business. Being a first-mover offers a company the advantage of penetrating an expanding market first and acquiring the best of what the market has to offer by way of opportunity. First-movers can also inadvertently break the trail for others who will use even more speed and learn from the first-movers' errors. Modeling helps companies ensure an optimal ratio of risk and sustained reward optimized for a period of opportunity, which is rarely static or open-ended.

Opportunities vary in size, lead time, and complexity. Predictive modeling helps companies identify which opportunities to prioritize, thus helping them ensure maximum efficiency in sales, production, and service. Predictive analytical modeling also greatly compresses time; you can acquire real-time results from simulations that would take place over extended periods of time in the real world.

Computational grids provide intelligence from numerous data points, significantly augmenting "what-if" dynamics. Certainly, the role of the computational grid is essential in such cases, and even the best databases possessed by companies would be applied in real-world and updated conditions. The role of applying future possible conditions based on the latest information would largely come from outside the company, as past trends have varying degrees of reliability relative to future events.

An additional thought on predictive analytics: Incentives often drive behavior. Accordingly, coupling personnel performance increases with incentives has proven effective in the adoption of real-time analytics. The best performance changes are those that can be measured. These metrics are unique not only to each company, but often within given time frames as priorities are adjusted to meet dynamic conditions both internal and external to the team and company.

Computational Grids and the Cloud

Mobile sensor systems and handheld devices are at their most useful and powerful when they are part of a computational grid. The scenario of finding an optimal restaurant with a smartphone is truly much more about the computational grid than the smartphone itself. We can hold the smartphone in our hands and admire its aesthetics, but the device is essentially a point of convergence and a user interface for the more important deliverable: actionable information.

In business, ultimately, as with all computational grids, the best and final decisions are made by managers but are based on high-quality, real-time information that is accurate and provided with minimal regard to physical location of the endpoints, including the user.

While sensors and endpoints may reside at various customer sites, the numerous key data points reside in an array of locations, many of which are thousands of miles apart. In the smartphone scenario, grid elements are in the user's hand, at a mobile cellular tower hundreds of feet or multiple miles away, in the GPS satellite info sourced from satellites circling approximately 13,000 miles above the Earth, and in data servers at various locations inside and perhaps outside of the United States.

The power of a computational grid is that many of the endpoints reside in what is called "the cloud"—data facilities from small to massive that reside all over the globe. These data "clouds" are connected by the Internet, and some of the more forward-thinking observers say that it will contain all the data you'll ever need. My view is that although most of that speculation is probably true, in a business sense, and even largely a personal one, the Internet will probably not include all the data most personal and important to you. Most of our vacation pictures and journals, for example, reside on our home computers, although it's certainly evident that more of that is moving into the cloud as well.

My point, however, is that businesses have an enormously powerful array of assets they can bring to bear and which reside outside their company. Synthesizing that intelligence and sensor network with their internal operations is a profoundly powerful combination that creates the most clear and compelling predictive analytics. And this is not a new approach. These systems have been online for more than a decade in key markets such as financial, agriculture, manufacturing, and many others.

The case used to be made that it was prudent to move server farms off premises, primarily for costs reasons. The reasons for doing so now are far more about sourcing massive amounts of intelligence from expert sources than the cost of purchasing and maintaining a server farm inside the company. There isn't enough expertise or financial resources in any single company to assemble even a fraction of the information readily available in the cloud.

Consulting and IT

These predictive analytical systems are included as part of the services package sold by premier IT consulting companies such as Accenture and IBM. The concept of augmenting predictive operational software with expert industry consulting and cloud-sourced intelligence and services is one of the most powerful combinations in business today. The consultants assigned to support customers from these specialized IT partners feature degreed industry veterans who truly understand not only the customer's operations, but also the market at large. They also know how predictive analytics can be best deployed for maximum effect. Expensive, yes, but you get what you pay for and then some.

My firsthand observation of the approach of expert consulting that augments the traditional IT deliverable is very favorable. The engagement sequence begins with the "why" portion of the discussion. I have thought for years that this was clearly a preferable path to maximizing both mobility and general IT assets. You're likely familiar with the old saw, "If you don't know where you're going, any road will take you there." When mobility and IT engagements begin with engineering discussions before identifying which operational challenge is being addressed, and before ensuring that the coupling between the technology deployed and operational issue resolution is in place, most roads will do just fine. It's my front-line experience over most of the past 20 years that this occurs much more often than it should.

The migration of mobility-enhanced IT assets from data pipes to computational grids should be the top priority for businesses. The evolution of the network as the primary business operations platform is non-trivial. This evolution is hardly new but is gaining in momentum and importance. As evidence of this, consider the major public joint announcement made by Accenture and Cisco in February 2009. The objective of the joint partnership is clear, given the following mission statement on the Accenture website: "Accenture and Cisco formed the group to let companies take advantage of IT as a strategic asset to help them further improve business agility, reduce costs, increase revenue and deliver superior customer service."

The direct references to unified communications, data centers, and additional technologies such as Cisco's Telepresence make it clear that mobility extends these capabilities and is therefore an essential element of the deliverable. More important is the reference to IT as a strategic asset; in my estimation, it is *the* primary strategic asset of a business.

Collaboration Tools Break Down Group Silos

The power of collaboration is more than just a sound bite. The antithesis of collaboration is that of a "group silo." The result of operating within a silo is the modern-day equivalent of being marooned on a distant island. That is likely the fastest path to becoming irrelevant, and irrelevance is not a condition well tolerated in business. I have begun to see the fallout of some old school colleagues who have struggled with the concept of collaboration. In the starkest terms, some no longer have a position with my employer.

While we respect all individuals equally and respectfully at every point of their career, there is little doubt that the workplace today is far different than anything we've experienced in the past, and it expects more from its employees than ever before. Considering the demands on many corporate jobs, collaboration has become a necessity. In today's job market, those who thrive through collaboration are much more likely to be the top performers consistently.

It's my view that businesses that are unable to build and maintain a living network of intelligence and assets will be compromised in its ability to succeed in today's competitive world. And this is as true in the labor force as it is in the corporate office environment: communication networks are a fundamental part of virtually every describable job in today's market.

Many tools can be used not as just collaboration tools, but as a powerful medium through which corporate objectives can be advanced.

Social Networks: The Moonshot of Collaboration

An example of a powerful collaboration tool is social networking. It's a topic worth not just a chapter but an entire book, though I'll highlight only key aspects here. Its relevance to mobility and IT is that it has profoundly reshaped the world of collaboration. Social networking is incredibly useful because it allows you to find the right people, markets, and information in real time on not only a broadly scaled basis, but on a very tightly targeted basis through the use of filters. It's also the primary medium for professional exposure now, which is a key element not only of making these connections, but of becoming an active part of the web of connections.

All smartphones currently on the market have social networking applications either shipped with the handset or readily downloadable through sites such as Apple Store.

Qualcomm's head of European operations chipset manufacturing stated at the 2009 Mobile World Congress in Barcelona the company has incorporated specific features and technologies better to enable social networking connectivity via smartphone. Smartphones such as Apple's iPhone will automatically connect via Wi-Fi when within range of a wireless LAN both at home and at work. Most of networking site Twitter's uploading is by smartphone, and indeed with its 140-character limit per upload, it was designed from inception to be accessed wirelessly.

It's not an overstatement to say that social networking is the moonshot of collaboration. Nothing in the realm of collaboration rivals it in scope, adoption rate, and impact. Social networking is the single largest, fastest-growing change in the online world since the development of e-mail.

Expertise at social networking will shortly become as important to most workers as knowledge of standard programs such as Word, PowerPoint, e-mail, and Excel.

Growth statistics from Facebook are impressive with a look at six-month growth rates (www.facebook.com/press/info.php?statistics):

■ Fastest growing segment: 35–54 year olds at 276 percent growth

■ Second fastest growing segment: 55+ demographic at 194.3 percent growth

■ Third fastest growing segment: 25–34 year olds with 100 percent growth

■ Largest demographic segment: 18–24 year olds at 41 percent; notably down from 54 percent over the previous six months

The growth rates indicated by Nielsen NetView in March 2009 reveal similar growth statistics, as shown in the following table (from http://blog.nielsen.com/nielsenwire/online_mobile/twitters-tweet-smell-of-success/):

Rank	Site	Feb 08	Feb 09	Percent Growth
1	Twitter.com	475,000	7,038,000	1382
2	Zimbio	809,000	2,752,000	240
3	Facebook	20,043,000	65,704,000	228
4	Multiply	831,000	2,394,000	192
5	Wikia	1,381,000	3,758,000	172

Social networking brings two key elements to the work world: information repositories and real time news without broadcast media spin. For example, sites such as LinkedIn, which are depositories for resumes, may now be more often used for providing professional profiles than for their traditional use as a job search tool. I've used LinkedIn to prepare for key meetings; the information there helps me better understanding the backgrounds of personnel with which I'll be meeting.

Knowing the basic types of social networking sites, their purposes, and how to leverage them provides professional exposure, which lends credibility, and also, on the receiving side, in terms of gathering intelligence on markets, it reveals trends and fast-breaking news. The amount of information exchanging hands in social networking is overwhelming. Although a considerable portion of it irrelevant to the workplace, filters do exist, and by using them with some care, you can receive the right amount of information on relevant matters of interest. These filters play a great part in optimizing this powerful tool.

The CIO and the balance of the C suite are increasingly likely to use social networking as a source of intelligence. If you're scheduled to meet with them, it's possible, if not likely, that they'll check your credentials, blogs, and other online publications prior to the meeting.

Many business problems have already been addressed and resolved in whole or in part by other professionals and organizations, and this arena is particularly where the repository aspect of social networking is valuable. Tapping into these data warehouses is important and appropriate. For example, I learned a lot about social networking at a memorable "webinar" at work, which featured new media expert Brian Solis, who I consider one of the leading thinkers on social networking. It was his presentation on social networking that I learned not only how powerful it is, but how to maximize its effects in the workplace. While I've had my profile on LinkedIn for years, Brian suggested that we use LinkedIn as a source for improving our understanding of people with whom we work.

My friend John Yrigoyen of NEC Unified, one of Cisco's top IT integrators, also taught me a lot about organizing social networking sites to enhance my professional endeavors. In a webinar, John showed me, along with a group of peers, how to harness the power of an array of social networking sites and how to maintain them without spending too much time doing so.

John emphasized that it's vital that we understand that social networks are linked together by every powerful search engine on the Internet. The more we participate in social networks, the more prevalent we become in the search engines. That's a powerful concept to realize, and also a sobering one, because our uploads remain "alive" for a very long time within search engines. This is why you should post nothing that would compromise you, your company, or the industry in any way. Your virtual presence should have the same polish and audience consideration it would have if you were speaking to a large live industry audience.

The following illustration, included by permission from John, includes a slight variation from one of the slides he used during that webinar.

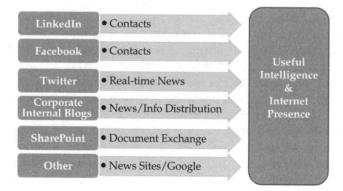

A particularly poignant moment in the presentation came when an audience member asked this question: "If you're doing all this to maintain your social network, doesn't it keep you from communicating with stakeholders?" John's response was a revelatory moment for many in the audience: "Actually, no. I use social networking to communicate with stakeholders."

Placing your objectives in the context of those you work with is an excellent communication technique. Knowing your audience is an essential part of any presentation. Reaching out to a group in advance of a meeting—at least by learning about the group in terms of performance, priorities, and achievements—will help you improve the quality of your presentation. For example, my manager and I share some common hobbies. We occasionally frame the reference of a focus issue in the terms of the hobbies we enjoy. Occasionally, a pattern within the hobby will be applicable to the problem at hand and can provide a key to the resolution. You can also reach out directly to a group by sending a very short questionnaire of two to five questions to prepare for a presentation.

Tools such as social networking, computational grids, and information sources for key issues are important, as is promoting corporate cultural change to embrace these tools. Developing expertise on an individual basis is something best led by a combination of willingness on the part of the individuals in a group plus exposure to mobility tools such as smartphones and voice picking, which allows workers to communicate with warehouse staff. As these great tools are understood, they can be quickly incorporated into day-to-day operations.

To extend the information network, a CIO can invest in mobile sensors, create analytics, and practice changes to bring the network to elements of interest such as equipment status and location, inventory volumes, environmental conditions within a building, and wireless video cameras for security monitoring purposes. Connecting the right combination of information sources with the right people in the right places in real time will help break down group silos. This specifically extends to incorporating powerful elements of the computational grid, such as social networking sites.

Most people adapt and improve over time because most people want to succeed. Collaboration and improvements are good things made much more possible by tools, policies, and perspectives that deliver collaboration, analytics, and positive change. When we improve in the workplace, we also take those skills and tools into our personal lives. We are therefore enriched by this at home as well as at work.

Improving Operational Efficiency

Efforts to reduce the amount of time and assets required to get a product or service to market are endless. Markets rarely remain static in their demands, in terms of volume, features, price, quality, and speed of delivery. Better companies move in harmony with macro market conditions, and the best of companies move in advance of changing external conditions.

Optimal timing in dealing with changing market conditions is difficult, because few future events are entirely reliable in their realization. Too long a lead time increases the risk of incorrect preparation; too little time to respond has its own apparent peril. Managing this timing is not an easy task, and schedule slippage is common.

Operational efficiency is the result of increasing profitability through cost reduction. *Efficiency* refers to a comparison of waste and velocity. Using wireless sensors and handheld devices enables companies to move the network to the element being measured in an efficient manner. By using agile sensors such as handheld scanners and smartphones, dynamic conditions such as inventory levels, location of personnel, and equipment condition can be more easily and quickly measured.

Operational efficiency can be significantly reduced when unscheduled events or other anomalies occur—from the production floor to the heavy duty environment of the mining industry. Consider the remote management of heavy equipment—a good example of managing operational efficiency by bringing mobility and the network to the equipment itself.

The concept of measuring vehicle dynamics is commonly called *telematics*. Caterpillar has incorporated this technology and connectivity into its equipment for years; in fact, I saw the first systems in development nearly 20 years ago. By including sensors in each piece of equipment and connecting these sensors to a network, Caterpillar enables fleet managers to monitor operations at numerous sites around the world via mobile cellular, satellite, ZigBee, WLAN, and other wireless links. Maintenance schedules can be included in management applications so that correct replacement parts are automatically delivered to the job site at precisely the right time to minimize the downtime of machines, which can cost hundreds of thousands of dollars.

The May 2009 *Government Fleet* magazine reported a case of a product fleet manager responsible for a massive Cat 5110 mining shovel (shown in the following illustration along with a sensor), who noticed an impending malfunction.

The malfunction was relatively minor in direct cost; however, it was affecting the machine's cooling system. The sensor network and wireless communications links provided critical information equipment status in real time to the fleet manager before any real damage occurred from overheating. Catching the malfunction and shutting down the machine before major damage occurred to the equipment saved the company nearly $100,000. Noteworthy is that these systems not only notify fleet managers of routine maintenance, but they can inform them of when critical operation parameters are exceeded. Preventive maintenance and the timely replacement of failed parts provides financial returns far in excess of the costs of the monitoring systems.

Managing the latency between when inventory changes condition or location and when the network is notified is an essential element of improving operational efficiency. Ideally, every significant change of status or location is recorded in real time. This is the prevailing principle of flow-based control: real-time management of assets in motion. Realizing and improving that capability is essential to steady improvement in terms of efficiency.

Operational efficiency now entails much more than flow-based control of the assets internal to a company. A company is considered an element of not just one computational grid, but many computational grids. A company is not part of one single supply chain, but many supply chains.

These days, smart CIOs spend as many cycles looking outward from their company as they do looking inward. They must realize the potential profitability that can be achieved by considering and making the best use of their company's role within the entire matrix of supply chains and computational grids. Successfully and consistently knowing where, when, and how to make the right investments, always within a limited budget, is a mark of the best CIOs. They must use and coordinate a wide array of IT technologies to maximize the analytical potential of the business world around them.

CHAPTER 4 | Virtualization and Mobility

Those of us who were present in the early days of mobile cell phones remember calling our friends and saying things like, "Hey, I'm calling you from my car!" Our friends and colleagues would be puzzled by that statement today; those born after the mid-1990s would likely think this statement very strange indeed. We have moved well beyond the point where mobility and Internet connectivity are novelties. It's easy to see that the world ahead will be far more connected in more ways than we can even imagine.

Virtualization has enabled what some are now calling *immersive networking*. The quality, pervasiveness, and reliability of mobile networking today is so good that we can now immerse ourselves deeply into the information provided by distant endpoints. It's somewhat like suspending disbelief in a good movie or book; you lose focus on the real world around you and begin to think in terms of the environment or information provided by the network endpoint with which you are connected. Could the connectivity today be much better? Of course. Will it improve vastly in the future? Very few doubt that.

While the incredible quality of sound and imagery afforded by the live pictures with Cisco's Telepresence systems are amazing and much better than HDTV or BlueRay, it will no doubt improve tremendously in time. Will 3-D images be the norm in the future? I believe they will. In fact, I spoke recently with developers of *4-D* animation—a system that will provide sensory feedback in terms of fragrances, and in some cases, mists and other tangible experiences directed at the participants. The reality of the technologies that will most amaze us in our lifetimes are barely even on the drawing boards, and the engineers who will bring them to fruition are probably not born yet. The best, most amazing, and most impactful technological changes are still ahead in our lives. It will be incredibly exciting to observe and participate in this.

Consider that 1000 Internet devices were in use in 1989—primarily e-mail reading devices for the newly launched MCI Mail system, and later followed by similar systems from OnTyme, Telemail, and Compuserve. By 1992, the number of devices exploded to 1 million as desktop computers began to be routinely connected to the Internet. In addition, the Worldwide Web rose meteorically, largely from the deployment of the Mosaic web browser. In 2008, the number of Internet devices in use was estimated at 1 billion. Connectivity is now as much about machine-to-human as it is human-to-human. And we are only now just beginning to become truly connected.

The age of exponential growth is well upon us. If, as many indicate, the amount of information on the Earth doubles every two years, this means that half of what a first-year college student learns will be outdated by their third year. Virtualization and mobility will, among many other things, drive collaboration and virtualization skill sets. For most of us in the industrialized world, we are very much connected; this can be a source of stress, but it can also be a very powerful tool that profoundly affects our quality of life. We can do so much more now than we could at any other point in human history.

The degree to which we can participate in the virtual world is proportional to how pervasive the network is and how well we untether one, both, or many endpoints of the networks around us. Virtualization is far bigger than the devices that bring information to us, because the value of what is delivered is far more important than the devices that enable it. This is partially why I work diligently to orient IT personnel to consider the value of what they're doing—in other words, to look way beyond the cost of an IT device to the advantages it will enable. (This set of value propositions and success metrics is the focus of Chapter 5.)

According to an IBM Global CEO Study (www.935.ibm.com/services/uk/bcs/pdf/the_r-o-i_of_globally_integrated_operations_-_white_paper.pdf) completed in 2009, the vast majority of business management executives have extensive plans and budget commitments for global partnership integration. In other words, stakeholders once unknown are now moving near the center of the decision-making processes. That an overwhelming percentage of managers in the IBM survey are involved in global partnerships is not surprising given the increased velocity of business; there is less and less time to recover from trial and error—and outright error.

In the larger context, it's important to recognize that the "why" of networking may be advancing even faster than the technical evolution. For example, networks are rapidly evolving from data pipes to computational grids, which rely heavily on both virtualization and collaboration to manage information, supply chains, profit, and competition. Computational grids, of course, extend well simply connecting network endpoints to the analysis of information from these numerous points of transmission and reception. While many endpoints are stationary, many others are in transit. Hence the essential role of mobility in this new evolution.

To virtualize is to gain the value of an interaction without being physically present. And the role of mobility is to ensure virtualization while in transit between two points. For the purposes of this chapter, the concept of *virtualization* is of particular interest to the world of mobility, because we gain acceleration and productivity by untethering applications and workers.

Virtual Meetings

The amount of time spent in meetings varies tremendously for workers, but clearly meetings have been a significant part of corporate life for decades. Microsoft released a 2005 study (www.microsoft.com/presspass/press/2005/mar05/03-15threeproductivedayspr.mspx) that indicated workers spend nearly one-third of their work week in unproductive meetings. Few, if any, reputable studies show a reduction in the amount of time spent in meetings since that time.

More than ever, projects are increasingly complex, expertise more varied, time more compressed. It's a positive development, therefore, that more meetings than ever are now virtual; collaborative tooling such as WebEx converts millions of travel hours to a few work hours. The productivity gain for this is enormous for businesses of every size. This type of virtual tooling dramatically reduces the expense, effort, and productivity losses caused by travel. In business and in work, mastery of virtual mobility tools is far more than a time-saver; it has increased productivity enormously.

Web 2.0 practices, WebEx, social networking, high-speed wireless connectivity, and virtual team meetings more than offset travel budgets, which are a fraction of those required not so long ago.

My story is similar to that of many others, though my manager has been insightful and well ahead of the virtualization curve. He has required that our team deeply embed virtualization and wireless tools into our daily work practices.

Of all the corporate and team meetings in which I now participate, few are live. This practice extends even to most of my external meetings. The notable element here is that although I travel only about 10 percent of the amount I used to, the key metric on which I'm measured—revenue generation—has not been reduced in the slightest. If anything, pressure has increased to perform at ever higher levels of productivity and impact. At many jobs, including mine, if you can't or won't perform at the highest levels, you will find yourself left behind at least, and released from the company at most.

During all this high-speed, highly complex, ever-changing activity, my physical presence at work is rarely imperative. It's routine for me to attend a WebEx meeting not only in my home office, but also with my laptop in my car while parked outside or near a Wi-Fi hotspot. Even better, I can also do this on my iPhone from almost anywhere, and I now do so routinely. My iPhone has also provided business resilience on the few occasions my home LAN has gone down. I have literally linked back into a meeting via my smartphone in less time than it took for my laptop to reboot from a blue screen. In my world, mobility has changed work from a location to an activity. It's also enabled tremendous productivity gains.

Because of virtualization and high-speed mobile connectivity, I now mix personal and professional meetings throughout my day. It's normal for me to participate in a wireless teleconference during my lunch break at a local restaurant. It's interesting to note that while I'm not physically present with my external contacts, I'm actually in much closer daily contact with them through wireless mobility and online tools such as WebEx. Given that most of my meetings involve a video element, my internal colleagues and many of my external colleagues can see each other. The personal touch is maintained in many instances, and in many other instances it has improved.

I routinely attend meetings with personnel across the country and in some cases from Europe and the Far East. On a recent work day, I resolved issues in four different areas of the major metroplex where I live. With equal ease, I also attended meetings with participants from Japan, Seattle, Boston, Raleigh/Durham, Grand Rapids, San Jose, Kansas City, San Francisco, and Los Angeles.

Ten years ago, I would have spent days on a plane and in hotels to achieve a fraction of what I now routinely produce. Instead of being worn to a frazzle from traveling to and from these global meetings, I spent the evening relaxing and laughing with my family. My productivity has improved, I'm less worn out, my employer saved thousands of dollars of travel expense from that day alone, our business partners retained their momentum, and, most important, I didn't miss family time. Virtualization with wireless mobility is a highly powerful business practice. What's not to like?

Virtualization with high-speed wireless mobility also provides an outstanding return on investment. For example, the list price of all the tools for my home office and my car fall well under $5000. My annual Internet and smartphone access fees amount to far less than that. As my home office features more than 10 Mbps of download speed, and my 3G phone can deliver speeds up to 3 Mbps, I can remain connected and working for a reasonable price.

Because my company pays a lot less than list price for equipment, especially for the network gear it provides to me, the actual cost of my connectivity is far less than the numbers shown. My *monthly* travel and expense budget alone used to be *multiples* of the list prices for the networking equipment in my home. And because of this connectivity, I'm far more productive and generate much more revenue for my employer.

This isn't to say that live meetings are a thing of the past. While incredible tools such as Telepresence do allow me to experience people's body language and other important nuances in a meeting, and WebEx allows me to collaborate on presentations, observe participants by video, and integrate with other productivity tools to reduce meetings and accelerate projects, there are certainly times when a live meeting is best.

Sometimes meeting in person offers more advantages than a virtual format. Live meetings are often the preferred medium when meeting key people for the first time or when negotiations are particularly fragile and require unusual levels of diplomacy. Ideally, a first meeting includes a meal, which in my experience strengthens and deepens relationships. And the time following a meal is often the best time to close a sale, resolve difficult matters, or expand professional relationships.

Perhaps person-to-person meetings are in line with an old proverb: "Business is socialization for profit." People often prioritize the needs of those they know best. In a business world, where most of what we accomplish comes through changing the behavior of those who do not report to us, building and maintaining a network of strong personal relationships is fundamental to success, velocity, and productivity.

All things considered, virtualization has not only saved my employer considerable travel expense, but it's also dramatically improved my productivity, saved wear and tear on me personally, and improved the quality of my family life. Mobility plays a mission-critical role in changing my work from a location to an activity. What's not to like?

Agile Workforces

Agile workforces are equally relevant to the concept of virtualization through business partners residing at various points regionally, nationally, and globally. Of the most common major industry types, not one has entirely sedentary workforces.

Agile workforces abound in healthcare, education, manufacturing, and retail, but they are also prevalent in every major industry type, such as the following:

- Kindergarten through high school (K-12) education
- Higher education (two- and four-year colleges and technical training schools)
- Healthcare
- Manufacturing

- Government (federal, state, local)
- Retail
- Professional services (doctor, accountant, and so on)
- Service provider (telephone and cable companies)
- Wholesale distribution (warehouses)
- Technical services
- Transportation
- Financial services
- Media/entertainment
- Hospitality/hotels and leisure

In many industries, mobility is mission-critical, and this is readily apparent in healthcare. But at least one industry, transportation, is all about agile workforces.

Where once laptops dominated as the mobile connectivity device of choice, smartphones are the norm in an increasing number of business meetings. Lugging a laptop to a meeting is less prominent than it used to be. I remember back in 1999, when people would arrive at meetings early to ensure that they could run an Ethernet cable to a hub. Conference and large meeting rooms sometimes had so many hubs and switches in place that the equipment fans' noise meant that the presenter had to speak more loudly. If you arrived late to a meeting, you didn't get to connect—it was a relief when our company deployed WLAN technology pervasively.

Mobile connectivity is not just handy; it's essential, as business cycles shorten and business velocity increases. Waiting to return to the office to plug into an Ethernet port is hardly an acceptable form of connectivity these days. And even wireless hotspots, though increasing in number, are becoming inadequate to meet the need.

Virtualization

Today, trade show presentations are conducted over smartphones that blend the realities of the trade show experience, the warehouse, and Internet channels. Virtual meetings include participants working from airports, offices, vehicles, and homes across the globe. With much of the virtual world falling clearly within the world of fantasy, such as that experienced in online gaming, the lines between what is virtual and what is real are becoming increasingly blurred.

In businesses and other operations, the concept of virtualization means quite different things to different people. Much of it relates to content servers that reside at a distant location, or services such as remote analysis, monitoring, and storage. As you read about virtualization and networking, you'll often see the term "cloud computing." Cloud computing describes a model for IT services based on the Internet and involves the provision of scalable and virtualized resources as a service over the Internet. A common cloud scenario is represented in the following illustration:

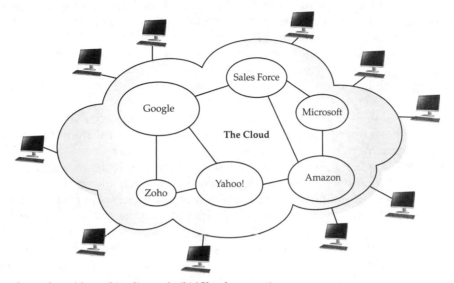

Source: http://en.wikipedia.org/wiki/Cloud_computing

Many IT experts believe that this cloud is an extension of an existing, trusted set of network endpoints. What's new is that the network endpoints may or may not exist within the intranet of the corporation at which the end users are employed. Several different types of clouds exist, depending on your industry view—but I'll leave that discussion to the true cloud experts.

It's not so much now about *having* IT assets; it's more about knowing *how to use* assets. Indeed, the concept of having assets is changing rapidly through virtualization. If you think about it, what businesses truly want is information, not IT assets. The network is the most critical platform in business today because it connects and enables every essential business decision—from intelligence gathering on market conditions, to real-time analytics, to managing inventory levels, equipment status, and lead times. There is little serious discussion as to whether or not a company, from the smallest boutique to the largest multinational conglomerate, will be online. Yet, the IT investment remains a business adjacency, in spite of its rightfully acclaimed mission-critical nature. Ironically, it's primarily an adjacency even for IT equipment suppliers; while my company and its competitors commonly use new IT developments in-house before selling them on the open market, we're not directly *about* IT ownership—we're about selling it to ensure customer profitability.

The issue of core versus adjacent business interests drives the issue of IT ownership. And core versus adjacency fuels the discussion and strategy of virtualization in any business.

Ownership of IT assets will not shift en masse from the current owners to virtual or third-party owners. There's simply too much legacy IT already in place. Consider, for example, Cisco Systems, which sold $165 billion worth of IT product and services worldwide since 2005. Cisco has a worldwide IT market share of 60 percent, and the amount of IT and services sold worldwide by all vendors combined approximates to $275 billion over the last five years. The conversion of that much IT ownership to third parties is not tenable by any reasonable thought.

Most analysts and IT blogs are more or less aligned in their belief that within the next couple of years, cloud computing will make up approximately 25 percent of all IT spending. With limited exception, most believe the trend will increase in size and relevance.

It's my opinion, for example, that traditional news services aren't much more accurate than most blogs, which tend to forecast well ahead of the traditional news sources and use expert industry analysts. Analysts tend to carry more weight as trusted sources, even though, interestingly enough, they rely to a large degree on interviews with equipment providers and bloggers. Getting the most reliable and accurate forecasts is probably found in the synthesis of reputable bloggers, formal analytical companies such as IDC and Forrester, along with some augmentation from the major news wires.

The business, architectural, and usage implications of network virtualization are non-trivial. Architectures are evolving because intranets now reach deeply into other layers, from the physical to the application layers—in other words, the entire Open Systems Interconnection (OSI) stack.

Most information these days is gleaned by layering analytics from one intranet on top of inventory control systems in another. The idea is to get information to every device or person with minimal regard to the endpoint's physical location. How we incorporate mobility, security, reliability, and business resilience through redundancy is altering how we sell, incorporate, and use these complex systems.

Untethering network endpoints virtualizes not just physical spaces, but also the reception and transmission of information. This extends far beyond devices such as smartphones; the very sequence of connectivity has changed. We now bring education, healthcare, and business intelligence to people instead of the other way around. Work and information have changed from a location to an activity through a myriad of wireless sensors. Productivity, business velocity, and operating expenses have been significantly improved as a result, and we are just beginning to tap into this potential.

Business and Social Networks

This is not just about bringing remote endpoints within our virtual grasp; it's also about extending our physical presence to many other locations. The fact that we can have virtual presence in an unlimited number of locations is a highly powerful productivity tool.

Consider LinkedIn, a website where professionals can upload and share resumes, backgrounds, and professional profiles. At the time of this writing (January 2010), web traffic indicator Alexa (www.alexa.com) rated LinkedIn as 39th in the top websites on the Internet. The context of this amount of traffic is apparent when compared to the popularity of the following:

- Microsoft: 20
- CNN Cable News network: 60
- Wal-Mart: 200
- Cisco Systems: 1111

According to www.domaintools.com, approximately 111 million websites exist as of August 2009. Considering this number, it's clear how powerful business networking sites like LinkedIn really are. For example, I have about 90 direct contacts on the site—individuals with whom I'm linked. The linked contacts from my contacts number well over 21,000. The contacts of those contacts number well over 2 *million*. This means that I'm only one reference away from more than 2 million business contacts—far more than I can practically use. LinkedIn is a powerful tool for presence.

Now consider the social networking site Facebook, ranked number 2 by Alexa right now. I thought long and hard about joining Facebook; I did so to learn more about people I work with and to reconnect with old friends. The following statistics (from www.facebook.com/press/info.php?statistics, as of January 2010) are impressive:

- Facebook has more than 350 million active users.
- More than 120 million users log on to Facebook at least once each day.
- The average user has 130 friends on the site.
- More than 5 billion minutes are spent on Facebook each day (worldwide)
- More than 35 million users update their status at least once each day.
- More than 2.5 billion photos are uploaded to the site each month.
- More than 3.5 billion pieces of content (web links, news stories, blog posts, notes, photos, and so on) are shared each week.
- More than 3.5 million events are created each month.
- More than 700,000 local businesses have active pages on Facebook.
- About 70 percent of users are outside the United States.

If Facebook were a country today, it would be the fourth largest on the planet. Five billion minutes of Facebook user time each day equates to more than 40,000 *man years* of work. These numbers are simply breathtaking.

According to statistics (www.textmessageblog.mobi/2009/02/19/text-message-statistics-usa/), the number of text messages sent in the United States alone *each day* in 2009 was approximately 2.5 *billion*. More text messages are sent than phone calls are made; the average number of text messages per person in July 2009, for example, was 357 compared to 204 mobile cell phone calls. According to www.intomobile.com in a April 2009 report, more than 1 trillion text messages were sent in the United States in 2008. Even if this data were incorrect by a factor of two, it remains a staggering figure.

Virtual Presence: An Enormous Movement

So what does all this mean? It means that virtual presence through mobility tools such as text messaging and cellular phone calls is an enormous movement; it's larger than phone calls and much larger than live visits or business meetings. Consider that a large portion of that virtualization occurs through untethered means such as smartphones or access points. Virtualization is tightly coupled with collaboration, and if you're not involved and in possession of considerable expertise in collaboration, by the time you read this, your professional livelihood will be in considerable peril.

The workplace directory at work now allows employees to list various areas of expertise and interests. By simply clicking one of those areas of expertise, I can quickly connect to people who have information of importance to me professionally and personally.

I've offered three suggestions to my professional peers with regard to enhancing their virtual presence:

- List your expertise in your directory listing.
- Get listed on LinkedIn or a similar site.
- Learn and understand how to use social networking tools.

There are many other ways you can create and manage a virtual presence. I spend only a few minutes a day maintaining my virtual presence. Most of the real-time information, logistics work, and research on people, corporations, and trends I receive come from this virtual network, and it has become an indispensable tool.

Workforce Mobility in Any Work Environment

Changing work from a location to an activity affects far more workers than those of us who work at forward-thinking IT companies like Cisco Systems. Technology is a common element of many jobs today, including both blue- and white-collar jobs. Few workers are without cell phones or e-mail accounts.

For laborers in manufacturing, healthcare, education, and retail, interfacing wireless technology has become the norm. A voice-activated system enables managers to send instructions to workers on the spot. Consider warehouse workers, for example. Voice-activated inventory control, also known as "voice picking," provides a powerful tool that reduces errors and order turnaround time. It's easy for workers to use: they simply speak into the headset to begin recording information; the latest generation of voice recognition no longer requires a speaker to "train" the system to recognize their specific voice.

To use the system, the worker dons a noise-canceling headset and logs into the system with a password. The system accepts the password and automatically gives the worker their assignment, including location and inventory to select. As the worker moves the inventory, they read the labels into the headset microphone. The system will verify correct load and, if necessary, direct the worker to other locations in the warehouse for additional items. Productivity is improved when real-time assignments are sent to the worker by the system, and it also reduces the need for meetings at the beginning and end of work shifts.

One of the larger issues in warehouse management is employee turnover. Studies have shown that warehouses with better technology, including voice picking, incur less employee turnover. Turnover means workers must be quickly trained, and effortless voice picking can help achieve this objective.

In addition, worker injuries are reduced as workers retain a "heads up" position while performing their jobs. Barcode scanning, by comparison, requires workers to focus on the label placed on pallets and containers. The headset provides the worker with a broader range of vision.

Though the worker, of course, must show up for work, they can receive assignments while working anywhere in the warehouse, quickly find inventory, and do it all with far fewer meetings. Managers spend less managing workers so they can focus on other management issues. As fewer managers can manage more people, this efficiency helps drive down the business costs.

Many retailers and other commercial interests find a significant portion of their competitive advantage in supply-chain agility. End users are placing increasing pressure on suppliers of every type to reduce shipping lead times and errors. Voice picking, which relies on both unified communications (UC) and third-party application software, plus mobility, enables a better response to delivery pressures. It also offers cash-flow implications, as the more times an inventory turns over, the more revenue is generated for the supplier.

If we take this one step further, it's easy to imagine a centralized location or various remote locations for managers and other warehouse personnel to direct workers without being present in the warehouse itself.

Social Networking and Mobility

In my entire professional career, the fastest and broadest change I've ever seen has been the explosive adoption of social networking (SN). It has, of course, been around for several years, including common interest sites such as user groups for cars, sports, and other topics. In it's broadest definition, SN is an ecosystem of 20-plus *types* of websites that provide fast-breaking, crisp news and trending sites such as Twitter and Utterz; blogs (pick your topic); Wikipedia, the encyclopedia with contributions from experts within the public domain; image storage such as Flickr; professional networking sites such as LinkedIn; and video aggregation such as YouTube.

Brian Solis and Jesse Thomas assembled a broader version of the SN world based on an earlier version called the "Social Media Starfish," developed by Robert Scoble and Darren Barefoot. You probably don't need all of it, or even most of it, to gain maximum benefit from SN. The following illustration helps to demonstrate how massive this movement is (source: http://scobleizer.com/2007/11/02/social-media-starfish/):

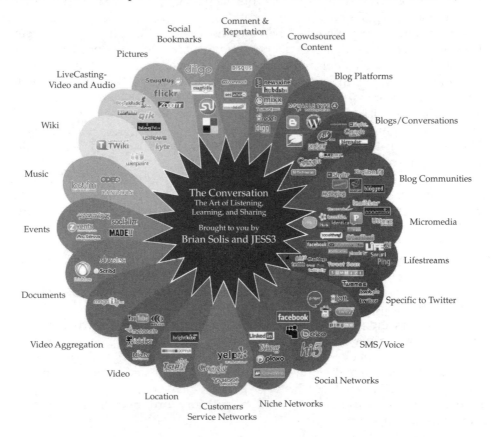

There can be little doubt as to the rapid adoption rate of SN sites, both for personal and professional uses. In 2009, www.mashable.com estimated that Twitter alone grew 752 percent in 2008, with well over 4.4 million unique users in December of that year alone (http://mashable.com/2009/01/09/twitter-growth-2008/). Twitter may be the most animated and broadly adopted form of collaboration. Millions of users contribute and/or spend time reading SN sites each day. The huge number of SN types and pages is indicative of the tsunami it has become.

Between the time I write this and you read this, much will have changed as to the names and importance of various SN sites. Hot sites today will become fads in a couple years, and new, relevant sites will appear that don't exist today. Nevertheless, collaboration is an essential practice in today's professional world, and SN is a way to do three things faster than ever:

- Catch fast-breaking news
- Track and monitor fast-breaking trends
- Connect with fellow collaborators

SN is helpful because it provides crisp bits of information—an important quality because of productivity pressures. Attention is the primary currency in the world of collaboration, so collaborators with the best information per the "three Rs" (Is it *Right*? Is it *Recent*? Is it *Relevant*?) are most valued. The best collaborators draw the best associations because people are attracted, of necessity, to those who provide the greatest value by being more "tuned in." Autonotification from SN sites will arm you with the best and most recent trending information and help you acquire late-breaking information in real time as events develop. By setting filters on your SN sites that will provide only trending and fast-breaking information relative to your needs, you have access to some very powerful data monitoring and harvesting tools.

I don't spend much time uploading SN information; I upload only the most valuable items relative to fellow collaborators. I don't want to trade the productivity I've gained with excessive uploading of quasi-useful information. It's a far more powerful practice to listen (or read) rather than upload copious amounts of material. I'm not advocating that you should not upload information, because the best collaborators give as well as take. But what they give is the product of what they've received, retooled with their contribution. It takes a lot more listening than transmitting to be effective.

The relationship between SN and mobility is profound; like unified communications, it's not the star at the center stage, but SN wouldn't be what it is without mobility. Ruder Finn released a study in February 2010 (www.prnewswire.com/news-releases/new-study-shows-intent-behind-mobile-internet-use-84016487.html) dealing with how people use their mobile phones. The study revealed that 91 percent of mobile phone users access SN sites versus 79 percent of desktop users. In fact, one in five people accesses the Web this way. This represents a 156 percent growth over the year 2008. And of course this trend is growing.

It would be very difficult to provide real-time SN breaking news from a scene, meeting, or event without a mobile phone. In my business life, I rarely bring my laptop to meetings anymore, except when I have to make a PowerPoint presentation. I migrated to an iPhone to upgrade my online access, to access SN tools, and to use applications that improve my quality of life, and I can do all this without lugging around a laptop.

(One notable user of SN is the Kogi taco truck in Los Angeles, which advises customers by Twitter 20 minutes in advance as to where they'll be stopping next. Customers arrive in advance at the site and grab a quick [and apparently quite tasty] meal. This is an easy venture for both the seller and buyer using smartphones.)

Many excellent smartphones are available, and the iPhone is simply one good choice in many. The key point is that if you haven't upgraded your mobile phone in the last two or three years (like me), you'll likely want to do so because you'll find the tooling has vastly improved. Companies of all sizes are filtering the enormous traffic on SN sites to find and market directly to customers. Considering the audience size and the specific targeting you can acquire through filtering and assembling followers who are customers, it's quite a phenomenon.

Borderless Networks

The ability to use SN and UC far beyond our traditional workspaces is a concept that has been dubbed by some as "borderless networks" and has greatly evolved over the past few years. In the past, few networks were deployed pervasively throughout a work facility, even in the healthcare industry, which was, in my opinion, the first industry to deploy Ethernet routinely throughout its buildings and campuses. This buildout was followed soon by wireless Ethernet, which of course became the 802.11 standard. In the most wired and wireless hospitals, as many as 11 different wireless protocols are employed, including the following:

- 802.11 (four protocols)
- Wireless medical telemetry (WMTS)
- Unlicensed 300 and 900 MHz
- Mobile cellular (six types)
- HART (Highway Addressable Remote Transducer)
- Zigbee
- Bluetooth
- Public safety radio
- Walkie-talkies

The concept of borderless networks goes well beyond simply removing geographical boundaries by carrying applications such as data, voice, and video over media from one endpoint to another, across miles, counties, and continents. It's challenging to state on a multi-industry basis as to whether more transmissions occur from licensed or unlicensed radios. That's really beside the point, though; most licensed radio frequencies (RF) cohabitate reasonably well most of the time—it's a foundational element of having a radio license in the first place.

The area of focus and concern is on loading a large number of unlicensed wireless devices in a common radiating space. Designs featuring lower output power along with better receivers and advances in optimal radio location points have enabled the tremendous amount of radio energy found all around us in modern urban settings. These systems work surprisingly well most of the time.

The issue going forward with regard to borderless networks is getting devices to use multiple radio frequencies and protocols elegantly and in parallel. We're accustomed to this already with the incorporation of Bluetooth devices into mobile cellular radios. Virtually every smartphone has global positioning service (GPS) incorporated as well. Even my car has five different RF spectrums or protocols: AM, FM, satellite (Sirius Radio), GPS, and Bluetooth. We should not be surprised, then, to see this concept expand into many more devices, thereby placing a single device onto multiple radio networks.

Most networking professionals who are pondering the concept of borderless networks focus more on the vision of connecting any device to any device, regardless of where the devices are located. The device provides a platform for an application. We generally care less about the technical merits of a smartphone than the device's ability to provide many applications to us in a reliable way. By January 2010, 100,000 applications were available for the iPhone (www.nytimes.com/2010/01/25/ technology/25apps.html). Hundreds of thousands of other applications are running on a seemingly innumerable number of devices at hospitals, manufacturing plants, vehicles, stores, and small businesses.

To enable this staggering plethora of useful software packages, we must install networks to transport these applications from one location to another. That's Cisco's *raison d'être*. We sell $40 billion in hardware and services annually in nearly every country on the planet. Build the network first, and wondrous things follow.

The network is a platform over which flows one of the most crucial elements of business: information. Every corporate process, policy, investment, asset, strategy, objective, metric, and communication flows over the network. Applications are carefully honed tools that provide specific kinds of information. At a higher level, applications serve as a way to maximize collaboration.

The use of these applications from device to device, regardless of location, is based on five key areas:

- The workspace experience
- The wireless network platform
- Third-party applications
- Technology partners
- Professional services

Borderless networks operate on the premise of converging on-premises wired and wireless networks, off-premises cellular networks, and long-range fiber networks, thereby enabling collaboration from any workspace.

Borderless networks are about maximizing collaboration. Enormously powerful ecosystems of tools, known collectively as social networking, provide highly valuable real-time information. They could not exist without networks evolving to a truly borderless condition.

Virtualization and mobility are augmentations of reality that add much quality to business and life. They don't replace reality; they expand it. They let us perform at far higher levels, enjoy a much richer and more healthy lifestyle, and affect so much more of the world around us. There are some who fear this; I say embrace it. We've been doing this a long, long time. Remember mail, the landline phone, radio, and television? They were but the earliest variants of something far more rich, far more connected and immersive.

See where it can take you in how we live, work, and play.

CHAPTER 5

Value Propositions and Success Metrics in Education and Healthcare

The concepts of *value propositions* and *success metrics* are so complex that an entire book could easily be written on each of the major 15 industries in which these services are applied. On the full enterprise-class side, only a few of the 15 leading verticals generate the bulk of the revenue generated by systems integrators and equipment manufacturers. More than $1 billion is spent annually in enterprise-class networks, with education and healthcare being the two largest verticals into which wireless systems are sold. This chapter focuses on these two industries. The value propositions and success metrics discussed in this chapter will help you expand the way you think about wireless beyond strictly a technological application to include the business implications of mobility.

Measuring Value and Success

The most successful engagements among customers, integrators, and technology equipment providers occur when business requirements are tightly coupled with the manner in which technology is deployed to address business concerns.

Industry equipment vendors and system integrators provide two major kinds of enterprise network account types: "value" accounts and "volume" accounts. The differences between the two are important: Value accounts are the major accounts that represent about 70 percent of revenues received from enterprise wireless engagements. Volume accounts are accounts of small office/home offices (SOHOs) and small and medium businesses (SMB). These smaller accounts represent about 30 percent of all the revenue generated by integrators and equipment vendors, but about 80 percent of the purchase orders—though the SOHO and SMB are much smaller, there are far more of them. Small business networks typically feature less complex architectures, fewer network nodes such as access points, and fewer clients such as smartphones and are therefore generally less troublesome to design, install, and maintain.

Historically, most integrators and equipment manufacturers have spent most of their customer engagements across all verticals, extolling the wonders of various technical protocols and their "speeds and feeds" data. Given the credit constraints of the macro market at this time, and perhaps more importantly for the long term, managers who have survived "the depression" tend to retain cash-flow retention practices learned during lean times. Cash-flow managers who survive significant downturns become more adept at ensuring returns on investments (ROIs) and the cash-flow benefits from those investments. They well understand the indirect dollar values and metrics for these investments: all are derived primarily from working with far smaller budgets while continuing to manage full-scale operations.

Value propositions and success metrics are essential to a manager who must make critical decisions based on ROI and benefits. A value proposition is a statement of *why* the investment is of value. Success metrics are the specific measurements of the value after the investment has been delivered. Both are important in an enterprise engagement, and they are interlocked. As integrators and vendors learn more about what their equipment and services can bring to end customers, the proposed value and the methodology by which the value is measured can evolve and improve.

The Value of End Users

Industry specialists know that it's far more likely that intriguing new uses for wireless systems will come from end users rather than the equipment vendors and system integrators. While some personnel commonly migrate between the three key business types—equipment manufacturers, system integrators, and end customers—specialists know that the experience of using the systems is deeper and broader when you live with it constantly as a primary element of your daily profession.

In the nearly 20 years I've worked in this industry, I can't think of a single case in which marketing and sales teams came up with a brilliant new strategy or use for wireless systems; the groundbreaking changes always came from end users. I'm confident that there are exceptions to this and that many startup companies were launched from new and clever ideas, but even after these ventures begin, the end users still evolve at a more rapid pace and continue to move ahead of even the most clever startup in terms of innovative applications of wireless and other IT technologies.

Measuring Vertical Solutions

Many of the key metrics for measuring value propositions are not initially indicated in terms of dollars, but using other increments of value such as lives saved, increased hours on the street (for law enforcement), and increased market share. Certainly these elements can be understood in terms of cash flow or pure dollar measurements, but the metrics used by major enterprise-class customers are often in terms most important to a particular vertical.

Value propositions often involve industry terms such as "shrinkage," which pertains to inventory loss through theft or damage, or "supply chain elasticity," which pertains to manufacturing and other verticals and refers to how suppliers respond to changing demands for products and pricing. It goes without saying that while many elements of both value and measurement are common across these verticals, such as productivity or operating expense reduction, many other value propositions and metrics are unique to a particular vertical. Understanding the context of information within a specific vertical is important, and it's why I've been encouraging integrators and equipment vendors for years to deepen their expertise in two to three verticals as opposed to broadly selling on an opportunistic basis to as many verticals as possible. I'm not suggesting we should abandon or ignore any sizable sale, however; I'm saying that most of the money made actually comes from only a handful of verticals.

Distribution of money generated from verticals is not at all homogeneous; some verticals generate considerably more than others. This varies from integrator to integrator, and of course from original equipment manufacturer to peer manufacturer. Being able to brand your business through case study–based deployments will accelerate the time-to-problem resolution at the customer level.

"Engagement drift" occurs when a sales team visits a customer and opens the entire portfolio of "what they can do for the customer." This approach can not only overwhelm the customer, but it can do the same for the team, as few sales teams indeed truly and deeply understand the technical, operational, and cash-flow basis of the everything in their company's portfolio. It's a far more effective and profitable engagement for an equipment vendor or system integrator to focus sharply on a handful of challenges within a specific vertical.

Technical solutions are horizontally oriented. The same group of products will work just about as well across nearly every industry vertical. Wireless remains wireless, routers and switches perform the same tasks, and so on. Value propositions, however, are vertically oriented; in other words, they address and satisfy very specific problems and challenges within very specific industries. Understanding the primary value propositions and success metrics in the top industries is not just the responsibility of the equipment vendors and system integrators; it's more particularly owned by those working within the vertical itself. Resolving inventory shrinkage in a hospital is the problem of each particular hospital, and the integrators eventually learn how to resolve those issues. Equipment vendors in and of themselves rarely design "box-level solutions" because "the boxes," with rare exception, are designed to resolve vertically oriented problems. Of greater value is the general technical architecture of the solution with regard to a specific vertical; the value proposition is exceeded only in value by the success metrics, because that is the element that not only assures the value proposition, but leads the evolution of the value proposition, the architecture, and box-level features.

The "IT Value Matrix" shown in the following illustration demonstrates the relative value both to the vertical industry and the broad horizontal array of industries in general. The matrix shows that the lowest values are placed on "box-level" features because they are the least adept at resolving industry problems that are specific and tightly confined to a particular vertical—such as healthcare, education, manufacturing, or retail. The highest values on a vertical basis are reserved for the value proposition and the success metrics.

IT Value Matrix

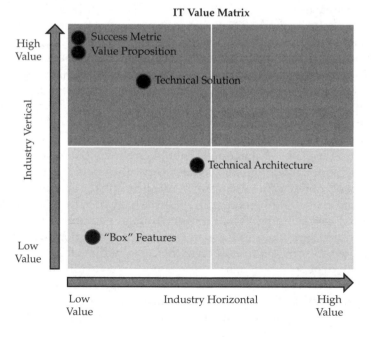

It is telling that most sales personnel, from both equipment manufacturers and system integrators, generally focus far more of the engagement on box-level features than value propositions and the success metrics that ensure them. The best companies, however, such as Johnson Controls, Accenture, and a small handful of others, not only prioritize the value propositions and success metrics but offer highly evolved financial models to forecast and assure the value propositions. They also offer something else that affords them tremendous advantages over competitive sales teams that sell box-level features: fiscal guarantees of performance.

The purpose of this chapter is to illuminate some of the most relevant value propositions and success metrics for the verticals, which generate most of the revenue for wireless equipment manufacturers and system integrators. While I'm not aware of a study that corroborates the revenue generated between wireless sales and sales for other technologies, it's been my anecdotal experience that they are more tightly interrelated than broadly understood. The verticals that are universally most recognized as the predominant verticals in the wireless large area network (WLAN) market may well be the most key verticals for sales teams who sell core technologies such as routers and switches as well as sales teams that provide advanced technologies such as wireless, voice, and digital signage.

Education Priorities

The education vertical is divided into two primary subverticals: K-12 (kindergarten through grade 12) and higher education (two- and four-year institutions). Many educational verticals cross over into other verticals—for example, the cafeteria in a school could be categorized as either retail or education, depending on the definition of the vendor or equipment manufacturer. Training centers for a major business are often grouped in the educational vertical as are some child day care centers and athletic training institutions.

K-12 Education Value Propositions

K-12 education has three overriding priorities:

- Smart classrooms
- Smart administration
- Safe schools

Smart classrooms are powerful assets for scaling both teachers and the education experience for the students. These highly evolved, modern-day versions of the schoolhouse provide an educational experience with great impact and velocity. The smart classroom features two primary multimedia interfaces: the interface between the students and the teachers, and the interface that occurs between the class and the Internet at large. The following value propositions offer examples of how this can be best accomplished.

Following are the value propositions for the K-12 space:

■ Wireless interface for students and teachers

■ Connectivity in the classroom

■ Student, staff, and visitor identification and access

■ Tons of paper to gigabytes of data

■ Web access for learning

■ Wireless video surveillance

Wireless Interface for Students and Teachers

By connecting the students to the teacher with multiple wireless technologies, a teacher can provide a richer and more interesting and comprehensive educational experience for the student through graphically rich media such as video, interactive devices, and remote learning. Students accelerate the rate at which they learn when the tools are more interactive.

We've come a very long way in education since I was in the K-12 system. Back then, nearly all of the information was presented by the teacher using voice or blackboard. It was a special treat to have filmstrips in class, manually rolled forward by a lucky student, and typically accompanied by a phonograph record for the soundtrack and a "beep" to indicate when to move the filmstrip from one image to the next. Of course, books were used as well and remain important today, although they are used primarily for homework as opposed to providing content in a live classroom setting.

According to a study and comments at www.edutopia.com, most high school students spend between two and four hours on homework each night. Approximately 30 percent of the school day is spent in homework outside the school campus. With 8 to 12 classes per day, students spend relatively limited time ingesting content from books on each course. These factors drive demand for richer media that can provide maximum information in a limited time setting.

Today's state-of-the-art classrooms have evolved far beyond blackboards and filmstrips to include the following equipment:

■ DVD players

■ Interactive whiteboards

■ Smart podiums for instructors and presenters

■ Student editions of laptop computers

■ Smart tables

■ Wireless tablets

Each of these devices requires connectivity between the student and the teacher, and virtually all of it can be wireless. The devices may connect directly with a teacher device or be routed to the teacher via the wireless infrastructure in the walls and ceilings of the classrooms, through the IT closet, and from there to/from a teaching screen like the one shown in the following illustration:

The importance of connecting a real-time, dynamic link between the teacher and student is an essential element of the educational process. Teachers—or, in the professional environment, presenters—are challenged to remain connected to each student and to understand whether they are mentally connected to the teacher—and, more importantly, whether they are receiving information in the impactful manner intended by the teacher. Educators today are using smart handheld devices to ensure that the communication link between the teacher and student remains constant. For example, Sento's wireless handset, shown in the following illustration, enables students to interface with the instructor in real time through quizzes, pop questions, and voting. The handsets can do more than that, however, by including student access curriculum, student grades, homework assignments, and logistics information such as upcoming field trips, school events, and holidays online and remotely.

The professional world, of course, has equivalents of this in high-productivity tools from interactive software by companies such as WebEx (owned by Cisco Systems), which allows for polling and allows audience members to "raise their hands" virtually to signal to the presenter that they have questions.

Connectivity in the Classroom

Instructors, administrators, and parents can easily connect with their children's educational process by using wireless technology. The amount of information generated, transmitted, stored, and remotely accessed by an average K-12 school rivals that accessed by most medium-sized businesses in the United States. Untethering that information and applications such as voice, video, and even student interaction is no longer optional at some schools.

> **NOTE**   A rapidly increasing number of IT and wireless sales are made to entire school districts as opposed to individual schools. These engagements can involve dozens of unique schools and several dozen support facilities such as school district headquarters, sports facilities, and maintenance depots.

The average number of access points (APs) deployed in a K-12 facility is between 10 and 20, although it's increasingly common to see K-12 AP deployments with double that number. This is a reasonably modest deployment in terms of node count (number of APs), size of wireless controller, relative distances between APs and the closest IT in which the controller resides, and the node density (how many APs per square feet of floor space).

What has changed significantly in the past several years is that school districts are now routinely pushing voice communication services to wireless 802.11 phones. In addition, there is a steady movement to push security video content to the same handheld devices. This requires much more design and design audit complexity than K-12 WLANs deployed in prior years in which connectivity was limited primarily to laptop PCs interfacing an autonomous (not centrally controlled) AP.

Security sophistication has vastly increased, driven by a strong requirement to secure not only student records and confidential information such as home addresses and medical conditions, but now also levels of security commonly found in retail stores, given the proliferation of debit cards and charge cards used in school cafeterias and in-school stores.

Classroom connectivity has also evolved to pervasive schoolwide connectivity. For this reason, the wireless interaction between APs requires specialized engineering so that very low radio frequency (RF) outputs retain high degrees of receive sensitivity. An AP residing in one classroom must reliably connect all the devices in the classroom without also connecting the devices in the classroom on the other side of the chalkboard.

Student, Staff, and Visitor Identification and Access

Long gone are the days when a parent or visitor could simply walk into a school building. Whether or not the amount of physical security deployed at most K-12 schools is excessive or deficient is a matter outside the scope of this book.

Today's schools routinely incorporate moderate levels of physical security in terms of devices that secure points of entrance. Policies have also evolved to support this increase in physical security, and they have an enormous impact in the quality and consistency of deployment and use of physical security devices such as electronic locks and video monitoring.

Wireless access enables administration staff and faculty to access images from anywhere in the school or on the campus where there is video coverage. These facilities also have fairly high degrees of physical access security through badges and video cameras. Few believe this level of security will decrease; most believe it will in fact increase.

Tons of Paper to Gigabytes of Data

Schools generate, store, and move literally tons of paper. Enormous storage facilities are required to archive student records, staff and faculty payroll, continuing education unit information, facilities maintenance records, materials purchasing contracts, and myriad other types of information.

Not only do student academic records require updating, storage, and access, but a school's extensive support staff of teachers, administrators, and faculty all have corresponding records. A school also uses a considerable amount of materials, from cleaning supplies to books, and from lightbulbs to pencils.

School compliance records include documentation for the following list of items, which is not exhaustive:

- Safety
- Cleanliness
- Adequate student academic progress
- Special education eligibility
- Student discipline
- Teacher certification
- Reports on funding usage

Schools report on these and other items to their school district and other agencies on a regular basis, commonly by school district management mandate and often by city, county, and law. Migrating literally small hills of this paperwork to silicon storage is important; having instant access to this information is equally important, because this information augments the responsibility and responsiveness of education administrators.

Providing remote access to a handheld client such as a smartphone adds even more return on the IT and wireless investment. Enabling a teacher to access a student's academic and, in certain cases, medical information quickly and wirelessly scales a teacher's ability to remain in the classroom while accessing essential information.

Having an online presence with connectivity to wireless smartphones and other clients also allows schools to notify parents and families of extreme weather conditions and other emergencies. This increases the safety of students and families alike, especially in rural settings where distances to and from the schools are typically much greater than those in urban locations.

Web Access for Learning

Schools connect routinely to the Internet for guest instruction and access to programs specifically created for the student education experience. A noteworthy example occurred when the space shuttle astronauts communicated with K-12 students during the February 2009 shuttle mission STS-119, with two former science teachers aboard. The shuttle included science experiments aboard, and the astronauts were interviewed by students. This created a truly memorable learning experience for both the NASA team and the students.

Another noteworthy example of web-based education is the International CyberFair (www.globalschoolnet.org), started in 1994 with the aim of connecting K-12 students from around the world to promote student collaboration on a global basis. An immense program, it now brings more than 2.5 million students together online from more than 115 countries. The students collaborate on story-telling activities that provide a local view into life in many countries, providing real-world experience and age-appropriate social engagements to students from all walks of life.

NOTE   Another of the excellent elements of web-based learning is the prominence of the same educational process in the workplace. It is common now for employees to receive ongoing training, counseling, and career enhancement training through the Web. Learning how to gain the most from online, self-paced tutoring is a vital skill for high-performance employees and top-rated employers alike.

Wireless Video Surveillance

Few issues seem to draw as much emotional attention in the K-12 space as physical safety. However, many, if not most, campus incidents occur after school hours, making 24-hour video surveillance a powerful tool for reducing crime and education costs. Video systems using cameras like those shown next, when integrated with remote monitoring and access control, act as a deterrent multiplier, because this technology convergence requires fewer security personnel. These systems also reduce crime rates as persons with ill intentions are discouraged from criminal activity because of the video surveillance. Remote monitoring enables a much faster response time to incidents, including fires, when the response team is triggered by events detected by the camera.

Remote monitoring, combined with real-time camera images, enables investigators to evaluate incidents on a post-event basis without reviewing the many hours of tapes compiled on the older VCR systems. State-of-the-art systems can monitor changes in temperature, movement, sound, and light, which trigger the system into a high-definition mode, enabling not only enhanced analysis of the incident as it occurs, but also far better forensics support on a post-incident basis. IP-based systems allow monitoring personnel to view images from handheld clients, such as smartphones, and to do so from any point of wireless connectivity within the neighborhood, city, or state.

An excellent example of such a system was deployed by Moss Point School District in Moss Point, Mississippi, which serves more than 3000 students in eight different schools with 250 teachers (according to a Cisco case study entitled "K-12 School District Improves Physical Safety" at www.cisco.com/en/US/prod/collateral/vpndevc/ ps6918/ps9145/ps9152/case_study_c36-508965.pdf). This school district is one of many that installed video surveillance not only on its campuses for outdoor monitoring, but also in its school hallways and in every classroom. The initial value proposition in the six K-12 schools was student safety by monitoring the doors and hallways, preventing unauthorized access from adults.

In the junior and senior high schools, the primary value proposition is to protect the property from vandalism, graffiti, and theft. Since deploying the system, vending machines, classroom computers, and other property destruction has been reduced. The school reported that cases of unsafe driving in the parking lots and front streets of the school were also reduced since the system was installed.

One theme remains common with video surveillance, both wired and wireless: the word quickly gets out among those being observed, and poor behavior diminishes in the area being monitored. People know if they're being observed, and few are willing to have their poor behavior videotaped as proof of their misbehavior.

It's not surprising that the system has also proven effective at reducing and stopping physical confrontations on the school grounds, a long-time problem at junior and high school levels. Given that most students won't divulge information to teachers and staff when incidents involving physical confrontation occur, a video system greatly enables staff to determine who was involved and what actually occurred during an incident.

Moss Point went much further than simply installing a high-definition video surveillance system. As this state-of-the-art system is IP-based, it is also integrated with the IP telephony system; the Internet access network; and the heating, air conditioning, and vacuum systems (HVAC) as well. This provides significant operating expense reductions for the school in addition to improving student behavior and incident resolution.

K-12 WLAN Success Metrics

The success metrics for the K-12 space can be summarized as follows:

- Improved communication and connectivity among students, teachers, administration, and parents
- Better communication within and outside the classroom
- Improved web-based methods by which to learn
- Higher teacher, staff, and faculty retention through reduced workloads by providing efficient wireless access, enabling an agile workforce
- More teacher hours spent in the classroom as opposed to absences while teachers perform administrative tasks
- Fewer unauthorized personnel on campus or within the buildings during or after school hours
- Reduction in costs due to vandalism and theft
- Reduction in physical confrontations by students

Higher Education Value Propositions

Higher education campus networks tend to be far larger, though not necessarily more complex than K-12 networks, especially when the campus network uses an extensive set of IP-based applications, as illustrated at the Moss Point School District.

Higher education networks tend to span much greater distances, commonly covering hundreds of acres on the primary campus and nearly that much again in satellite campuses.

The value propositions for higher education are different from those of the K-12 space:

- Competitive advantage
- Building-to-building wireless connectivity
- Increased revenue generation
- Maximized use of restricted budgets

Competitive Advantage

Colleges now compete heavily for the best students and faculty. An enormous amount of money is at stake, commonly running into the billions of dollars for major four-year institutions, from revenue generated not only from student admission, but from alumni donations. Some college athletics programs generate millions of dollars for the school from television, radio, and other broadcasting revenues.

Students attending two- or four-year colleges fully expect not only wireless access on campus, but pervasive high-speed wireless for their mobile cell phones, laptop computers, and PDAs. Relatively few of today's college students attend college without these handheld devices. While the most recent cell phone usage data is not readily available, it doesn't require much observation to recognize that cell phone usage among colleges students has been pervasive for more than five years.

Wireless connectivity considerably improves collaboration among students, allowing them to post joint work projects and to access them from virtually any place where mobile cellular or WLAN is available. In urban areas where colleges are prominent, it's no surprise to find an extensive array of WLAN hotspots at local coffee shops, sports venues, and certainly on the college campus.

This connectivity, of course, allows more than just mobile contact for an agile student population; it allows access to changes in curriculum and lecture location changes, classroom assignments, and homework, and offers remote access to enormous libraries. Real-time connectivity with college professors has taken the place of many in-person visits to a scholar's office. Texting is nearly as common, if not more common, than a voice call, both over WLAN and mobile cellular networks.

Most college students find that the smartphone or cell phone provides significant additional safety factors while in transit to and from parking lots and in between buildings during class sessions. At the same time, however, handheld device usage also contributes to accidents while students are driving and even walking. Incredibly, it's not uncommon for a person texting to step off a curb and into moving traffic. As a result, cell phone use and texting are often banned in school zones.

It's not just the students who require pervasive wireless coverage, but also the professors and staff, who need both cell phone and the much higher-speed WLAN formats required to do their jobs. In fact, wireless mobility is demanded by educational institutions to attract the top teaching talent, which attracts the largest amounts of research money. That research money is of major importance to schools.

Few, if any, faculty members access the network by Ethernet cable alone. While much research is completed on high-performance computing systems that are often tethered by vast fiber-optic systems, a great deal of project administration, lecturing via PowerPoint slides, and note-taking is achieved via laptop computers, nearly all of which today include a WLAN interface for connectivity.

Building-to-Building Connectivity

There can be no doubt about the superior capacity and reliability provided by fiber-optics over every other commercial wireless network available today. Fiber-optics is simply the fastest and most reliable medium for connecting multiple points on a network.

However, fiber-optics networks are time-consuming to plan and deploy, whether the lines are placed in trenches or in parallel above ground with telephone or commercial electrical delivery systems. Trenching for fiber is disruptive, expensive, and time-consuming. In states such as California, studies and bureaucracy required prior to installing fiber connectivity is non-trivial and can take five years or more before the trenching even begins. Above-ground systems are generally deployed much more quickly unless the lines call for new towers or support poles.

When two or more buildings need to be connected, it's hard to beat the speed of installation and general performance of a wireless bridge, shown in the next illustration. Within half a day, a team of half a dozen or fewer technicians and engineers can install a wireless bridge with 54 Mbps (megabits per second) of connectivity with voice- and video-quality reliability. Licensed wireless bridges can deliver ten times that speed, and optical wireless bridges that use laser light as the medium instead of the more common RF can achieve speeds up to 1 Gbps (gigabits per second), also with voice and video quality of service.

Today's bridges are very cost-effective, especially when compared to the enormous cost of a 54 Mbps link. Bridging technology typically does not involve monthly connectivity fees; this value proposition is commonly referred to as "toll bypass." They involve no right-of-way issues—which occur when a fiber link crosses a road or property belonging to another entity—to negotiate, and distances of up to 20 miles, with reduced transmission speeds, can be covered as long as no significant obstructions block the path.

Increasing Revenue

Mobility changes work from a location to an activity, and it has the same impact on education. Today's educational goal is to bring the classroom to people in addition to bringing people to the classroom. This concept extends well beyond the approach of online distance learning; education is now made available wherever a wireless connection is available—in the home, at the local coffee shop, at the library. This brings more people into the education process simply because they can make time in their schedules for the investment and effort of education provided they aren't required to drive across town, park, find their way across a complex campus to a building and room that typically aren't all that well marked, and do all this in the limited time between when work ends and class starts.

By attending a class remotely via wireless connection to a laptop, students can spend less time commuting to class and more time learning and collaborating. Distance learning is becoming a major market segment; in a 1998 MIT study by Glenn P. Strehle (www.ingenta.com/institute2000/strehle.pdf), 55,000 distance learning courses were being offered in the United States, and the rate at which these courses were becoming available was growing at 30 percent per year at that time. Given the disparity of income between those who have college degrees and those who don't, it's not surprising that during these economically troubled times a decade later, many people are pursuing additional education.

According to the National Center for Education Statistics, enrollment at two- and four-year college institutions increased at a robust 26 percent, from 14.5 million to 18.2 million, between 1987 and 1997. Approximately 34 percent of this growth was from full-time students. Of considerable interest is the total enrollment for students in nondegree institutions such as industry certification and adult continuing education facilities, with 447,000 students (http://nces.ed.gov/fastFacts/display.asp?id=98).

The education market is no longer limited to traditional education, in which a person completes high school and then a basic college education. A considerable market exists in job-based training, and today, few high-performing white-collar workers go without regular educational enhancements. The higher education market that centers on adult education—be it part-time, full-time, degree, or nondegree curriculums—is an immense market.

It's essential that educational opportunities continue to be available for people in fast-paced, high-paying jobs. One of the unique elements of a high-paying job is that it involves many changes that can happen quickly. Staying in touch with macroeconomic conditions, industry trends, technological advances, and new and brilliant uses of existing technology all require a part-time and perpetual exposure to education. Much of this can be achieved via smartphone these days from almost any location. While I'm waiting in line at the grocery store, or waiting for a haircut or a takeout order from a restaurant, it's wonderful to be able to catch up on the latest trends and news from my smartphone via a connection I've establish with a local hotspot or free WLAN.

Maximizing Restricted Budgets

It can be argued that nearly all budgets are restricted—that is, by definition, what a budget is, after all: a specified allocation of funding over a period of time. Wireless provides an excellent ROI due to the cost-effective connectivity between two or more points that can cover large areas versus connectivity at a single point such as an ether jack.

In addition, wireless requires substantially less cabling than Ethernets. Cabling is labor intensive to install and easily makes up a third to a half of the entire scope of a wired network deployment.

Cables are generally more prone to damage and deterioration from weather than a wireless link, primarily at the points where connectors are used, but also at any point where chafing of the cable housing or exposure to the elements can occur. Although a wireless link has its own share of cables and connectors, these runs are much shorter than those of cables, and the longer the cable run, the greater the likelihood of wear or mechanically induced problems such as pinching or chafing.

Wireless connectivity allows users to change locations without the necessity of rewiring ether jacks and managing ether ports. Ether ports are commonly left "open" and unsecured, posing obvious potential liabilities for security and access. With wireless coverage, the user simply moves from the old location to the new location and receives coverage from the WLAN in real time upon arrival at the new location. A single access point can cover most rooms with ease; this makes pervasive coverage a cost-effective choice for users who move frequently, as it's easy to regain connectivity upon setting up at the new location or while at a temporary location.

Higher Education Success Metrics

The success metrics for the higher education space can be summarized as follows:

- Market share increase and penetration from students and staff who expect pervasive wireless coverage

- Capital expenditure reduction in connecting campus buildings

- Operating expenditure reduction in connecting campus buildings

- Operating expenditure reduction through toll bypass

- Network connectivity to/within protected buildings

- Increased revenue generation from distance learning, adult education, community projects, and paid access

Healthcare Priorities

Worldwide, healthcare is an enormous industry. According to the U.S. Bureau of Labor Statistics (or BLS), the U.S. healthcare industry features an impressive summary of key facts, including the following:

- As the largest U.S. industry in 2006, healthcare provided 14 million jobs—13.6 million jobs for wage and salary workers and about 438,000 jobs for the self-employed.

- Seven of the 20 fastest growing occupations are healthcare related.

■ Healthcare will generate 3 million new wage and salary jobs between 2006 and 2016, more than any other industry.

■ Most workers have jobs that require less than four years of college education, but health diagnosing and treating practitioners are among the most educated workers.

Nearly 600,000 unique business establishments made up the U.S. healthcare industry in 2006. As in most industries, most employees work in small enterprises—in fact, 77 percent of healthcare workers are located in the small offices of physicians, dentists, and similar practitioners. We may see a shift in experienced employees from the larger hospitals to the smaller urgent care facilities, in part to work hours more parallel to the 9 to 5 hours for most workers and schools.

Wireless IT value propositions in the healthcare industry can be incredibly important. In 2005, the U.S. Joint Commission on Healthcare released a white paper entitled "Healthcare at the Crossroads." The report reviewed 2500 injuries to patients and found that, among other key factors, poor communications between medical caregivers was one of the top five contributing factors to patient injuries (www.jointcommission.org/NR/rdonlyres/167DD821-A395-48FD-87F9-6AB12BCACB0F/0/Medical_Liability.pdf). These unexpected healthcare events, in which a patient's death or serious injury occurred and was not directly related to the patient's medical condition, was one of the key focus areas for improvement. There can be no question that advances in IT communications systems featuring wireless mobile technology will help reduce injuries or deaths to patients in healthcare facilities.

In conversations with some of my colleagues, doctors have concurred that the study's findings were realistic. They were passionate about the challenges they face in their work environment and the power of effective communication with co-workers in real time, especially in critical healthcare situations.

Healthcare Subvertical Overview

While most of us think of hospitals when we consider the healthcare industry, hospitals are only part of the picture, as shown in Table 5-1. About 42 percent of all healthcare facilities are walk-in facilities such as a doctor's or dentist's office. Almost every small town has at least one doctor's office, making healthcare one of the most pervasive industries that operates on a continual basis.

Most of the IT industry's efforts in the healthcare system is focused on large hospitals—as it should be, because those are the largest IT networks and the largest WLANs in healthcare. In the United States, about 2500 hospitals with more than 250 beds each exist in the United States.

Industry Segment	Employment (%)	Establishments (%)
Physician offices	17	37
Home healthcare services	7	3
Dentists	6	21
Other health practitioners	5	19
Outpatient care centers	4	3
Other walk-in healthcare services	2	1
Medical and diagnostic laboratories	2	2
General medical and surgical hospitals	33	1
Other hospitals	1	0.2
Mental health hospitals	1	0.1
Nursing care facilities	13	3
Elderly care facilities	5	3
Residential mental health facilities	4	4
Other residential care facilities	1	1

Table 5-1.   Employment and Facilities Within the U.S. Healthcare System

However, as shown in the table, the center of mass for the industry is not large or even medium-sized hospitals, but the smaller clinics and doctor's offices for the following eight specialties:

- Chiropractors
- Optometrists
- Podiatrists
- Occupational and physical therapists
- Psychologists
- Audiologists
- Speech-language pathologists
- Dietitians

In 2006, the BLS indicated that 86 percent of nonhospital establishments employed less than 20 people, as shown in the following illustration. About 29 percent of the healthcare workforce was employed in facilities with less than 20 employees, and 31 percent were employed in facilities with less than 100 people on staff. Nearly 40 percent of all hospital staff are employed in institutions with 100 or more staff, according to 2006 BLS statistics.

Over 85 percent of nonhospital health service establishments employ fewer than 20 workers.

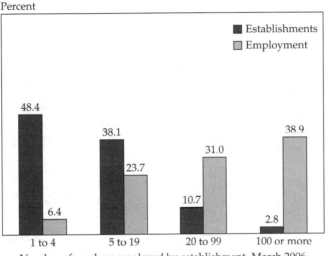

Number of workers employed by establishment, March 2006

Healthcare Value Propositions

While the health care industry, with its numerous subvertical markets, is enormous, there remains a common theme for industry priorities: pervasive wireless transport. In other words, extending the value of mission-critical medical applications such as patient records, admission processes, and human resources applications such as payroll, benefits, and so on, relies on having a wireless network deployed pervasively throughout the facility.

In my view, none of the top industries that view mobility as a necessity place a higher priority on the concept of untethering applications than the healthcare industry. This foundational principle holds true throughout healthcare, whether it's a small doctor's office with a total staff of five or a major teaching hospital with thousands of employees.

Considering all the major industries that use mobility, there is no larger agile workforce than that of healthcare. Some are tempted by the argument that the U.S. military is the largest agile workforce and indeed the largest employer outside the federal government, but despite its size, the military workforce including direct combat personnel is dwarfed by that of the healthcare industry, which expects nearly three times the number of personnel *in new hires alone* between now and 2016, according to the BLS. U.S. military spending averages about 4 percent of U.S. gross domestic product (GDP), and healthcare is four times that, according to the 2008 Trend Watch Chartbook, one of the most respected data sources on trends affecting hospitals and healthcare (www.aha.org/aha/research-and-trends/chartbook/2008chartbook.html), as shown in the following graphs (from www.truthandpolitics.org/military-relative-size.php):

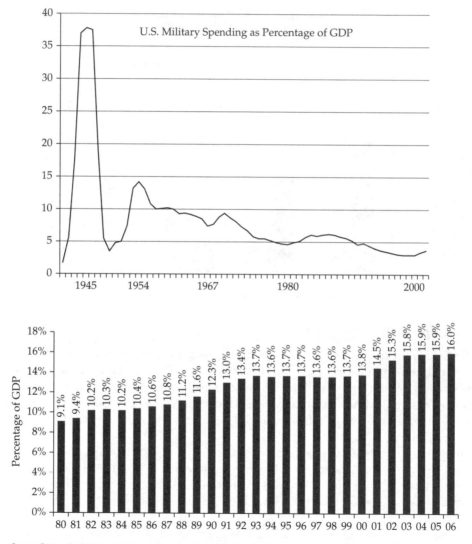

Source: Centers for Medicare & Medicaid Services (CMS), Office of the Actuary. Data released January 7, 2008.
(1)   CMS completed a benchmark revision in 2006, introducing changes in methods, definitions and source data that are applied to the entire time series (back to 1960). For more information on this revision, see http://www.cms.hhs.gov/NationalHealthExpendData/downloads/benchmark.pdf.

Approximately 75 percent of the medical industry workers are considered part of the *agile workforce*—doctors, nurses, and direct caregivers are in near-constant motion while on duty. Administrative staff, such as human resources, facility managers, admissions and records staff, and similar, make up the bulk of the remaining 25 percent of healthcare staff.

Three main value propositions for healthcare are discussed in the following sections:

- Connectivity
- Untethered collaboration
- Location

Connectivity

Pervasive wireless connectivity is as essential to healthcare facilities as electrical power, air conditioning, and physical security. It connects devices throughout the physical facility, be it a handheld smartphone, a high-end computer on wheels (COW), or major medical equipment such as CAT scanners or MRI imaging machines. Wireless is the preferred medium for agile workforces that are constantly on the move, not only throughout each facility, but outside the traditional hospital environment as well.

Connectivity involves much more than connecting devices; it's about pervasive access to crucial information, such as a patient's case history or data on similar cases to provide the healthcare worker with a broader understanding of the scope, possibilities, and options available for a particular patient.

Of all the IT programs under way in the healthcare industry, few have the visibility of electronic medical records (EMR). Using EMR, all patient medical records are immediately available electronically—as opposed to paper files that require enormous physical storage space and physical handling, so they are prone to being lost or misfiled and occasionally are rendered incomplete or unusable due to damage.

One of the most powerful elements in EMR is the ability for authorized personnel to access data remotely using tablets or handheld devices such as smartphones. When EMR systems are linked with hospital policies, data on dangerous drug interactions, and new and emerging prescriptions and treatment practices, the total care deliverable to the patient is enormously augmented. Reductions in days of treatment, healthcare, and insurance profit margins increase and, most importantly, quality of patient care and safety are enhanced. Mobility untethers the best of those possibilities by providing access to authorized users wherever there is a wireless connection.

The concept of pervasive wireless infrastructure should not be considered as simply "lighting up" healthcare facilities. Mobility now relies entirely on the same premise of all other networking technologies: the ability to get the entire Open Systems Interconnection (OSI) stack to be transported reliably, at high speeds, and with suitable ranges between the endpoint devices and the wireless access point. The variations of endpoint clients is vast, especially considering how clients run generations of software, firmware, and even hardware such as processors, radios, antennas, and other physical structural elements.

Each of these aspects, on an isolated basis, contributes significantly to the performance and reliability of the wireless link. When these elements or changes are additive—in other words, when the processor is upgraded, plus the software, and other elements—the only way to determine how well the system works is to turn on the link and observe performance. At this point in the deployment project, senior engineers begin to enter the deployment phase, which centers largely on isolating specific problems and resolving them one by one. A typical problem is that the link is either inoperative, unstable, or significantly lacks performance. The elimination of problems typically begins with configuration changes on the client and infrastructure side, and not uncommonly, with specialized software uploaded into the access point, security, client, and controller software for the larger deployments.

While it appears a daunting task to deploy pervasive coverage at a healthcare facility, you should realize that much of the existing infrastructure has been deployed during the last five years. My own estimation, based on my observations, a combination of calculations based on my employers' annual mobility bookings, our percentage of market penetration, and industry data on hospitals, indicates that large WLAN coverage exists in about a third to a half of the patient care floor areas in hospitals with more than 100 beds.

More interesting, and less defined, is WLAN coverage in nonhospital settings. These structures make up 99 percent of the healthcare structures in the United States with about 60 percent of the healthcare workers of all types—from degreed medical professionals to cafeteria workers and groundskeepers. Many of these facilities are known colloquially as "doc-in-a-box," but more formally as urgent care facilities. These structures are typically 10,000 square feet or less, and most are less than five years old. The aging of these structures is an important consideration, because very few, if any, commercial buildings are commissioned without extensive wireless coverage. Most facilities do not include the full spectrum of high-end medical equipment found in major hospitals, but these smaller facilities commonly include high-end equipment for specialty patient care such as CAT scanners, 3-D imaging equipment, MRI instruments, and dental equipment, according to the specialization of the facility.

Untethered Collaboration

Collaboration well and truly impacts the primary focal points of quality healthcare: responsiveness and patient safety.

Consider, for example, an emergency procedure that is about to take place in an operating room. All the personnel but the anesthesiologist are present and ready to go. The treatment requires anesthesia and minutes are essential. The ability for the medical team to reach the anesthesiologist is very much enhanced through wireless links, especially considering that 75 percent of the healthcare workforce is constantly on the move, and the odds are slight that the anesthesiologist is sitting at a desk.

A call is placed to the anesthesiologist, who is currently working on a critical case and can't leave for ten minutes. The anesthesiologist forwards the call to the secondary anesthesiologist, who is contacted in real time. Within seconds, the backup anesthesiologist is moving toward the operating room (OR) with the patient ready for the emergency procedure. With literally only minutes to spare, a life is saved. Similar scenarios occur around the clock in thousands of emergency departments.

Collaboration is not always a matter of life and death, but in healthcare, it's nearly always connected to quality of care for the patient and reduced operating expense for the institution.

Consider another scenario, which, though not as critical as the first, could become serious if not dealt with early and correctly. A patient with an unusual series of symptoms visits a doctor. His smart handheld device includes a database of symptoms and conditions, so she checks the information to narrow down the possible diagnoses and treatments for the patient.

This scenario is far from unusual; quite to the contrary is true, in fact. A 2005 study, for example, published by the *Journal of the Medical Library Association,* discovered that 87 percent of physicians use a smartphone or PDA for patient encounters. Of the frequent PDA or smartphone users, 85 percent said that the device influenced their overall clinical decision-making and 73 percent altered treatments because of information received from or via the device.

Given that the study occurred in 2005, we can expect that even more doctors are using these types of devices today.

The current generation of handheld medical devices is powerful. ePocrates (www.epocrates.com) provides the following application for nearly every smartphone available:

- Health plan formularies
- Drug interaction checker, medical calculators
- Pill identifier, pill pictures
- Medical news updates
- Hundreds of brand-name over-the-counter drug products
- Infectious disease treatment guide
- More than 600 alternative (herbal) medicines
- IV compatibility checker
- High-resolution disease images
- Diagnostic and laboratory tests

Another collaborative scenario involves the same doctor, but this time with another patient with a more serious condition. The patient is new to this doctor, and before prescribing treatment, the doctor consults in real time with the former doctor, who is in transit between his private practice and a large local hospital. Within minutes, the two physicians collaborate and concur on the best treatment regimen for the patient.

Another collaborative scenario involves the concept of training new medical personnel. Approximately 3 million new healthcare workers are forecast to arrive in an industry where mistakes can be fatal and, less important, can incur lost revenue to major facilities through errors highlighted by the news media.

It's clear that in any industry, much less a vital one like healthcare, collaboration and communication between newer personnel and more experienced and full-credentialed personnel is important. Adding to the complexity of the scenario is the workforce agility element. Being able to collaborate in real time as the newer worker gains experience is essential for scaling both the experienced person and the new hire. Smart handheld devices, such as Motion Computing's C5 medical tablet, which incorporates imaging, radio-frequency identification (RFID), and 802.11 connectivity, enable physicians and medical technicians in remote locations to monitor and assist in patient point-of-care scenarios.

Not only do devices like the C5 allow for barcode reading (shown in the next illustration) and patient ailment photography, but they also offer high-resolution video abilities, handwriting recognition, and voice technology. The voice technology is a tremendous staff multiplier, because it allows the care professional to discuss patient conditions and treatments to a single remote support person or to a conference room with support staff, greatly increasing patient safety, treatment outcome, and reduction in healthcare operating expenses.

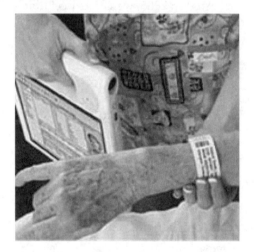

Another less documented, but highly valuable, element of effective collaboration tooling is employee satisfaction. Healthcare workers, understanding firsthand the shortage of qualified personnel, are exercising increasing amounts of discretion with regard to where, how, and on what they'll dedicate their professional time.

As indicated earlier in the chapter, large facility healthcare workers may begin an employment shift from large hospitals to small urgent care or specialty practice facilities. Part of this future shift may result from job satisfaction as tight teaming through collaboration is generally far better with smaller teams—at the smaller urgent care facilities. These teams also tend to experience a lot less turnover than at large hospitals, which can vary greatly by shift and by day. Effective teamwork with colleagues one enjoys and respects definitely has an impact on employee turnover.

Few layers of administration lie between the employee and the owner or general manager of a smaller facility. Flatter organizational hierarchies also tend to have less employee turnover. This is in part because the scope of collaboration goes well beyond daily task loads to include, importantly, career management, compensation, grievance resolution, and exceptional consideration for extraordinary life events such as family death and illness.

Collaboration has significant productivity implications. This is critical to acknowledge and manage, as most forecasts indicate an increasing shortage in nursing staff, according to a 2004 healthcare workforce analysis that was published in the 2008 Healthcare Trendwatch Statistics.

The following chart indicates an increasing and significant shortage of full-time equivalent (FTE) of registered nurses, showing that there will be significantly increasing workload on nurses, which in turn means that productivity and efficiency will be a critical element in maintaining high healthcare standards and metrics.

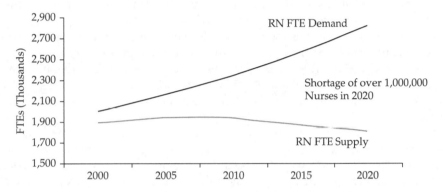

Source: National Center For Health Workforce Analysis, Bureau of Health Professions, Health Resources and Services Administration. (2004). *What Is Behind HRSA's Projected Supply, Demand, and Shortage of Registered Nurses?* Link: ftp://ftp.hrsa.gov/bhpr/workforce/behindshortage.pdf.

In my opinion, mobility will be so impactful in this regard that nurses, doctors, and other technical healthcare staff will select their employers in part by the quality of their communications infrastructure. The correlations between employee satisfaction, productivity, burnout, and turnover will be ever more closely linked with the effectiveness of collaboration.

Wireless mobility will play a frontline role in managing this critical healthcare issue. Wireless collaboration is essential; it greatly augments collaboration by untethering the communication links. In what may be the most agile major workforce on the planet, untethering allows mobility for healthcare workers.

Location

A healthcare worker has three primary elements of concern with regard to their being able to support a real-time point-of-care scenario:

- Physical location of supporting personnel and equipment
- Status: available or unavailable
- Distance to event

Most healthcare workers have fairly tightly subscribed physical domains in which they perform their tasks. In a hospital, many specialists and generalists roam from department to department and floor to floor, but nurses work primarily on a single floor or within a certain section of the floor. Doctors spend approximately half of their time outside the hospital, and administration staff generally do not roam outside the office environment. Of course, there are numerous exceptions to these generalizations indicated, but they remain fundamentally true.

Personnel and equipment location awareness is also of utmost importance. Knowing a person's location is essential, as indicated in the preceding example of the anesthesiologist in an emergency room scenario. And knowing that the person is currently subscribed with another patient is as important as knowledge of the person's location.

The combination of location and status is a powerful knowledge tool in healthcare. Though location and status are related, they're not the same. Knowing the status of equipment, for example, generally requires more sophisticated tooling.

In addition to considering use status of medical equipment, equipment refurbishment must also be considered. For example, an infusion pump might be currently in use with a patient, and it will be refurbished by cleaning and other reclaiming operations after it is no longer being used by that patient. Much of the refurbishment occurs on site at a large hospital; in smaller facilities, the unit is often refurbished by an outside vendor, generally off premises.

Now consider, for example, wheelchairs, which are ubiquitous in a hospital setting, as most hospitals require that any person being discharged be wheeled outside the hospital. The reason behind this policy is simple: the number one cause of injury in a hospital isn't misdiagnosis, incorrect medication, or surgical errors; it's patients falling down. Wheelchairs commonly take 15 to 30 minutes to procure. During this time, the patient and their family and/or friends are kept waiting. This leads to a reduced patient satisfaction score and ties up the facilities for an unnecessarily lengthy period.

Knowing the location of wheelchairs, ensuring they do not leave the healthcare facility with the patients, and reducing the cost of repairs that occur commonly to wheelchairs when they leave the healthcare facility are important for healthcare providers. Knowing the location and repair status of a wheelchair improves the perception and actual quality of care, reduces operating expenses, and reduces frustration among healthcare workers. Improving employee satisfaction helps minimize worker turnover, training of new employees, and costs from errors from new employees. This demonstrates that managing the location and status of equipment and personnel is highly cost-effective for healthcare providers, and wireless systems can play a major part in this.

Healthcare Success Metrics

The success metrics for the healthcare industry can be summarized as follows:

- Operating expense reduction through increased productivity
- Decrease of employee turnover
- Increased accuracy of patient care; reduced injury
- Operating expense reduction from location services

CHAPTER 6 | Wireless Network Assessments

W ireless network assessments are one of the most powerful tools available today for not only end customers, but for systems integrators and IT wireless equipment providers. On an industry-wide basis, the assessment tool is greatly underutilized; this is unfortunate, because a wireless network assessment ensures that your wireless IT investment resolves your most critical business operational issues.

It's my experience that less than 10 percent of all WLAN investments are tightly coupled with resolving top business operational problems. This isn't to say that mobility has failed to resolve some of the most important operational problems; indeed, it has been a powerful tool for businesses of every size. The point is that relatively few mobility deployments originated with this intent in mind, mostly because the majority of mobility deployments were based on sales engineer–to–customer engineer discussions instead of deployments firmly rooted in the functional requirements as set forth by a broad-based team of customer, integrator, and technology provider stakeholders. The best deployments enable the best outcomes, which are nearly always fundamentally based on reducing operational costs and increasing specific corporate functions such as sales, quality assurance, and so forth.

Having worked on wireless deployments with roomfuls of customers, engineers, and IT sales account managers for the last 20 years, I rarely discover more than one or two professionals in a group who routinely link wireless deployments to C suite operational priorities before the project begins. It seems that few integrators and technology equipment salespeople are in tune with the C suite that reside as the business leaders at end customers.

Sales people are talented, hard-working individuals who are passionate about their employers, their business, and their careers. When presented with the concept of wireless network assessments and the methodology for ensuring cohesion with top operational priorities, most professionals use this information to the stakeholders' advantage.

As you know, IT assets are used to manage information dominance over competitors and even customers. While it may sound condescending to assert that integrators and technology equipment providers should have information dominance over their customers, the best-performing providers of products and services should know more about what customers need than the customers themselves. This is not a position of arrogance when services are delivered to the customer in a humble and helpful manner.

Most customers are far more adept at core business issues than IT issues; in other words, they know a lot more about their business than about harnessing the power of IT. Maximizing how IT augments a business is an expertise that generally resides in the domain of the system integrator and to a lesser degree the technology equipment provider.

When a customer fully understands the value of IT in the business, the discussion shifts from a deliverable benefits engagement to ensuring that the customer point of contact is in line with their objectives. In other words, the integrator role would be to ensure the success of the point of contact. Possessing the best situational information allows the service and product provider to understand its role in the customer relationship before the net deliverable discussions occur.

In the best customer/supplier relationships, the supplier manages the relationship carefully in every engagement. Top suppliers and salespersons execute very quickly on knowing what role to play, and how to play it, in customer engagements. No two customer relationships are identical; information dominance allows the supplier to adapt to each customer's needs with the best possible information on how to close the deal. This format best serves the customer, the company, and the salesperson. The fewer the cycles prior to deploying, the sooner the investment begins to provide solid returns, and the sooner the customer, integrator, and technology provider can move to the next engagement phase to improve other customer operations.

Network Assessments as Performance Predictors

For most companies, mobility IT improvements are one of the final stages in operational process improvement. However, as the return on mobility is better understood and used by the end customer, mobility investments tend to move upward in the allocation of corporate resources. The sooner a customer understands that IT is central to every critical business process, the sooner IT investments are not only prioritized in terms of timing, but also in terms of total corporate resource allocation.

In real terms, well-deployed mobility approximates 15 percent of the total IT investment. On average, however, across the enterprise-class market, mobility represents something closer to 5 percent of the total IT investment—and often less than that. Of course, this is a broad average, and it is higher in education, which has been the perennial earliest adopter of unlicensed wireless for more than a decade. Healthcare has been the vertical with the second-most wireless deployed.

When the customer has evolved to the point at which mobility is in the 15 percent range of total IT investment, a very noticeable performance improvement results with regard to taking advantage of dynamic market trends, reducing operating expenses, increasing employee satisfaction, reducing employee turnover, and increasing cultural agility that includes a propensity for collaboration. Where mobility is broadly deployed at customer sites, corporate success metrics of nearly every kind improve, regardless of whether or not the customer has a predominantly agile workforce.

Customers who engage system integrators on wireless network assessments tend to upgrade their core IT investment heavily to allow greater speeds, reliability, and reduced cost of maintenance. Although I can't reveal the names of the Cisco customers that have invested in network assessments, I can say that you'd probably recognize many of them as high-performance companies. These customers have weathered the macroeconomic meltdown much better than the average IT customer; some have indeed prospered quite well when their competitors were descoping operations.

A coincidence? Not at all, in my view. Companies with the highest degree of collaboration through mobility and network asset utilization have consistently been top performers within their respective fields. Collaboration has been mission-critical to my career success, but quality of deliverables for products and services, system integrator performance, and end user return on investments are also important.

At least 60 percent of my daily tasks involve collaboration; it's nearly impossible at my company to gain measurable and sustainable impact without having strong collaboration skills. The output and performance of my co-workers are simply tremendous, largely due to collaboration tooling and a culture that has learned to collaborate effectively. Fewer boundaries between departments exist within our company, and groups that never used to interact, such as finance and marketing, now do so routinely.

While numerous clever and thoughtful academic studies have shown mixed results with regard to increases in productivity and parallel investments in "computers," many factors are relative to productivity. Connectivity and collaboration are as much corporate cultural issues as technology issues. Where mixed results are experienced, studies generally fail to characterize the quality of employees relative to their skills. Having strong fundamental skill sets are a critical precursor in predicting productivity through collaboration, because a commensurate relationship exists between level of basic and advanced skills and the ability to accept, use, and forward collaborative information.

One reason why mixed results are shown from IT investments and productivity is the pervasive citing of "computers" versus the total IT suite. "Computers" are more about data crunching, content generation, and storage than they are about connectivity and collaboration. "Computers" tend to be linked with the precollaborative era of social networking. The larger, more powerful, and physically heavy the computer is, the less elegant it is as a collaboration tool, however. Obviously, whether or not the "computer" is tethered also has an enormous effect given the value of mobility.

Connectivity resides within the realm of IT; collaboration resides at the transport level within IT, but far more importantly it resides within corporate culture. A company can use the latest, most pervasive, and most powerful collaboration tools such as WebEx and smartphones, but the amount of collaboration that occurs is proportional to cultural drivers that sustain it and the fundamental skill sets of the collaborators. Collaboration resides best on a foundation of strong basic customer skill sets.

The tendency to collaborate based on a strong basic skill set may be one of the single largest factors in why high-performance companies typically have the broadest deployments of connectivity and collaboration through IT tools. In short, the best customers purchase the most IT resources.

The predominance of collaboration within a company is fundamental to the network assessment process. Companies and integrators that are well versed in collaboration quickly realize that their network needs to deliver more performance while users are in motion, and on a more pervasive basis with greater levels of reliability. This observation holds true whether collaboration is new or not so new in a corporate setting. Network assessments elegantly provide the delta between what the IT network should do and what it can do.

It's also noteworthy to consider the quality of the integrators that routinely perform network assessments. Cisco partners with literally tens of thousands of companies;

you'd expect that from a company with $35 billion in cash and annual sales in the same range. Most network assessments are performed by Cisco partners who are consistently "the best of the best." I know this because I've evaluated Cisco mobility partner bookings performance and compared it to how often these partners provide network assessments. These same partners feature not only top-level performance with regard to how much technology they sell; these partners tend to have highly evolved internal processes and larger numbers of certified and credentialed engineers who have also completed some of the largest and most complex wireless deployments in the industry.

The results are abundantly clear: top-performing mobility partners perform many more network assessments than nearly all of their competitors. If the integrator proposes a network assessment, it's likely the customer is working with one of the top-performing and therefore one of the most capable IT integrator partnerships in the industry.

Bill of Materials or Multiyear Engagement?

It's tempting to believe that a network assessment results in merely a bill of materials, but it's far more than that. For the salesperson, an assessment is a powerful sales tool that defines the scope of products and services that may be sold to solve important customer business problems. For the end customer, this tool and methodology ensures maximum return on an IT investment. The best salespersons illuminate untapped possibilities from an investment in mobility, drawing on their experience from customer peers while disclosing only information from an industry experience perspective.

The best customers quickly pick up best practices from their industry peers, which strengthens and improves their operation. The best suppliers are key providers of this information; the cross-pollenization they provide is an important supplier role, remembering at all times that protection of sensitive information is an element of relationship longevity. No customer possesses every best practice. Having a network of trusted information sources injects intelligence into the operation. Incorporating emerging best industry practices is an important part of the network assessment deliverable.

Ideally, a network assessment occurs not just once but on a recurring basis. That which is measured tends to improve. Initially when a network assessment is performed, the gap between top operational priorities and network capabilities is usually wider than anticipated. Because IT investments compete for a customer for limited priorities, closing the gap between what the network should deliver and what it can actually deliver often takes up to three years.

Even when mobility is prioritized, it can take two or more budget cycles to deploy entirely in most enterprise-class deployments. This is nearly always true when the decision has been made to migrate from hotspot-type wireless coverage to pervasive wireless coverage. In larger enterprise operations, it's not just about fiscal allocations, it's also about manpower allocations.

The untethering of IT investments requires careful advance planning, auditing, and maintenance. IT and mobility upgrades are also disruptive; the temporary delays in customer production during the upgrade to expanded mobility access need to be accounted for and carefully administered as part of process improvement. By its nature, infrastructure improvement is disruptive, whether it's a stretch of freeway or an IT improvement. The outcome, however, is long-lasting, impressive, and very much worth the pain of the transitions.

Not only does the physical process improvement require interruption, but it takes time to change processes, even though mobility likely provides the greatest amount of process and operational improvement with the least amount of disruption—if planned and deployed correctly. Never trivial to achieve in complex environments such as healthcare and manufacturing, untethering provides incredible amounts of business acceleration.

This acceleration tends to be slower at first and is tied to the amount of fine-tuning mobility required to provide its full measure of potential. Once the bugs are cleared off and employees are lightly trained, the acceleration of productivity, collaboration, and connectivity is impressive. Employees quickly find new ways to communicate and quickly add new types of information both to transmit and receive. Application providers step up shortly thereafter with refined software that makes mobile collaboration and connectivity more relevant, reliable, simple to use, and productive.

Capitalizing on these changes typically requires more than one budget cycle, because the improvements afforded by mobility require investments not only in wireless access points and controllers, but also in clients, security, applications, training, and maintenance. Untethering applications involves a whole lot more than simply installing some antennas; every layer of the OSI stack is affected. It also profoundly affects the way a business is operated, secured, connected, and managed. The full scope from initial proposal to maintenance certainly takes multiple calendar quarters, if not more than a year, in major enterprise deployments.

From the technology integrator's perspective, the issue is not simply one of changing a customer's IT approach to include wireless. Rather, the net deliverable to be gained from wireless network assessments is to improve the customer operation constantly and continually. IT is not a static investment, because by its nature, business operational development changes and continually improves; it evolves and adapts to capture changes in how the money flows within the customer target markets. The best integrators propose multiyear visions of that, which maximizes market capture and customer management for the customer. The focus is always on closing the gap between the top business operational problems and the manner in which the mobility investment resolves those problems.

Most customers can be shown significant ways in which improved mobility can further enhance their operational processes. The wireless network assessment enables this through an engagement sequence that not only identifies the delta between the customer's top operational problems and actual IT capabilities, but also includes the acquisition of emerging industry best practices and a plan for continued coupling of IT investments against ever-changing market conditions.

Wireless Network Assessments Procedure

Following are the primary steps for assessing a wireless network:

1. Assess business operational priorities
2. Assemble mobility resolution metrics/ROI
3. Plan network assessment with customer
4. Perform network assessment
5. Present assessment report and review
6. Plan for recurring assessments and next-generation IT investments

These elements begin with a foundation for understanding the operational priorities. From there, the stakeholders should determine what success looks like. These steps involve analyzing the delta between what the network should do and what it actually can do. The sequence ends with a loop back to reassessing what is truly important in the business and redeploying the entire cycle on a forward-going basis to ensure that the IT investments evolve in parallel, or ideally ahead of, changing market dynamics.

Assess Business Operational Priorities

Before any meaningful operational assessment can occur, all stakeholders must be identified and brought into the process. My experience is that most major project delays occur because an individual was either brought in too late or not at all into major project meetings. While business executives are generally chartered with top operational priorities, the execution of these priorities requires the full support of the individual contributors and midlevel managers in a company. The value of having the right number and types of stakeholders involved early on is difficult to overstate.

A measurement is meaningful only if it's compared to something important. In this case, the operational priorities set forth by the executive leadership of the customer are the important factor. The best-run companies are open in their communications about operational priorities.

My employer, for example, recently made it clear to the media, industry analysts, and every employee that we had to reduce the cost of doing business. Waste had to be reduced and efficiencies increased. Every significant expense was carefully examined, and any nonessential expenditures were re-examined and/or reduced. Each employee who routinely traveled was informed of expense limits. As a result, our company met its objectives, and this point was recently declared publicly by our CEO.

Knowing what was required made it easier for us to hit our targets and make contributions on an individual basis for the greater good of the company; it also showed that Cisco employees care about the company. The same standard can and should be declared with every company that has significant IT investments. In this day and age, that would include almost all companies operating in highly industrialized countries.

Knowing the top operational issues for a customers is essential prior to a wireless network assessment. These priorities across each major industry that uses wireless mobility can typically be identified in one or more of the following four categories:

- Workforce connectivity
- Real-time business analytics
- Untethered collaboration
- Reduction of product/services time to market

Obviously, some operational priorities may be unique to certain industries, such as warehousing, where high employee turnover is a key issue. Improving employee satisfaction would be a priority, as well as improving productivity, which would enable profit sharing to the employees and can be a powerful incentive for employment longevity. In other industries such as law enforcement, priorities might include increasing patrol officer hours on the street through paperwork reduction—that is, officers could do some paperwork from their patrol cars while on the street, using electronic forms and wireless communications.

Generally only a handful of "top" priorities exist; it's not feasible from an expense, manpower, or disruption basis to have more priorities than a few. The more top priorities a technology can address, the more likely the technology will be deployed. A quick review of the top priorities such as those posted earlier quickly highlight the fact that mobility enables or improves every one of them. While mobility is certainly not the answer for every operational priority, it can help in any number of ways.

Assemble Mobility Resolution Metrics/ROI

Once the top operational priorities have been resolved and distributed across the entire stakeholder team, the next step is to determine what success looks like. This requires not only a set of metrics, but also an investment and reporting of the metrics.

The metrics are derived from the top priorities. Using the common priorities outlined earlier, the following success metrics could be considered:

Priority	Success Metric
Workforce connectivity	Reduce patient response time by 30 percent by providing credentialed emergency department staff with handheld VoIP phones with voice, electronic medical records, prescriptive services, location, and voice mail services to all handsets.
Real time business analytics	Provide real-time inventory levels through wireless barcode readers that update the system in real time through wireless backhaul.
Untethered collaboration	Increase sales by 10 percent by enabling all sales personnel to attend meetings without leaving the sales field by including WebEx on their smartphones.
Reduction of product/services time to market	Decrease warehouse fulfillment time 30 percent through a wireless voice picking system within 30 days of deployment.

The metrics involved should include clear statements that can be measured by management. These metrics don't always involve a direct dollar cost but will always have a value understood by the company deploying the mobility technology.

The ROI, or return on investment, is a more complex calculation but highly appropriate to understand and measure. The technology system integrator and equipment provider can provide a valuable ROI. For example, if hospital managers know that a wireless location service can reduce losses of wheelchairs being taken off premises by patients, they can accurately predict how much they will save and how long it will take to pay off the location-based service.

The value of investments in mobility and other IT assets can entail a straightforward discussion with a financial senior manager. The integrator might demonstrate, for example, that the cost of a mobility technology—such as a location service—will pay for itself in about 12 months. And that would interest a financial manager who knows that the cost of a location-based system could be amortized over three years—in other words, the system would provide a legitimate tax reduction over three years, even though the system will pay itself off in one, by eliminating or greatly reducing the number of lost and damaged wheelchairs. The more attractive and realistic the success metric, the more likely it will be a purchase priority. This emphasizes the value of engaging the customer in terms of value proposition as opposed to merely the pure technical merits of a system.

Put another way, it's a more compelling story for the customer if you tell them the system will pay off in 12 months, versus telling them the system can track any wheelchair on the premises within ten feet. The wireless network assessment should therefore focus on how the mobility investment will reduce operating expenses versus how much the mobility technology will cost. The better the ROI modeling, the shorter the sales cycle, because the customers have only limited funds and other resources in which to invest in process improvement. Interestingly, it's often not the best technology that wins the lion's share of IT investments on a purely technical basis; it's the technology that is the best outlined in terms of financial benefits.

Plan Network Assessment with Customer

Once the stakeholders have been assembled, the top operational priorities established, and the metrics for success defined, the next phase is to perform the actual network assessment. The planning phase is a joint discovery and documentation stage typically between the end customer and the system integrator. As few networks are well documented enough that any professional could evaluate them across the OSI stack, the close participation of the customer engineering team, along with any third parties that may be managing the customer network, is imperative.

One of the primary elements required to ensure a successful plan is that the wireless mobility element be properly assessed. The evaluation must go well beyond straightforward evaluation of the areas covered by radio frequency (RF) to include how traffic and applications function from the clients to the network core. Security is also a key function to be included and requires a representation of that expertise as well. Third parties, specifically application suppliers and developers both in-house and subcontracted, will need to review not only what is currently in use, but also the releases scheduled for the next 12 months.

The wireless network assessment is more than a snapshot frozen in the moment of the evaluation. Instead, the plans for network upgrades across the entire OSI stack for the next 12 months should also be considered to ensure that the planned direction of the IT evolution is consistent with the impending changes in business operational priorities. Most operational priorities are fairly stable over a 12-month period, but up to 30 percent of them can and may likely change over the 12 months following the actual wireless network assessment.

Another key element of a wireless network assessment is to balance the depth and scope of the evaluation versus cost and resource investment. The most granular assessment would continue in perpetuity, and to some degree that's what occurs with real-time security and overall condition monitoring. However, real-time monitoring should not be linked too closely with an assessment; the difference is that the assessment evaluates the delta between what the network can *actually do* and it *should do* to resolve the most important business operational problems.

The network assessment should take about one working day per 20 access points. This rule of thumb holds true up to networks involving 100 to 500 access points. For enterprise-class networks with more than 500 access points, a reasonable estimation for an assessment is about one working day for every 50 to 75 access points. These are massive networks, though they make up only about 1 percent of all WLANs deployed.

Little documentation at present correlates the size of network with whether the delta is large or small between actual and ideal network capability. Both small and large networks tend to deploy about the same state-of-the-art technology, though obviously there are unique issues for larger networks in terms of scaled manageability, security, and the degree to which the network is heterogeneous or homogeneous (from a single technology supplier or multiple technology suppliers).

Accordingly, then, the plans for a larger WLAN will be more comprehensive. The sample sizes in terms of total traffic count and scope of areas or VLANs evaluated will generally be much larger. The larger the network, the more varied the types of success— for example, warehouses, bullpens, and outdoor areas will likely have unique metrics.

Prepare and Prioritize

While it would be theoretically beneficial to have an exhaustive assessment that covers every conceivable element of the wireless network, it's not practical from a cost or manpower resource perspective. Having a limited amount of time and resources is actually a good thing, because it forces the customer and integrator to focus on what is truly important and relative to the greater well-being and advancement of the customer's operational objectives.

For this reason, carefully planning the assessment as a joint partnership between the integrator and end customer is important. Careful assessments take several weeks to cue up; often access is truly feasible only during late night shifts when traffic count is reduced or when certain network functions such as major data backups and transfers occur.

The timing and sequence of key operations, traffic, and employee flow are information owned and best understood by the customer. The integrator typically brings the specialized tooling and evaluation talent to deep dive into the assessments.

Prioritization is a key element for the most impactful assessments. Not every physical area will be measured on a broad enterprise-class deployment simply because there isn't enough time to achieve this. Sampling, therefore, is important in terms of quality. Not all physical areas, wireless domains, applications, and users have the same value to a customer. It's also true that these areas, domains, and user priorities will normally shift and cycle through the normal course of a business day, week, or month. Knowing when to assess the most important wireless network elements to derive the most important recommendations, both now and in the foreseeable future, assures that you and your partners can understand the delta between what the wireless network actually can do and the most important business operational problems the IT investment is intended to resolve.

Perform Network Assessment

As indicated, it's important that you focus holistically across the entire OSI stack when performing the actual wireless network assessment. The fundamental items the wireless network assessment should cover would include, but are not necessarily limited to, the following:

- RF
- Security
- L2–L7
- Roaming
- QoS
- Applications (voice, video, RFID)
- Increased node count and traffic

RF Assessment

The foundational work will of course be with regard to the three primary elements of how well the RF coverage is performing, and these three items make up what I've long called the "triumvirate of RF." For many years, I've been asked, What speeds can we expect? My response has been that RF coverage is a triumvirate of not just *speed*, but of *range* and *reliability*, too. A change in one of these elements will almost always affect how the other two elements perform.

Today, however, a fourth element has become important to consider with regard to RF: *coverage*. In particular, you want to assess the quality of the RF coverage in terms of maximum range between the access point and the client, the minimum speed at which you need the RF link to operate because it will vary with range and reliability, and the reliability of the RF link at the outer edges of a predesigned cell size.

Of equal importance is the concept of *knowing where cell nulls exist*. Coverage areas should be well documented, not just for the active cells, but also for null locations. Nulls are areas with little intentional RF coverage. They're rarely completely devoid of RF energy, but a null can be defined as an area in which there is insufficient intended RF coverage to allow a client to perform within normal operational parameters.

Nulls are not necessarily bad; RF coverage should be available only in areas where you want it, and it should not exist in substantial amounts in areas where you don't need it. This may sound counterintuitive—that is, many people believe RF coverage should blanket an area from wall to wall and floor to ceiling. Most of those well-intentioned folks do not fully understand the physical paths that clients routinely take—that is, most clients reside in very specific physical domains and on highly repeatable pathways. Clients generally don't take random physical paths; they follow workflow and transit routes between points of workflow. Of course, it can be argued that certain kinds of clients such as voice devices are used more often between points of a workflow, but the larger consideration here is that clients nearly always reside within certain well-defined physical areas. It's a good thing to engineer a proper RF blanket in those areas, and, to the extent practical and possible, minimize the amount of RF energy in areas where clients don't currently reside.

This view is held in part due to the massive proliferation of clients in place, which will greatly accelerate over the next few years, a time in which most of today's infrastructure and RF coverage plans will exist. Each new client will need the least amount of interference to enable clients to perform at optimal levels of speed, range, and reliability.

Security Assessment

When you discuss security with network security professionals, two themes become apparent: complete security is more of an illusion than a reality, and the purpose of security is to maintain a difficult enough target that the bad guys will migrate to a softer target.

Security is perhaps one of the most evolutionary elements of a wireless network. A plan and review should necessarily then focus as on the forward-looking plans and security agility as well as which protocols, practices, and depth and types of security are used.

WLAN on the whole went through several major phases from the early 1990s to the present day. Initially it was about reliability; the prevailing question in the early '90s was about maintaining fundamental connectivity. Most customer engagements centered on convincing the customers that the system was fundamentally reliable. The next major phase was the security scare around 2003 or so; most customer engagements were focused on convincing customers that WLANs were as secure as any other network access methodology. Many government institutions even today have not been convinced of this, though it's generally far less of a problem than it used to be.

Security is a vital WLAN element, whether the WLAN is used in a home network or the world's largest enterprise-class WLANs that now connect via 802.11 versus Ethernet ports. Security works in layers, so a wireless network assessment should evaluate the layers of security as opposed to that which resides only at any single point in the WLAN.

L2–L7 Assessment

The key assessment point regarding the OSI stack is to ensure the entire stack operates at the client device in the WLAN. Applications, security, roaming, speeds, reliability, and other key performance contributors all have to work harmoniously up and down the OSI stack. In truth, very few if any wireless network assessments will involve testing discrete layers of the OSI stack; a likely best way to test this is to ensure that the application runs properly on the client.

Some security experts believe that the higher levels of the OSI stack cannot be secured if security breaches occur at the lower levels of the stack. I'll leave that debate to the experts, but I can say that there are have been considerable advances in securing both the physical layer of the stack, partly through RF security intrusion detection and prevention, and recent enhancements in securing the data link layer.

WLANs are much more about what happens at L1 and L2 in the network, though the premise of the entire stack operating efficiently and reliably for more challenging applications such as video and location-based services are very important in today's networks that routinely include wireless access.

Roaming Assessments

Some engineering and system integrator circles debate what truly happens with regard to roaming in terms of how many access points a typical user associates with during the normal course of a workday. Many believe most roaming occurs only within one RF cell that belongs to one access point. I agree that this is likely the most common form of mobility for most deployments in manufacturing, retail, and the K-12 education markets. That said, the rule is probably the opposite for highly agile workforces such as healthcare, public safety, and higher education. The more agile the workforce, the more roaming should be a prioritized issue for evaluation.

Roaming is important, especially when latency-sensitive applications such as voice and video are concerned, but also certainly with regard to location-based services (LBS). The concept of a client in motion while being tracked for real-time location isn't the same as the classic definition of roaming—which is changing the client association from one access point to another—but in LBS scenarios, how and where a client moves has a great deal to do with accuracy and repeatability in terms of understanding the client's position.

Roaming from one access point to another requires a myriad of software and firmware adjustments to ensure a smooth transition all along the route in which the client is moving. Roaming is one of the first sources of end user complaints in a WLAN that isn't fully stable and reliable, exceeded only in technical support calls by users who are unable to associate and log in to a WLAN. To keep this network dynamic in check, not only for now, but as the network expands and evolves, it must be managed ahead of the curve rather than retroactively.

QoS Assessments

Quality of Service (QoS) is an inherent part of voice and video traffic, and indeed every network where applications, personnel, clients, or location is given priority over other traffic. It's important because it provides assurance for priority traffic. Bandwidth, delay, jitter, and allowable levels of packet losses are part of what QoS implementations manage. Evaluating not only QoS mechanisms on the network but also how QoS policies are determined is vital to affording the best-performing and most reliable WLAN possible for an investment.

QoS has perhaps a special role in the world of WLAN, because wireless networks are more prone to contention as data packets travel through free space; the potential for collision, contention, and degradation is arguably more pronounced in a wireless network than in a network where the packets travel more reliably inside jacketed copper or fiber mediums. An unlicensed wireless network such as 802.11 affords perhaps even more value for a QoS implementation, given the great number of radiating unlicensed devices and how they are less likely to be configured in a noninvasive manner regarding neighboring wireless networks.

Applications Assessments

As with assessing the OSI stack, assessing applications such as voice, security, and location requires specific tools and uniquely deep understandings of those specialties. One key assessment would be to ensure how well the applications perform at the client level, given that most clients operate on elegant power structures, such as handheld clients that typically feature smaller processors and less RAM and ROM, and they sip as little electrical power as possible to help with battery longevity. This makes them, in general, less able to overcome application and other OSI stack glitches by using pure processing power or memory. If an application works well on a handheld client, it nearly always works well on the network infrastructure side.

Applications are critical in wireless networks and networks in general because each application itself is being used to perform or augment valuable tasks. Most of the applications you enjoy reside in the background—for example, there's a whole lot more to a security application than matching the username and password. The same is true for voice, location services, and so on. While we see only the very tip of the application iceberg, we know it works when we attempt to use it in a normal production format. Tooling and evaluation by experts allow insights into far more of the stability and functionality of the applications.

Increased Node Count and Traffic

In performing network assessments, it is essential that you keep in mind not only the present state, scope, and use of the network, but you must also retain a view of the network three years in the future.

Networks undergo substantial evolutionary changes as they grow in node count and the amount of traffic distributed to various endpoints, and with the significant increase in end points. Presently, by far the largest increase in networks is the number of network endpoints that are smartphones. Smartphone integration into networks now represents a significant contribution of additional data; in the case of service providers such as AT&T, Verizon, and others, smartphones have increased 3G data traffic by 5000 percent, according to AT&T CTO John Donovan (*MacDailyNews*, November 18, 2009).

Most networks aren't experiencing that much data traffic increase from a single new type of endpoint device, but few, if any, cases of decrease in network traffic have been documented in healthy and growing businesses. Indeed, the Visual Networking Index forecast of traffic between 2008 and 2013 is impressive; it shows that the Internet will be four times as large in 2013 as it was in 2009 (see www.cisco.com/en/US/solutions/collateral/ns341/ns525/ns537/ns705/ns827/white_paper_c11-481360_ns827_Networking_Solutions_White_Paper.html.)

Understanding where future nodes will reside as well the nature of the endpoints such as building automation, RFID, physical security, or a wide variety of other devices is vital. The closer to the core of the network, that is, the largest switches and routers, the greater the need to consider increased future traffic not just in terms of pure bandwidth, but also in terms of quality of service if future considerations include voice systems for inventory control, wireless cameras for video surveillance, and similar devices.

Discussions should also necessarily include a view into the future in terms of large acquisitions by the company, such as the acquisition of a competitor or a company that ventures into new sales and marketing ventures that are not part of the current operating business. Examples of such ventures on a small scale might include a bakery that purchases a small trucking company to make deliveries and transport raw materials, a car rental company that purchases an auto-body repair facility, and so forth.

One of the largest implications for the consideration of nodes and traffic count is relative to the borderless networks phenomenon that, in part, is where endpoints owned and maintained by one company may reside in a completely different company, perhaps even on a different continent. This scenario has been around for some years now in the example of large retail companies that want to monitor and manage the supply chain of goods more closely and at every point between the retail floor: the transportation elements such as truck, rail, and ship, and the original manufacturing sites; and well into the subcontractors of the manufacturing sites.

While the scope of what may be incorporated into a network beyond the three-year time frame can be difficult to predict accurately; there is a considerable amount known about what may happen in the next two years. Incorporating these possibilities into how the present-day network may be affected allows for much improved network planning, resource allocation, and ultimately, reduced cost of operations as well as increased corporate resilience and competitive agility.

Present Assessment Report and Review

A best practice to consider during the final assembly of the wireless network assessment report is the balance between a report that truly stands on its own—that is, it requires relatively little cross-referencing to other documents—yet it remains small and features crisp content that most stakeholders will understand regarding the best ways to ensure the wireless IT investment meets the needs of the business.

In the final assessment report, you should include an explanation of terms to describe technical and other networking jargon, as most report users will be nontechnical types. As IT stakeholders, they'll need to be conversant in basic networking terms and should well understand what their network can, and should, do. But the wireless network assessment report will have far less value to far fewer stakeholders if it is filled with indecipherable technical jargon. Where appropriate, such jargon can be reserved for the engineering section of the report, written by and for engineers. Semi-technical and nontechnical stakeholders are the ones who'll be making the budget recommendations for upgrading the network. The technical assessment personnel will need to ensure that the report is eminently digestible by those who control the budget purse strings.

There are as many forms for an optimal wireless network assessment report as there are teams performing the work. That stated, the best and most meaningful reports will likely include the following key elements:

- Top operational problems statement
- Network migration statement
- Migration high-level design, audit plan, deployment, maintenance
- Bill of materials
- Cost and amortization statements

Top Operational Problems Statement

Beginning the wireless network assessment report with a statement of the top operational problems is essential because it fosters a discussion on those same points. It's my experience that less than 5 percent of enterprise network stakeholder teams fully understand these problems.

If these discussions have not occurred or the issues have not been disseminated from the executive officers, initiating this dialogue is a healthy and productive corporate practice. Chances are, if the executives have not communicated the top corporate problems to the operational staff, the operational problems will not likely have been addressed.

Another interesting development occurs when these dialogues are initiated. In my experience, duplicate funding for projects is found about 25 percent of the time when IT stakeholder groups are first established. The first time I experienced this, I was parachuted into a large account for a government agency. The potentially large project had become bogged down with interdepartmental differences. I agreed to speak to the customer on two conditions: that the customer would agree to all parties participating in one room at one time, and that I would be allowed to paint a broad picture to the entire group of what was possible from certain wireless network upgrades.

The meeting was remarkable; I spoke for only about 20 minutes before turning it over to the stakeholders. They had a wonderful, animated, frank, and revealing discussion that lasted nearly two hours. Following the meeting, a number of agency people approached me, complimenting my employer and me for one of the best meetings of the year.

The truth was they did nearly all of the talking and were quite able to sort out the coordination and objectives among themselves. The project budget nearly quadrupled, as it was determined that multiple duplicate budgets had been set aside. The project was very successful and was one of the largest wireless deployments of the year. To the best of my knowledge, that stakeholder group remained intact for many months after that meeting.

No master list of top operational problems existed before that meeting, but the stakeholders were more than capable of understanding and prioritizing the top problems. The untethering of applications and enabling real-time mobility through voice and location were essential elements of resolving their problems. And it continues to be for many other organizations in similar meetings.

Network Migration Statement

One of the most important elements of an assessment report is an overview of where the network is technically evolving: the migration statement. Some of the gaps between what the network can do today and where it can improve to meet the business operational priorities may already be closed through normal technical upgrades. In my experience, 30 to 50 percent of the time, fairly major network upgrades are already scheduled and budgeted.

The statement should also include information on the manner in which the network *should* evolve. This is a critical summary that highlights changes that should be made to reduce the delta between what the network can do and should do. This portion of the assessment report is likely to be the most read portion of the document; most of the other elements exist to support the migration assertions.

Migration High-Level Design, Audit Plan, Deployment, and Maintenance

This reference pertains to the high-level design, audit plan, deployment, and maintenance of the migration plan, not the existing network. As stated, only a small percentage of existing networks are well documented, primarily because documentation is highly labor intensive and because most enterprise-class networks are in a perpetual state of evolution, so maintaining up-to-date records would require expensive overhead, additional meetings, and a reduction of the migration velocity. Anyone technically savvy enough to document a migration fully and carefully without extensive interviews of the migration team would likely be applied as a resource to the actual migration as opposed to the migration documentation. This is apparently why most network design resides in "corporate memory"—that is, in the minds of those who've performed the migration and work.

This is hardly specific to the IT industry. Next time you're walking down the sidewalk and you see a telephone company truck parked on the curb next to a large gray cabinet with open doors, ask the technician staring at the bird's nest of wires if the cabinet's contents are well documented and enjoy the gales of laughter. Each local telephone repair person adds changes or subtracts lines over a period of time that becomes decades. Most of the technician's time is spent isolating the wires he or she needs to work with.

The same is true in enterprise-class networks, except in this environment, myriads of boxes reside on numerous racks with dozens, if not hundreds, of code, hardware, and software variants. In this scenario, time is spent in isolating issues—the repair is usually not as challenging as determining the source of the problem.

The challenge is that networks, unlike local phone exchanges, are growing vastly more complicated. Even a modest enterprise network that supports 250 employees with wireless access has an eyebrow raising number of technology issues to contend with. The opportunity to document the migration will baseline not the technical maintenance, but the budgetary maintenance required going forward. It therefore does not need to be as up-to-date or comprehensive in nature. It does, however, need to outline a multiyear network evolution trajectory for which budgets can be spoken for months, if not a year, in advance. The result is a wireless network that more nearly ideally resolves the top operational concerns of a customer's network.

Assessment Report Bill of Materials (BoM)

The BoM is an essential element of the assessment report because it specifies the network elements to be migrated and outlines the budgetary allocation going forward; another optimal variant of the BoM is one that is phased appropriately to capture not only the correct amount of manpower required, but also the correct amount of financial resources necessary to purchase, plan, audit, deploy, and maintain the upgraded or new wireless elements.

The BoM can also consider not just equipment that is available on the market today, but versions or releases of the equipment that will become available during the multi-month or multiyear migration. This kind of knowledge comes from a close association among the end customer, the system integrator, and the technology equipment provider. To accomplish this, state-of-the-art equipment may be better suited for early adopters such as higher education customers. Healthcare, on the other hand, has been far more reserved, and appropriately so, on how close they get to the edge of technology development with regard to networking equipment.

These assertions hold up fairly well on a generalized basis, though I recognize there is a spectrum of risk acceptance and aversion in every wireless market. The larger point is that the technical evolution should be considered as an element in the assembly of bills of materials for wireless network assessments.

Assessment Report Cost and Amortization Statements

If you're receiving a wireless network assessment as a customer, you're likely dealing with one of the elite mobility partners on the planet. If you're a technology partner to an IT equipment vendor, you're one of the most valued partners of that technology provider. That compliment duly paid, one of the most common errors I see in network assessment reports is the focus on cost versus amortization schedule.

The great secret that most integrators have yet to discover is the superior caliber of an investment in mobility. The critical bridge between that truth and the bookings that flow from it is the amortization statement included in the wireless network assessment report.

There is no sidestepping the issue of cost when evaluating network performance and how it meets the business's top operational considerations. All decoration aside, at some point a purchase order must be created for the equipment, and that fee is paid to the integrator and ultimately the IT equipment provider. This affects the cash flow of the customer that is placing a bet on getting a good return for the money spent on a mobility investment.

And that's another key point. If the technology integrator indicates only cost and does not include estimated amortization statements with the report, two essential elements will be lacking:

- The justification for the investment
- A delay in closing the transaction due to missing or incomplete ROI modeling

More than just including cost and amortization of the mobility investment, it's a shrewd move for the integrator to include financing from the technology equipment provider or the integrator itself. A long-term lease program is attractive for many customers because it eliminates the need for a lump sum payment, which eases customer cash flow and, more importantly, preserves cash flow until the investment begins to pay off.

Further, a lease program ensures a perfectly predictable cash-flow scenario over the term of the equipment lease. Predictable cash flow is very attractive to a CFO and their department. The CFO team takes a lot of effort to ensure a healthy cash flow in the business; little else it does has more importance to the health, growth, and longevity of a business than the critical issue of cash flow. In every sense, it is the lifeblood of the organization and is an excellent predictor of hard times or business expansion ahead.

One of the other advantages of leasing is for the integrator: equipment that is leased is less likely to be replaced by a competitor because leases are expensive to terminate early, and early termination involves additional contractual review and negotiations. Most integrators have gross profits on hardware of only a handful of percentage points; an early buyout of a competitive lease can erode most of that for an incoming competitive integrator. If there are delays in deployment from a slightly misjudged sales process, or there is any other factor that delays deployment, the incoming competitor is further compromised. It cannot sustain a great deal of these kinds of engagements without significantly straining its own cash flow and credit resources. Financing through leases is therefore a powerful competitive mitigator.

In addition, most IT equipment leases benefit the integrator because the equipment passes directly from the technology provider to the end customer. The integrator does not, in that scenario, usually have to purchase and then resell the equipment, which ties up capital, fills physical space, undergoes delays through shipping, and increases management overhead to enable the transaction. Even better, the integrator receives a lump sum payment from the technology provider or lessor, which is attractive to the integrator on a cash-flow basis.

Another benefit to leasing may or may not be relative to the amortization statement included in the wireless assessment report: At the end of the lease, the customer can renew the lease for something on the order of a single additional payment. In many cases, an additional payment can be negotiated or divided into the total payments of the new lease. What this means to the customer is that it retains current equipment in its IT infrastructure on a forward-going basis with its attendant reduced initial costs, reduced total cost of ownerships, enhanced security, and improved performance and reliability.

The concepts of highlighting the amortization statement and illuminating the cash-flow implications of a mobility investment are truly important. This is why I have so passionately committed my efforts over the last five years to expand mobility discussions from an engineer-to-engineer basis to include the C suite and the IT stakeholder team.

Unbeknown to most system integrators, final purchasing decisions are often totally separate from the technological merits of the sale. This is an amusing contrast, because most IT equipment vendors and integrators use most of the engagement to discuss technical merits. Yet, more often than not, the decision is made in the quiet confines of the financing department that is advising the C suite on where to make the smartest investments with limited amounts of capital.

I love engineers and often jokingly refer to myself as "a recovering engineer" because I spent so many years as a wireless network engineer and engineering manager. It's clear to me that customer engagements that feature engineer-to-engineer discussions are very nearly always smaller deals than engagements in which the C suite is included in the discussion, and this demonstrates how an investment in mobility is one of the best possible investments a customer can make. Mobility has a powerful impact in how well a customer operates. It also impacts how profitable the integrator can be, because it has a high service bookings per product dollar and it often pulls along other technology and services such as security, voice, location, and remote network operations services.

If an integrator is not truly conversant in amortization statements, they can nearly always receive support for this deliverable either from their own finance or leasing department or in many cases from the customer finance department. Ideally the integrator will lay out the general terms of the financial benefits from their own finance department before fine-tuning the details with the customer finance department.

Amortization statements are not complex to assemble or understand, and the assessment report has considerable additional leverage when it includes a statement from the customer finance department on how well the prospective investment in mobility performs as a financial option. It's that very department that typically gives the green light, or not, to the company C suite regarding the prospective purchase. Shaping the assessment in terms of the quality of investment makes it easier and faster for the finance department to recommend the project be funded.

Plan for Recurring Assessments and Next-Generation IT Investments

One of my regular discussions with elite mobility partners covers how to increase service revenues. The catch there of course is how to do this while creating additional value at the end customer. Most integrators make most of their money from services, not by reselling hardware. Most enterprise-class customers reduce the total cost of ownership of their IT assets when they carefully subcontract IT engineering to third-party firms such as technology integrators.

As IT equipment evolves, a few clear trends are revealed, including the concept of total cost of ownership (TCO). Reduced TCO is a main reason we're seeing major IT migrations such as cloud-based networking; centralized management of wireless networks; and smarter, more powerful, adaptable RF systems that maintain client links at greater distances and in more challenging RF environments.

The value of recurring network assessments is important to the end customers, the integrators, and the wireless equipment providers. Although no major wireless technology developments are emerging at this time, how wireless is being used is of perhaps equal, if not greater, value than migration to 802.11n. That said, the adoption of 802.11n has been more rapid than any other unlicensed wireless protocol in the last ten years. This is because it reduces costs, increases reliability, and improves performance, both on the access point and the client side of the RF link. This, along with a cross-pollination of industry best practices, is among the many reasons an annual recurring wireless network assessment is beneficial to the end customer, the integrator, and the wireless equipment provider.

CHAPTER 7 | Optimal Project Sequencing

uthor James Thurber once said, "It is better to know some of the questions than all of the answers." For wireless network users, integrators, and IT technology providers, the right questions are brought about by Optimal Project Sequencing (OPS), an important strategy that provides the right questions to help them enable project discipline on wireless network deployments of all sizes. Many questions serve as the leading components in the steps required to plan, deploy, maintain, and migrate a wireless network.

OPS provides an optimal sequence for larger and smaller WLAN projects. This WLAN deployment methodology will ensure the fewest project delays, the lowest cost of deployment and maintenance, and the greatest likelihood that the deployment will be tightly coupled to the top operational priorities of the end customer.

OPS was born as a result of experiences in some of the most complex WLAN deployments on the planet, plus many other deployments that weren't nearly as complex. In the aggregate, they provided enormous insight into the project management side of deploying WLANs.

I've taught OPS to hundreds of partners and customers over the years, and it has consistently yielded excellent results in terms of improving the quality of deployments and, critical for integrators, reducing the cost of deployments. This improves both customer and system integrator profit margins and frees human and fiscal capital to pursue more projects earlier in the sales cycle. OPS will continue to be an essential development in the years ahead, as both engineering and sales teams will experience considerable pressure to improve their productivity and financial output in major ways.

Much of the value of OPS is derived from first asking this question: How does this deployment best resolve the top operational problems of this customer? In considering the question, you must carefully consider who is involved—not just from the integrator and technology equipment provider, but most importantly at the beginning phase of the project, the customer.

Stakeholder collaboration is "ground zero" for wireless network deployments; it's also, therefore, ground zero in OPS. When the right stakeholders ask why they are doing this, the deployments are nearly always completed with much more velocity, and the deliverable generates value more quickly because it's coupled tightly with the top operational priorities set forth by the C suite. These benefits free up capital and human resources to resolve top operational issues in other important ways, such as training personnel in using the new technology, confirming policy changes, improving collaboration methods, and staking out new sales and competitive territories.

OPS has its roots set deeply in the hands-on world of the planning, deployment, maintenance, and migration of some of the world's largest and most complex WLANs. In one five-year period, for example, Cisco parachuted me into major WLAN projects around the world with the intent of unscrambling engagements that had gone awry. I kept notes on the key elements we used to resolve these engagement issues. I was shipped to sites around the world obstensibly to apply my RF and WLAN engineering experience to customer and integrator sites to resolve wireless technical issues, in particular those regarding RF design and propagation. I soon realized that the resolution tools and core issues I encountered were far different from anything we expected.

As I reviewed my post-engagement notes, I noticed that significant portions of the project challenges had clearly recurring themes: stakeholders were either late to the project or, in most cases, stakeholders were completely absent from the projects. I could see the correlation between stakeholder involvement and quality of not only the outcome, but also project velocity, access to critical physical areas, total budget allocation, and the speed with which a myriad of other logistic, technical, and quality issues occurred. In addition, I realized that other sequence elements were either deficient or missing entirely from the process.

Key WLAN Projects: The Foundation of OPS

I have evaluated the common elements of engagement resolutions for many WLAN projects around the world. A handful of projects stand out because they contributed unique and key illuminations that augmented today's OPS process. Without disclosing the actual customers, here's a list of some milestone projects and the key OPS element they brought to the forefront:

- Nuclear power plant design: Meet customer requirements.
- Very large aircraft manufacturing project: Gain access to complex facility equipment.
- A (very) large retailer: Gather input from facilities managers.
- Nuclear submarine fabrication facility: Use the locals.
- Shipyard coverage: Account for ground zero effect.
- Classified aircraft fabrication facility: Consider legacy systems.
- Muni projects: Find the money.

Nuclear Power Plant Design: Meet Customer Requirements

I was brought into this project at a late stage—in football parlance, it was a "hail Mary" play—because we were advised that the work was awarded to a competitor. In fact, the purchase order for the project was already printed and awaiting a signature. The competitors were staged and ready to begin that week on this large project.

A site survey had been conducted, costing an astounding amount of money; at that time, nearly all site surveys were provided for free by the integrators. This was a big ticket cost to the customer and was larger in pure dollar size than nearly any other WLAN deployment that year, including hardware and engineering costs. The site surveys in those days were a far cry from today's sophisticated and digitally documented engagements; this fact emphasizes the outrageous expense charged for this site survey. The customer was not likely to write off that expense and start the project over again with another WLAN company.

I arrived at the nuclear power plant the afternoon the purchase order was to be signed. I met with the customer project manager and asked if we could provide one final deployment review. The customer graciously agreed, and we reviewed the project as it was about to be awarded. Obviously, no confidential details were revealed about the competitor, but we were able to review the drawings and site survey results.

The design appeared to be sufficient to sustain nominal amounts of data traffic, though I did have some concerns about RF coverage with the antennas selected and power output. The meeting was moving to a close, and I had not found a way for us to displace the competitor—until the last few minutes of the meeting, when the customer mentioned in an off-hand way that he was excited about how this WLAN was going to allow wireless voice conversations from anywhere to anywhere within the nuclear plant. I realized then that the design was inappropriate to support voice.

In those days, we had two RF designs—one for low latency designs such as voice, and a more standard "data only" design. The design that I had just reviewed was clearly for data only. The spacing of the access points and other design attributes and configurations showed no consideration for voice-level connectivity, roaming, or Quality of Service (QoS) in the design.

"You realize," I mentioned, "that this design won't sustain voice traffic, right?" The program manager recoiled. "No, we never discussed this with your competitor. We simply assumed they knew we wanted to run voice over the WLAN."

Many voice traffic considerations had not been incorporated into the design I reviewed. The RF design would not allow roaming between access points, and it did not provide contiguous coverage down corridors and between major pieces of equipment from which clients would need to operate reliably. The design was a "hotspot" design—in other words, the end users would have to walk to a place where the signal was strong enough to sustain client traffic.

That problem, combined with other issues, allowed my company to recapture the project, especially because we had vastly more knowledge about voice traffic, from the RF and client elements all the way back to the voice control managers and router/ switch configurations.

While I'm not a voice expert, I have designed and audited many WLANs that carry voice. One of the differences between designs provided by a radio company like our competitor and a networking company like Cisco was the array of considerations that we know must extend from the clients to the core switches and routers. One of our first tasks was to sit down with stakeholders to discuss the voice traffic the next-generation WLAN was to carry.

The project ended up being one of the largest WLAN deployments in the industry that year. I learned only a few months ago that this design has served the customer very well since that date—in fact, it was expanded from approximately 700 access points to more than 2000. Voice traffic was also being augmented with real-time video traffic and other sensors deemed important to the nuclear industry. It was tremendously rewarding to learn that the network had served as an indispensible tool for this high-profile customer, and that the scope of the deployment was being tripled.

Both the customer and Cisco learned a valuable lesson with this project—one that I've applied in every major project I've supported since that time: *Ensure that you know what type of traffic will be deployed over the WLAN.*

Aircraft Manufacturing Project: Gain Access to Complex Facility Equipment

This project involved deploying one of the largest WLANs in the world, on a cubic-foot basis. Unusual at the time, nearly all this project's WLANs were designed to cover floor areas only. This deployment required highly reliable coverage from the floor to an elevation of nearly 70 feet, with a coverage area of 27 million cubic feet.

The stakeholder discussions and design were challenging but well within the range of our capabilities. At the correct point in the project, a team arrived on site from various points around the country for four days of design audits and site survey work. As part of the audit, we needed to verify RF coverage at not just the floor area where workers operated, but at various points throughout "the cube," which is how we referred to the total space being covered.

The most remote portion of the cube was near the top of the coverage area some 70 feet off the floor, at the aircraft tail fin area. We requested a scissor lift to proceed with measurements at that height, but the customer refused to allow employees outside the company to access these lifts. As we had not instructed any of the customer's employees on how to audit our design with complex RF measurement equipment, and the customer could not allow us onto their scissor lifts, the project ground to a halt. We could measure only about 15 percent of the total area required. The vast majority of the coverage area audit would not be completed on that trip, and we had little to show for the considerable portion of the project travel and expense budget used.

Although the travel and expense portion of the project was already used, there was no way we could abandon the inspection of approximately 85 percent of the cubic space the design covered. The customer was unyielding on this point, as was our engineering team. Not being able to measure most of the space where the WLAN existed, through which would pass one of the world's largest aircraft, was too great a design risk. We would have to reassemble the team and return another time.

The resulting meetings to resolve this matter took nearly six months, and we did in fact end up deploying the system satisfactorily. It was an extraordinary delay that slowed the customer down, incurred significant costs for us because we could not ship or deploy the WLAN and because a considerable number of sales, customers, and engineering cycles were invested in resolving the issue.

Lesson learned: *Arrange major pieces of equipment and, as required, gain advance permission for access into restricted spaces. Identify and resolve these issues near the beginning of the RF design planning phase, not at the beginning of the audit phase.*

Retailer: Gather Input from Facilities Managers

At the distribution facility of a major retailer, we were asked to deploy outdoor RF coverage. In this facility, retail goods were received from across the world and then palletized for shipments to retail stores across the United States. Such warehouses are massive, approximately 1 million square feet or more in size. To provide some perspective on how large that is, a 1 million square foot warehouse is equal to about 17 football fields, all under one roof. The rooms can be so large that most of the far walls can barely be seen; all your eye views is floor and ceiling. The outdoor areas that surrounded the warehouse were far larger yet, and the largest trucks on the road surround these buildings on every side, with hundreds of loading docks around the building.

The project was highly compromised and it seemed clear we were not only about to lose the account, but we would also be liable for considerable cost overruns. Upon my arrival, the facilities manager had just completed an uncomfortable meeting with the integrator responsible for installing the outdoor WLAN equipment sold by my company. These outdoor access points (APs) were being mounted on the light poles in the paved area surrounding the warehouse—a good architectural approach to covering these kinds of areas.

The problem was getting power to the APs during the day. The plan was to take the power supplied to the pole to run the night lights, which is also an appropriate architectural approach in many cases, but the integrator noticed that the power to the poles was shut off during daylight hours. This is not much of a surprise to many, but it was to the integrator on this project.

The integrator knew that daylight power was available at the building and that the APs needed to be mounted on various light poles that were a considerable distance away from the building. The integrator decided to hire a trenching company and run buried power cables from the main building to each of the poles selected as mounting points for the outdoor APs.

The trenching was completed on the day the facilities manager returned from a two-week vacation. As the last of the trenches was being paved over, the facilities manager wondered why his brand-new parking lot was being paved over in strips between the building and dozens of light poles.

The integrator was proud of the fact that the power problem had been resolved and added "only" about $80,000 to the project cost. The facilities manager, however, knew that $80,000 was close to the entire budget allocation to extend the WLAN to the light poles. At this point, the project had gone over budget by a factor of two and was not yet completed. After hearing the reasoning behind the trenching, the facilities manager indicated that a daylight power junction box was located inside the facility and could have been altered for about $2500, which would have supplied power to the base of each of the poles during the daylight.

All that was needed to remedy the situation in the power poles was a small daylight power junction box and sensor at each of the poles to ensure the APs would have power during the day. I arrived on the site minutes after the heated discussion occurred between the facilities manager and the integrator. After more heated discussions between the customer, the integrator, and my employer, the cost overrun and route to project completion was resolved and completed. The project runs well today, and it was a painful if not effective and memorable lesson on the importance of including the right stakeholders at the right time.

The lesson: *Facilities personnel are key stakeholders in complex WLAN projects. Facility operational knowledge is critical in large WLAN deployments.*

Nuclear Submarine Fabrication Facility: Use the Locals

A modern nuclear submarine is immense in complexity, beauty, and size. The latest submarines are referred to as the "Virginia class," and they're impressive to see in person at 377 feet long, 34 feet wide, and displacing 7800 tons of water. Think of a long, black, stealthy shaped machine that covers more than the length of an NFL football field, about half of its width and as tall as a five-story building at the sail. It's actually larger in person than you can envision.

Our project was to compete against another company for a project to cover the entire final assembly area of these submarines, along with some adjacent buildings and areas. Whenever possible in a competitive "bake-off" scenario, which occurs when you test your equipment against competitive equipment to determine which is theoretically better, I try to play the odds by requesting to go last. I want the competitors to blaze the trail for my team in certain ways—learning where the AC power is, how to attach the APs to elevated heights, how to acquire access to facility areas, and how many personnel are required to complete the test.

Going last was a good idea. The younger and more eager RF engineers often haven't learned that an excellent engineer can get more out of modest 802.11 equipment than a poor engineer can get out of excellent 802.11 equipment. When you combine a senior engineer's excellent technology and some hard-earned experience, younger eager beaver engineers nearly always finish second or worse in technology contests. In this case, I learned through casual conversation that a certain RF channel simply would not work in the test environment, which was an area that surrounded the final assembly tooling around the nuclear submarines.

I didn't have time to sort out why that was occurring; I only knew that our competitors had decent gear and that this channel didn't work. I also noted the types of antennas and power setting they were using. Our competitors could barely get a reliable signal down to the handheld clients used by the production assembly workers. This was partly due to their antenna selection, but more importantly they completely ignored the handheld client path routes. In other words, their equipment did a terrific job of radiating the area—40 feet above where it needed to be.

I took the time to ask the fabrication technicians where it was they needed to use the handheld clients. They were only too happy to spend 15 minutes showing me the exact areas that needed to be covered, and which areas were more important than others. We took our turn during the bake-off and ensured the RF coverage was precisely where it needed to be. This, along with some terrific work by my colleagues in other key areas of the engagement, ensured that we handily won the contract.

Lesson learned: *Use local knowledge when deploying systems. Including representatives from the actual end users is mission-critical to ensure that design intents are properly characterized and verified. Restated, it matters what problems the C suite is attempting to resolve with WLANs. It's just as important to speak to the blue-collar team about exactly how the equipment will be used to ensure maximum value of the deployment.*

Shipyard Coverage: Account for Ground Zero Effect

Shipyards that build large military or commercial crafts are immense in size, and this Louisiana facility was no different. The huge deployment, which occurred a few months after Hurricane Katrina, was under way and going well. I was brought on site because the RF propagation challenges were considerable. The size of the area covered, the available mounting points for the APs and electrical power sources, and the fact that very large structures weighing tens of thousands of pounds swung through the radiating area by cranes all contributed to very complex RF coverage issues.

As we toured the facility with the customer team, we discussed how the WLAN would be used, including the various outdoor environmental conditions the users would face year-round. We saw firsthand the extent of the damage from the hurricane, and specifically how deep the water was when it washed over the entire facility. What was not discussed during any of the previous meetings was the value of the sparse WLAN that was in place during the storm. It had played a key communications role during the worst part of the event.

It became very clear, not just to my team, but also to the customer, how valuable the WLAN was as they shared stories of how it was used. To the best of my knowledge, it was the first time these experiences had been shared openly by the customer; we were privileged to hear from those who were actually there. It was decided that the WLAN would and should play a key communications role in the next major storm event. What's clear to those who live their lives on the ocean is that the storm you just survived is only one ahead of the next one coming at some point in the future. It's not a fatalistic view, but is rather quite a realistic one.

The original design for the WLAN was nowhere near what it needed to be in what we called a "ground zero event." The usages, clients, power sources, and physical security of the wireless elements from the weather all required considerable rethinking and redesign. The outcome was a design that would be far more serviceable in the event of heavy weather or other macro-disruptive scenarios.

Lesson learned: *Consider how IT assets perform in heavy weather or other major incidents that have a major impact on customer operations. The network traffic, reliability, capacity, resilience, and other critical conditions are very different in emergency scenarios than in normal day-to-day operations. It may be appropriate to incorporate ground zero considerations into the network design for wireless access.*

Classified Aircraft Fabrication Facility: Consider Legacy Systems

If there's a common military theme from these lessons learned, it's purely unintentional and largely coincidental. Interestingly, government projects rank in the top five of the industry's WLAN customers, but they just barely make the list. They are unusual and memorable if only for the facilities themselves, as most ordinary citizens don't get to see these facilities. Working inside the final assembly facility for one of the world's latest, stealthiest, and most capable combat aircraft would certainly rank among those rare experiences one remembers for the rest of their life.

It was also the site of one of the best pranks I've seen in my professional life. During a tour of the hangar area, a light rain began to fall. One of the stealth aircraft was just outside the hangar door, and the ground around it remained dry. Someone had just moved the aircraft a few moments prior to my colleague and his guest rounding the corner where the jet sat only moments ago.

My colleague asked his guest if he could see the jet. "No, I really can't," said the guest, at which point my colleague asked the guest to remain standing where he was, while my colleague walked up to the area where the jet had been and began to pretend to pat the jet where it once stood, the dry ground below marking the apparent location. "Our stealth technology is so good," my colleague added, "that you can't even see these in broad daylight when they stand right in front of you. We lose these all the time this way." The guest was deeply impressed, and to the best of my knowledge he was never told it was a prank!

RF networks are somewhat like that: if you don't know what you're looking for, your eyes can readily deceive you. In the case of this facility, I arrived to tour the facility and lead the RF design because of the size, environmental variation type, and propagation complexity. While touring facilities like this, I often run a laptop-based program to sniff the air for RF energy, including possible sources of interference. We were told at the onset of this project that this was the first WLAN this group would install. My instrumentation showed anything but that; I could clearly detect not only a preexisting system, but five existing legacy systems.

Upon revealing this to the customer, he was quite surprised but had some ideas as to who the owners might be. Further investigation revealed that five separate operation groups within this large manufacturing facility had designed, tested, and deployed, and were maintaining their own systems. Each system was layered on top of the other. When the customer group with which I was working wanted to install a facility-wide WLAN, careful coordination would have been required to minimize interference between each of the five systems.

These five preexisting systems were fairly far apart from one another. This is what kept them from interfering. Installing a macro WLAN that would have overlaid them all would have likely resulted in degraded performance for both the legacy and new WLANs. Meetings were called, budgets were combined, and a small team was assembled from the various groups to lead, test, and manage the new system. All five systems, plus the new macro system, were to be managed under one umbrella team.

Handheld clients, applications, and management tooling was standardized to reduce overall cost to the customer, simplify training, and enable workers to transfer from one working group to another because they were familiar with the RF handheld clients; perhaps more importantly, the system operated on a seamless and complementary basis, allowing handheld clients and applications to roam from one cell and WLAN to another with quality and reliability suitable for voice. This allowed them to consider upgrading from their legacy walkie-talkie system to IP voice wireless handsets that allowed a wide array of applications to be pushed to the handheld client instead of push-to-talk voice only.

Lesson learned: *Consider that legacy systems may be in place even if your particular customer group is not aware of them. These systems will also identify key stakeholders who need to be part of the overall stakeholder team. Combining budgets and creating umbrella teams will not add bureaucracy; instead, they'll enable a synthesized approach to a company-wide WLAN that will perform seamlessly and allow roaming for various applications such as voice and, in the near future, handheld video. This collaboration will reduce operating costs and greatly increase the value of the wireless transport as additional applications are added.*

Muni Projects: Find the Money

One of the most exciting news stories around 2005 was the possibility of providing a coast-to-coast unlicensed wireless system. It seemed nearly every major metropolitan area and county government wanted to get in on this project, which some of us in the WLAN industry identified fairly quickly as a fad—one of the few in the wireless industry. Like all fads, it was consigned early to certain failure, though not for technical reasons. A small group of us in the industry believed something was far more important than technology to a business or city or county government, and that was cash flow—or rather, in this case, the lack of it.

The project type was called "muni-wireless." The idea was to provide Internet access to the poor in particular and to the public who were visiting each of these cities. It was theorized that by providing "free" Internet access, more people would live, work, learn, and play in these cities because they would have more of a connected experience.

It was during this craze, which was adopted by hundreds of city, state, and county governments, that one of the world's largest advertising companies had an even bigger idea. It wanted to install a wireless network on each of its roadside billboards so it could install immense LCD screens and change the advertising based on end customer, holiday seasons, local specials, and the location of the end customers who might be near the billboard and have the billboard push special offers and coupons to the retail customer's cell phones. These billboards were not counted in the hundreds or even thousands—in fact, hundreds of thousands of them were located across the country, all owned by this same advertising company.

It was a grand idea, and an enticing one. These meetings were led by a senior vice president from this prominent company who was absolutely convinced that this was the wave of the future. The project would cost tens of millions of dollars to design and deploy, and it would require thousands of installation technicians and hundreds of subcontracted companies. Not quite a lunar lander for scope and cost, but getting toward that end of the cost and scope spectrum.

I learned an important lesson from muni projects, however. When it came time to pay for the projects, no money could be found. Indeed, there wasn't a single responsible party who was offering to take sole responsibility for the design, deployment, and, equally importantly to my employer and the system integrators, the payment for the services and hardware.

What I learned for the first time was how deeply fractured city and state governments are on a political basis. That observation may seem logical and should not come as a surprise to many, but as technologists, we were simply looking to solve a problem with wireless IT.

Further investigation of the matter revealed that even if the money were somehow found, the greater portion of the cost would be in maintaining the wireless networks. The natural state of an IT architecture is that it will eventually stop working if it's not maintained. The same is true for automobiles, homes, and even people. The challenge with the muni projects was even more troubling: there was no cash flow to sustain the program.

The concept of whether the underprivileged people should have jobs and shelter versus Internet access is a debate best left to others. My position was that if the program was not generating more cash than it cost to maintain, it simply would not survive very long. It would only be a matter of time before a storm or a car hitting a pole would knock out one of the wireless nodes. It would be expensive to repair and replace, though the larger cost issues would be deliverables such as a help desk when someone could not connect or had difficulty creating a new login. Other issues included security: how would the cities keep those with bad intent off the networks?

The fad for muni networks featuring access to the poor and free access to all died a natural death in approximately 2007. Astonishingly, to me, some networks had actually begun to be built. In the excitement of the opportunity, some integrators offered to begin building the muni projects before the billing process was resolved. City and county governments agreed to "find a way" to pay those companies. Unfortunately, this rarely if ever occurred.

As for the very large advertising company that wanted to connect hundreds of thousands of billboards wirelessly? The project ground to a halt when the executive from the advertising company realized he could not fund the project. His attempts to get my employer to underwrite the project were denied. The executive himself left the advertising company not long after this project was attempted. I have to give him ample credit for thinking big; he was on the right track. At the same time, fiscal sustainability is more than just a good idea with regard to WLANs and all IT investments; it's the life blood of the system.

Lesson learned: *The larger the project, the sooner you'll want to know how it's funded— and if it's funded at all. The efforts by the system integrator and technology vendors to sell their vital deliverables should not get too far ahead of the funding. The potential of the project is proportional to how well the cash flows through it. WLANs certainly carry various types of traffic, and, if well understood by all parties, they will transport knowledge. The knowledge WLANs transport is carried on the current of cash flow. The better the cash flows, the better the entire system operates from inception to migration to next generation of technology.*

Optimal Project Sequencing: Three Prevailing Concepts

In the years OPS was assembled, three prevailing concepts became apparent with regard to the methodology of sequencing of WLAN projects. These prevailing concepts underpin the OPS methodology:

- Quality is conformance to functional requirements.
- Nontechnical project elements are nearly always more challenging than technological issues.
- Optimal project sequencing requires a synthesis of technology and nontechnology issues.

Quality Is Conformance to the Requirements

You might remember a famous book, *Zen and the Art of Motorcycle Maintenance*, written in the mid-1970s by Robert M. Pirsig. The book was in fact about neither Zen nor motorcycles, but was an inquiry into values. In this book, a struggle is ensued to define quality. I was fascinated by this book and how challenging it was, at that time, to define quality—not simply to list the attributes of quality, but to state the very definition of quality itself.

I had the good fortune to build astrophysics spacecraft about ten years after this book was published. My manager, Earl Powell, was one of my greatest mentors as a program manager and also about how to pursue the quality of life itself. We often spoke of how to develop and maintain quality in various projects; you can only imagine the intensity with which quality is pursued in an aerospace program. The pursuit of this key factor is achieved at levels uncommon to most industries. Precision is everything for structures such as spacecraft, which must perform flawlessly and relatively autonomously at distances of hundreds if not millions of miles from the people who built it.

Earl and I were having lunch one day when I mentioned the popular book. After listening to me carefully for some minutes about how difficult it was to define quality, Earl mentioned with a smile that the definition of quality was easy: it was conformance to the requirements. I loved that definition, and I still do. It instantly settled the matter for me.

Quality is conformance to requirements. This statement is brilliant and fundamental to the OPS methodology. It also explains the vital need to assemble stakeholders and to guide them to define the definition of quality for an upcoming WLAN deployment.

When the stakeholders have not been assembled for a new and large deployment, I am often asked how the agenda should look. The agenda's objective is to define the requirements of the WLAN. It rarely takes long for the stakeholder group to catch this vision of its mission. Where no preexisting stakeholder group exists, rarely is there a broadly held understanding of the top business operational priorities. Possessing those top priorities, and occasionally being charged with the task of defining the top operational priorities of a project, quickly leads to the establishment of the requirements.

Functional requirements are the type of requirements that allow engineers to define the WLAN in terms of design, testing, and maintenance. These requirements are the foundation on which engineers design WLANs and pretty much everything else. Functional requirements sit on the foundation of top operational business priorities. This hierarchy sequence is required for the WLAN investment to return the maximum value in dollars and other key success metrics that are vertically dependent—such as lives saved, time reduced to market, and so on.

Functional requirements are a set of brief statements for engineers—such as, "ensure voice level quality throughout the warehouse" or "enable wireless video traffic to handheld devices from any place on the fifth floor." They are simple statements that allow engineers to define technical specifications, such as which 802.11 protocol to use, which voice call manager to use, which security mechanisms to use, and so forth. Functional requirements drive the RF design by defining the mounting locations for APs, RF energy output at the APs and clients, stability specifications at cell edges, client density, and many other technical design elements necessary to deploy a WLAN in the most orderly, reliable, and best-performing manner possible.

While the engineers will provide assurance of the deployment through the site survey and final test phase of the deployment, the best engineers always close the deployment loop with a final check to ensure that the deployment meets the functional requirements, which are in turn set deeply into the top operational priorities as set forth by the customer.

The following illustration shows the hierarchy necessary to achieve maximum ROI made in the WLAN.

Challenges of Nontechnical Project Elements

I have generally found technology issues fairly straightforward compared to nontechnology issues in a complex deployment. This isn't to say that today's wireless technology isn't complex. I've struggled with the marketing premise of "engineer in a box" that in part implies that virtually anyone could find a reasonable location to place an AP, plug in an Ethernet cable into the back, plug it into the wall, and voila, instant wireless access.

The reality in enterprise networks is quite different, however, as a rapidly increasing complexity exists in every element of today's WLANs. Security, RF propagation, controller configuration, and client integration are so complex that engineers are increasingly being driven into small and smaller subspecialties. In 1999, most engineers knew virtually everything there was to know about an AP; today's descendants are vastly more complex, carry far higher speeds, and are expected to carry virtually any traffic an enterprise-class network might routinely transport.

Yet, with all this complexity, there remains a realm of WLAN deployments and maintenance that is even more complex and which fewer people are capable of managing. I'm referring to nontechnical issues. My experience in working with many customers with enterprise-class networks and the system integrators who perform the bulk of the WLAN installation and maintenance is that the key nontechnical issues are challenging because they deal with the following necessary elements:

- Organizational
- Budget
- Communication
- Political boundaries

Organizational issues are always prevalent in companies. I've yet to see a perfectly organized company entirely populated by personnel who universally believed the company was well organized and capable of tackling all operational, market, and technology issues in its current format. Organizational excellence is an approximation at best, imperfect in reality, but the better run companies with the best-trained, experienced, and motivated personnel are responsive enough and flexible enough to manage most issues both internal and external to the company.

Budgetary issues are important to recognize, mostly because that even in this day, most WLANs are sold by engineers to engineers. While this necessary phase must occur, the better and more complex deployments are nearly always handled with greater speed and a more optimal outcome when the stakeholder group combines its budgets for a common and greater cause.

Communication inside departments and, more particularly, between departments is a key element resolved by OPS, because this methodology relies entirely on a diverse group of stakeholders to collaborate on a common cause—to untether key applications in their network and to enable this more pervasively throughout their corporate organization.

In most companies, effective communication is rudimentary inside departments, and is probably more of the exception than the rule between departments. This isn't to say there isn't a tremendous amount of e-mail and other communications flowing among departments. The key issue is that of meaningful collaborative exchanges among departments.

Collaboration requires a much higher form of communication, understanding of prevailing issues, and the ability to put the team ahead of individuals and departments. Not so easily achieved, but when you see it in the best-run companies, it's hardly any wonder that those teams are typically industry leaders.

Political boundaries are a definite reality where enterprise-class networks link one end of the business to the other. There is simply no getting around this phenomenon. Political boundaries don't always have a negative impact on organizations; it's only when groups isolate themselves by not collaborating effectively with adjacent stakeholders and political groups that politics become problematic.

This is often the most challenging of issues to resolve where OPS is introduced, because political boundaries tend to be deeply historical to a group, person, or company. The key here is often to soften the boundaries through collaboration by illuminating the possibilities of greater reward for all parties concerned. My experience is that this very issue is the true core issue of why stakeholder groups have not been created prior to OPS. Getting key leadership figures and groups to migrate from "what's in it for me" to "what's in it for *us*" is generally the most rewarding experience for me.

When stakeholder groups are created where collaboration did not formerly exist because of political boundaries, I believe the customer's future is likely to be considerably brighter. My great passion as a "recovering engineer" is to see the right amount of technology deployed in such a manner that it has the greatest positive impact for the least cost to the customer. My heart and soul, however, reside in the realm of changing the way people work together, and OPS is a vehicle for this collaboration and customer business acceleration.

Synthesis of Technical and Nontechnical

While I enjoy the human collaborative process more than the pure technology issues, there can be no doubt that the synthesis of both technical and nontechnical issues is required to achieve the greatest amount of good for the customer.

The quality of the collaboration provides the correct wireless technology to solve the customer's operational issues. Like a good car on a long driving vacation, the more well suited the rig to the needs of the group, the better the overall experience. Collaboration, planning, budget, and an orderly social hierarchy are necessary to ensure the right vehicle is chosen and the right resources are in place to keep the machine running perfectly so that the focus of the trip is on the vacation, not the car itself. If people return rested, happy, and enriched through new experiences and relationships, the car performed its functions to the maximum expected.

When customers collaborate well and use a wireless network best suited for them, they are enriched through the achievement of important business objectives. While I believe the greatest happiness is achieved at home with family and close friends, I believe that work can also, and should also, be a rich source of experiences and rewards. The right synthesis of wireless technical and nontechnical issues will greatly enable the best experiences affordable in the workplace.

OPS: The Sequence of Success

Like most effective programs, OPS is a straightforward methodology to understand and execute. It involves eight essential steps:

1. Ratification of functional requirements by all stakeholders.
2. Project phasing ratified by all stakeholders.
3. RF coverage model presented to stakeholders.
4. Pre-deployment audit to verify RF coverage plan.
5. Deployment.
6. RF test and post-deployment audit.
7. Final RF node adjustments.
8. Automated maintenance and management.

Ratification of Functional Requirements by All Stakeholders

This first step is the most important of all the OPS methodology elements. Recall the pyramid illustration earlier in the chapter, which showed how the operational priorities are the foundation of the functional requirements that are the basis for site surveys and verify the design through audit. The foundation of the entire process is the stakeholder group.

The quality, velocity, and expense of the project are nearly always proportional to the quality of the initial stakeholder meetings.

Functional requirements are always *cartel-based* in enterprise-class WLAN deployments. They are fairly straightforward to deliver once the stakeholders have a firm grasp on the top operational problems. The functional requirements are set forth by engineers in the forms of brief statements such as "Deploy wireless voice to handsets for every healthcare worker on the fifth floor," and are tied to complex business operational priorities. The complexity of the business operational priorities can be difficult to comprehend by a single person or even a single department. The cartel approach is about the collaboration of numerous stakeholders who view operational issues from unique perspectives.

Each complex business priority selected by the stakeholder group commonly involves a number of underlying concerns. In the case of a large hospital, these concerns may include a long list of issues like these:

- Inability to handle patient load due to nurse shortages
- Excessive employee turnover from burnout
- Increased cost from prescription errors
- Poor customer service from lack of wheelchairs and administrators absent from their desks.

The discussions by stakeholders, from nursing administrators, finance, human resources, the IT team, training teams, and others, would quickly agree that this operational concern is expensive to ignore. All would likely agree that getting wireless information to the nurse on the move would increase productivity because the worker would not have to return to the nurse's station numerous times each shift. It would mitigate the burnout experienced by nurses from excessive workloads and the constant, high-pressure nature of nursing.

Pervasive wireless deployments would enable automated prescriptions to be delivered to patients, perhaps robotically, and would ensure that the prescription was carefully dispensed to the correct patient by confirming each patient's identification with RFID or a laser scan of a wrist bracelet. This RFID or laser scanner interface would be wirelessly connected to the larger hospital healthcare network as well as adjacent providers such as medical specialists, doctors, and pharmacies operating in concert, both on and off the hospital premises, to help improve the patient's health.

In a similar manner, the quality of patient care would improve by having a wheelchair available when necessary to transport the patient to and from various hospital departments as well as assisting in the checking in and out of the patient in a timely manner. Wireless can facilitate all of this.

Stakeholders

The list of appropriate stakeholders is often more comprehensive than many believe, especially in complex and large enterprise-class deployments. Review Chapter 1 for a list of stakeholder personnel and technologies.

To ensure that the right stakeholders are included, ask the key stakeholders to invite others as appropriate to participate in the project. Not every member of the list shown in Chapter 1 is appropriate for all WLAN projects. Often subsets of team members should be included as well, especially in the realms of applications, security (physical site and IT), and facility managers.

Project Phasing Ratified by All Stakeholders

My thinking on the concept of phasing deployments has expanded considerably over the years. As I have participated closely in many large and exotic WLAN deployments (and a great many that were important but in more routine environments), the concept of tackling a major WLAN deployment remains daunting. When you stand on the floor of a 1 million square foot warehouse, a new sports stadium, or one of the world's largest manufacturing facilities, it's very easy and quite normal to feel overwhelmed by the prospect. The same happens when I visit healthcare provider facilities; I quickly realize the outcome of my work affects real people and real families. It's sobering, and the drive to give my very best is strong.

When faced with these immense projects, and even far smaller ones, breaking the project down into subphases can be a great approach. Not all areas of WLAN coverage are equal in value or provide the same rate of return to the end customer. For example, it's likely much more important and valuable to the warehouse customer to have real-time inventory updates as trucks are being loaded on the docks than providing employee connectivity in the break room.

Project phasing is another example of the importance tightly coupling the top operational priorities to the WLAN design and deployment. Possessing the knowledge of top operational priorities will often provide clear direction in terms of which physical area to cover with a WLAN.

On a more expanded basis, large areas of coverage will generally also have various and unique values to the customer. You need to identify in which physical areas the WLAN will provide the greatest value and therefore ROI. The customer often knows what's needed, but the system integrator can add special value to the engagement by bringing their prior experience to bear. The best integrators will have received not only feedback from previous customer deployments, but will have remained in the feedback loop in terms of how well the deployed systems are performing in reducing operating expenses and other critical metrics of success, such as employee satisfaction, retention, and so on.

The prioritization of which area to cover may or may not be related to the size of the area. Where possible, you may want to begin on the smaller areas of coverage and deploy the WLAN in the larger areas later. By completing one or a few small areas first, you'll provide a more manageable break-in period for the team—a synthesis of integrator, customer, technology provider, application provider, and other teams. Working together well takes a while; focusing on a smaller physical area may be a preferred strategy for getting the team to pull together in unison and better collaborate on the deliverable.

It's not only area size that could or should determine the phasing of a project. The project may have a new application or new personnel to connect on a priority basis because of the higher value they provide. The case of migrating end users from push-to-talk walkie-talkies to IP devices that allow voice and a host of other business-specific applications may have a greater priority than which physical area is covered. Some employees can need a higher-priority connection, such as forklift drivers, warehouse workers, and truck drivers. The point is that the customer and the system integrator collaborate to deploy the WLAN so that the highest-value priorities are completed first.

Because major and minor project phases can take weeks or months from inception to completion, the ROI begins sooner in the overall project roadmap. On very large projects where the total deployment can take a couple years, getting the best return sooner in the project is important because it frees up more capital and human resources and moves the end users through the disruptive portion of the deployment sooner.

This is similar to investing portions of your own money, when you want get into the best-performing financial vehicles as soon as possible to harness the time value of money. We should give the same consideration to our customers by thinking and planning where we deploy wireless connectivity first. Wireless connectivity provides enormous benefits to the customer stakeholder groups and the ecosystem in which the customer resides. Deploying it where it will do the greatest amount of good the earliest is a great way to maximize the value of the investment.

Lesson learned: *Phasing both small and large deployments is important because it enables the earliest ROI. Prioritizing where the WLAN should be deployed could be based on the size of the deployment area or the value of the productivity within an area. Other prioritizations may be based on the value of a new application such as real-time inventory tracking or medical equipment location and status capabilities. Priorities may also be given to certain high-value personnel or physical assets such as trucks, forklifts, or other equipment.*

RF Coverage Model Presented to Stakeholders

One of the most important elements regarding WLANs is RF coverage. Although many other technical issues must be resolved to deliver the full value and technical capability of a WLAN, if the RF coverage model is deficient, little else in the OSI stack or user experience will work well.

For this reason, the RF coverage model requires a close collaboration between the end customer, the system integrator, and the WLAN technology provider. In the many designs I've completed, even with the best of input from the customer, invariably the customer will say something like, "Oh, I forgot to mention we don't have any power sources within 100 feet of that area we need to cover."

I advise what's commonly called a CDR, or critical design review. This review can take place anywhere, including virtually, through productivity tools such as WebEx. The optimal sequence in which to complete this phase begins with the design engineers completing the design and then reviewing it with senior engineers. From there, a knowledgeable customer representative is involved for a closed-door session with the system integrator. That phase typically results in discovery of additional deficiencies in the design, usually in the form of undocumented site information such as power sources, walls not shown on the floor plan, and similar factors.

Following the closed-door session, the design should be presented to the entire stakeholder board, keeping in mind that the more important premise is that the RF experts on the stakeholder team have reviewed and accepted the design. Most of the stakeholders won't have sufficient working knowledge to review the design critically, so it'll be important for the presenters to present their design with the appropriate level of complexity—some for the RF experts and some for the non-RF experts. With the correct review, onsite audits will still be required, but most of the larger design liabilities and assumptions will have been accounted for and incorporated into the RF design.

Pre-deployment Audit to Verify RF Coverage Plan

The next step is to verify the design assumptions on site. This is typically completed by temporarily mounting the APs in their proposed final location and then taking RF and traffic measurements between the APs and laptops or handheld devices with "sniffing" and traffic analysis hardware and software.

I like to see between 5 and 10 percent of the design change based on feedback from the site survey results. Most of the time, the changes are made in real time and then verified before the as-built documentation continues to be assembled. Most of the changes should include the following items, and ideally in approximately the following order:

1. RF output power
2. Antenna selection
3. Access point location

At each step, these changes become progressively more complex and costly. In addition, in terms of predictability, it's generally easier to predict antenna type and even general AP location as opposed to the optimal setting for RF output power. There is no perfect way to predict environmental dynamics 100 percent of the time. Estimates based on items such as range, speed, and general environmental conditions allow you to set the RF output reasonably correctly most of the time. Of course, for many environments such as carpeted bullpens, I recommend allowing the controller to set the output power and channels. "Trust but verify" is a phrase made quite popular by former President Ronald Reagan, and that concept applies here as well, even when a controller is used and trusted for getting these settings well within normal operating parameters for speed, range, and reliability.

RF Site Surveys and RF Designs

After ranking stakeholder inclusion, using the RF audit (site survey) is easily the second most common reason WLAN projects run into difficulty in large-scale enterprise-class deployments and more modestly scaled deployments in more complex environments such as manufacturing.

The common misconception held for years by those new to WLAN work, or those with only modest experience in complex WLAN deployments, is the notion that an RF audit is the same as an RF design. But they could not be more different.

If the system integrator is designing and auditing the design in the same pass, they can miss the extensive discussions on top business operational problems and functional requirements. I've redesigned many WLAN deployments in which well-intentioned system integrators combined both the RF design and the audit in one pass. I recognize that there is a fair amount of devotion to the approach by integrators to combine these two project phases; this approach is commonly used to save the integrator money, not to ensure that end customer requirements are considered and incorporated into the design from the onset. This technique can be used in less complex designs or where the radiating environment is very stable and straightforward, such as carpeted bullpens, but I'd generally advise against it.

Deployment

Two of the most important elements to arrange weeks, if not months, before deployment are

- Access to specialized high-elevation equipment such as scissor lifts
- Access to restricted areas

The importance of these elements were hopefully made clear by the aforementioned events that taught me years ago to pre-stage heavy equipment, clearances, and personnel with unique institutional facilities memory when the facilities aren't carefully documented. My experience is that well under 10 percent of all facilities are carefully documented in terms of their as-built records. Construction designs change, plan details are misplaced, and management and facilities personnel change positions or leave the company altogether.

The deployment should be carefully scheduled with customer personnel meeting with the integrator during the deployment and learning about the detailed design changes that include the final WLAN changes for important elements such as output power, AP location, and specific radiating area unique characteristics such as whether or not major doors open or close, whether large structures are moved through WLAN cells, and so forth.

The average time allocation for a deployment varies tremendously from project to project, but if the APs are mounted less than 15 feet from the floor in elevation, they have relatively easy access, and the cabling for power and signal can fairly easily be brought to the AP, an average amount of installation time, including the audit, is approximately one hour per AP.

The actual deployment of the APs and associated controllers and other network devices is only one part of the customer engagement when equipment is uploaded on their network. The completion of the deployment does not always involve loading up the trucks and returning to the head office for a round of high-fives, however. Several more critical deliverables are required before migration to the next generation of technology begins again with the sales process.

RF Test and Post-deployment Audit

Site survey measurements are snapshots of time, space, and elements in motion. Given that the elements within a radiating area typically change a constant basis, a second snapshot will often provide significant assurance that the deployment satisfies most of the design intent and, more importantly, the operational outcomes intended by various stakeholders. Another reason for completing the additional site survey at this phase of the engagement between the integrator and customer is that amending coverage problems after the deployment team departs costs 5 to 20 times more than it would if caught before the WLAN is turned over to the customer.

It's a best practice by the top WLAN deployment teams to expand the scope of the audit to include all layers of the OSI stack, not just the RF. The RF audit points generally don't change between pre-deployment and post-deployment, but walk-through tests with actual clients running production software is an imperative. This full function test should be carefully documented because this data will become the baseline performance test against which any future problems can be evaluated.

Final RF Node Adjustments

Some integrators make final node adjustments to the APs while they have the lift equipment in place. This is often the way I've approached this on major deployments, because elevation equipment tends to move vertically much faster than it does horizontally—that is, from one location to another. The outcome tends to remain high in quality whether or not the integrator returns to make the final node adjustments or completes them right after hanging the AP.

The one exception to this occurs when the AP and client densities tend to be very high, as in complex manufacturing environments. Most interference comes from native radios—that is, radios the customer has already installed. Some WLAN controllers will cascade power output and channel settings, and in some cases the timing of radiating environmental changes can coincide in ways with the controllers that tend to "chase environments." In other words, most controllers operate in reactive mode versus proactive mode with regard to environmental dynamics. To be candid and fair to the technology providers of controllers, it would be prohibitively expensive and complex to incorporate technologies and methods that would allow controllers to adjust APs ahead of, or favorably timed with, major radiating environmental changes.

For that reason, in highly complex radiating environments, I prefer to see how the entire WLAN operates once the entire thing is lit up and almost ready for production. To prevent controllers from chasing environmental dynamics in complex radiating environments, I prefer designs in which the RF output and channels are locked down. I recognize that some technology vendors will disagree with this approach, but my own experience supports it. This is, however, a technological evolution for which we should expect to see continued improvement. As the technology continues to improve, we may expect to rely on automated RF power output and channel selection. In the few years just ahead, however, "trust but verify" is an excellent assurance methodology.

Ultimately, whether the integrator has made the final RF node adjustments during the installation of the APs or shortly thereafter, the more important consideration is that the WLAN have a final and comprehensive checkout prior to turning over the network to the customer. One of the best checkout procedures is to use production version applications running over actual wireless clients. I use the client with the lowest level of performance and reliability as the baseline unit from which the final tests are completed, using the entire OSI stack. This ensures that even the lowest-performing client will operate successfully and reliably in the new WLAN.

It's important to the end customer, the technology provider, and of course the system integrator to ensure that the WLAN is operating at full specification prior to the integrator leaving the deployment premises. It typically costs from 10 to 20 times more to return to a WLAN to troubleshoot and resolve WLAN performance and reliability problems. Notably, the customer typically experiences a decrease in confidence in the technology provider and the system integrator in these scenarios.

Much of my work has involved the restoration of confidence with the integrator and the technology provider. Many customers will abandon one or the other after only one deficient deployment experience; it's imperative to ensure the WLAN is performing very well and to demonstrate to the customer that all systems, options, and features are operating reliably. When the customer is fully satisfied, you can return to the office for high-fives and advance planning for the next evolution of the WLAN.

Automated Maintenance and Management

A WLAN is a dynamic asset because the radiating environment is dynamic. The natural state of a WLAN is for the performance to deteriorate over time due to changes in complexity in the radiating environment, increasing latency-sensitive applications such as voice and video, increased traffic count, and increased node count. All contribute individually to far more strain and load on the network and the wireless access portion of it.

Mobility is far more than a "nice to have" network option in today's commercial environments. When the network goes down, it is an operational imperative to have it repaired and back online at the earliest moment possible. One of the greatest contributions of automated maintenance and remote management is that these assets can monitor deterioration that is as often gradual as it is sudden.

For this reason, automated maintenance and remote management mechanisms are cost effective because, rather than repair systems remotely or in a fast response mode, they can make adjustments to the network and implement backup systems or technologies. More than anything, automated maintenance and remote management repair and maintain WLAN elements *before* they fail.

It's important then to integrate these systems as part of the original design in not only larger enterprise-class networks but increasingly in the mid-market–sized networks and even small office and home office networks.

The right combination of automated mechanisms, from controller-based intelligence and client-based audits, enables two valuable assets: resolving problems before they become expensive, and assuring a smoother technology migration to next-generation systems.

Often, a solid relationship of trust exists between the remote managers and owners of a network system, and that's also true in today's WLAN environments. These managers are well placed to advise the end customer in which technologies, policies, vendors, and system integrators will best enable the reduction in not only the operating expense of a network but also the remote maintenance and management of a WLAN and other key network elements such as security, voice, and video, to name a few.

In critical industries such as healthcare, police and fire departments, and emergency medical services, it's somewhat of a surprise to learn how limited the resources are, not just for planning and deployment of WLANs, but also regarding maintenance. Often, the customer IT teams are so fully subscribed simply deploying the next technology that they have precious few cycles remaining to maintain systems before they break or require significant upgrades.

Optimal project sequencing is a terrific methodology for both larger and smaller WLAN projects. Using these steps and this sequence will help bring order, the protection afforded through collaboration, and quite often increased budgets through the combining of common goals and objectives within the same customer. This ensures that the maximum financial return and other success metrics are considered, and indeed even mission-critical, in the ever more rapidly evolving realm of wireless networks.

CHAPTER 8 | Finance Strategies for Wireless Mobility

Change is an important indicator of the health of a business. At its most fundamental level, business is about delivering change to people who need it. Businesses change the way people look, the way they eat, the way they travel, and the way they work.

Change always requires motion, either directly or indirectly. It's not only people who are in motion, although people are the most essential element. Business operations actually involve three primary kinds of motion:

- Goods and or services
- Information
- Personnel and physical assets

The common thread among these three types of critical business assets is information technology (IT). Wireless networks untether IT—in other words, wireless enables business endpoints such as people, equipment, and products to be tracked while in motion and through policy and/or equipment to decrease the time they are not in motion. It is essential that these movements are tracked and that the elements in motion are connected reliably to the IT network. The amount and proficiency of such connecting technologies are disparate between highly industrialized countries and less industrialized societies.

The role of a WLAN, and in fact all of a business class IT network, is inextricably linked to how well the business performs. IT assets are incorporated into every business decision that affects operations. It's hard to conceive of a business decision without short links to operations. Business operations are decisions, policies, and procedures that direct the "motion" of a business.

There is no more fundamental role for IT and the mobility assets than to ensure profit and positive cash flow in a business. Profit and positive cash flow are the twin princes of business. Even in non-profit institutions, cash flow is carefully measured to ensure that business demands are properly planned for and met. While non-profit businesses such as community hospitals, schools, churches, and civil services don't track profit, they do track how much and how well cash is flowing through the operation. The very survival of both for profit and non-profit operations rely entirely on how much and how well cash flows through the operation.

If It Matters, Meter It

There is wisdom in the teaching "that which we measure tends to improve." Two of the things being measured in business today far more carefully, in far more ways, with vastly improved tools, are profit and cash flow. Simply put, the best managed and most successful businesses have the greatest rates of profit and cash flow. Not coincidentally, they nearly always tend to have more cash and cash equivalent reserves. A robustly healthy business with positive cash flow, profit, and cash reserves has more options for growth and can take on risk from new ventures with far less potential harm to the business.

Exploration of new business opportunities can take a business to markets with far less competition, thus further enhancing growth, profit, and cash-flow potential. The result is an even more robust company. My employer is a prime example of this: with zero debt, $35 billion in cash reserves, and the tooling, procedures, and culture with a synthesis of cash conservation and appropriate risk taking, we tend to gain the most market share when our competitors are weakened from macroeconomic conditions or poorly executed risks.

Restated, robust companies grow the most when the economy is down because they have, among other assets, the cash and other reserves that allow them to be more aggressive than competitors that are necessarily focused on preservation of cash and cash equivalents. Cisco enjoys a massive presence in its chosen industry, but the principle remains the same for any well-run businesses: market share between competitors tends to change more in a depressed macroeconomic cycle than in a bull market. This is in part because competitors with the most cash and cash equivalent reserves, among other assets, are much less constrained to broaden their services, increase their presence through marketing, and create opportunities through attractive financing.

The concept of rapid growth in down markets is an integral part of U.S. history. Many of America's wealthiest families rose to the pinnacles of affluence during the Great Depression, for example. A considerable amount of wealth didn't disappear during that time; much of the tangible assets remaining from the crash of the stock market simply changed hands from the unprepared to the prepared. Profit, cash flow, and financing had everything do with what happened before, during, and after the Depression.

In the 1990s dot-com era, for example, some of these fundamentals were replaced with the belief in metrics—such as how many customers viewed a website (eyeballs) or how long they stayed on a website (stickiness). Billions of dollars in credit and virtual wealth change hands at breathtaking speed based on those perceptions. In the end, these new principles couldn't be sustained. The entire dot-com industry went down in a manner reminiscent of the *Hindenburg*. It took some years for the IT industry to recover. The result is a return to success based on the sound principles of profit, cash flow, and the optimal use of financing.

Financing Wireless Networks

Cash-flow and profit best practices have evolved and developed enormously since the Great Depression and took their rightful place again after the technology crash of 2000. Tools allowing transparency and highly granular views into operational transactions while simultaneously protecting corporate strategy and best practices are commonplace in well-run operations of today.

Of particular interest is the optimal role of ownership and debt in IT. Increasingly large portions of IT assets are shifting to being not only managed but fully owned by third parties. Companies such as Perot Systems (purchased by Dell), Accenture, and others generate considerable sales by adding value to their customers with this transition of IT ownership and management. The bases for these transitions are often complex, but in every case, the cash flow and profitability of the enterprise are at the root of the change.

The likelihood of IT and wireless assets becoming virtualized is directly correlated to how well the profit and cash-flow models are portrayed and understood. In my estimation, there can be no greater reason in business for change of ownership through virtualization than that of cash flow and overall profitability of the business.

At this point in enterprise-class networking, virtualization is not a strategy most businesses are prepared to undertake, though a change is under way. Financing is a highly appropriate alternative to the virtualization of wireless and other network assets for enterprise-class wireless network owners. However, in today's business environment, it remains much more common to focus on the technical merits of IT "boxes" than financing. Far more meetings are held to discuss technology features and specifications than how the latest WLAN standard will affect cash flow and profitability.

The incorporation of how mobility and IT technology in general affect profit and cash flow will largely decide the future of IT. This isn't to say that the future of IT is in jeopardy; in fact, the opposite is true. IT and mobility have long been embedded intrinsically into business. Ask a doctor, soldier, or salesperson if they could give up their wireless connectivity. Ask an operations manager if they'd like to clear out their IT closets and return to paper-and-pen based ledger sheets for accounting.

The better we know how to use a tool, the more likely we'll be able to shape it for use in the future. Emphasis should be placed on advancing the cash flow and profitability of the mobility customer regarding which specific wireless technology they plan to deploy. One key litmus test of how well cash flow and profitability are considered in a mobility plan involves whether financing is as carefully planned as the wireless deployment itself. Financing the mobility investment is a primary strategy in improving business operations. Whether the costs of the mobility assets are paid from the profits of the business or borrowed is a *critical* mobility decision to consider—it's every bit as relevant to the discussion as which mobility technology will be deployed.

While taking on debt should never be a trivial consideration, it is a highly appropriate business tool. Knowing when and how to use funds sourced from outside one's business is a true hallmark of quality business management.

Few, if any, businesses are completely resilient to every macroeconomic cycle. Yet the pressure to remain not only competitive but to grow the business never ceases in business. Cash flow, like most flows, is much more of an "ebb and tide" situation than constant, smooth, and steady flow. It works that way for most families, midsized businesses, and even the largest businesses in the world. One of the CFO's key functions is to keep the ebb and flow as manageable and predictable as possible. Inevitably—and, in fact, on a repeated basis—there is a convergence of cash-flow shortage and a driving need to invest in wireless and other IT infrastructure. The ability to finance mobility and IT assets allows the customer to manage vital business investments on their time frame as opposed to dealing with conditions imposed by cash-flow issues.

Many if not most businesses *react* to the up and down cycling of cash flow instead of *managing* their businesses into a more *cycle resilient* condition. The very best CFOs manage cash flow through a combination of financing, debt and cash flow management, and political savvy internal to their corporation.

In a perfect world, budget allocations for wireless deployments and other essential tooling investments are even, fair, and well timed. The reality is that most budget allocations are tied to the political acumen of the department heads, and in particular regarding wireless deployments, the political and balance sheet acumen of the IT director or CIO. (By *political acumen*, I am referring to the ability to influence another person's thinking or actions. Some are very adept at this within a business, while many others are less so.) If the IT director or CIO fails to outline the advantages to the business clearly and simply in terms of cash flow, market share increase, and profitability, the odds are significantly reduced that they'll receive all the budget allocation they request. That can lead to mobility designs that are stretched to the limit to maximize service coverage.

Businesses have a wide range of constant and heavy demand for capital and resources. The investments in IT are only one of the many ways for a business to reinvest in itself. The idea is to provide the best possible return for an investment and to maximize overall profitability and cash flow. IT competes for internal budget resources against every other business department, and mobility competes against other IT investment opportunities. But mobility and IT are corporate investments that can be financed in every phase of the macroeconomic cycle, thereby creating a far smaller financial footprint.

Third-party financing replaces a large capital expenditure (one large check) with many smaller and generally identical cash outlays. It's generally easier to fit in a request for a smaller monthly payment than a single large outlay of cash. Committing to three or four years of nearly identical payments is a better long-range predictive scenario for the finance department than asking for a single payment of a large amount of cash.

Preservation of cash during slow market conditions is a critical management marker. The ability to time the financing of assets shrewdly so that they will best improve the competitive nature of a business in every part of the macroeconomic cycle is essential.

Timing the purchase of equipment with special offers from technology vendors and integrators is also advantageous to the end customer from a total cost perspective. Some of these offers are not just for reduced cost of the wireless equipment, but also offers for the financing itself—such as 90-day interest- or payment-free periods to help drive sales for technology providers and, in the case of the largest system integrators, to help promote their services. Negotiating for non-interest or delayed payment periods is a quite normal, though underused, option.

The Most Common Integrator Complaint

Not only can the wireless equipment be financed, but the engineering required to design and audit (site survey) the WLAN can also be financed. I'm often asked to intervene by company partners who say, "We can't get our customer to pay for a wireless design or site survey."

It's not a matter of "getting the customer to pay for the design and site survey," however; it's a matter of value proposition and financing. I used to say that "if a customer believes a site survey is expensive, they should see how expensive it'll be *without* a site survey." The costs associated with not performing an audit (site survey) are non-trivial. The costs of returning to a deployed site can be 2 to as much as 20 times the original cost to deploy an access point because of the costs of adding or moving APs, losing production time, identifying analytics, planning, and securing the resources needed to resolve the problem; these are typically managed by the most expensive system integrator engineers. Deeper analysis of the problem shows that more often than not, customers forget to include, or vastly underestimate, engineering costs in their budgets for deploying WLANs.

Most customers have a preset budget—a ceiling figure—that can't be crossed easily, if at all. When the system integrator provides a detailed proposal for deploying the wireless network, the customer is typically surprised that the deployment includes significant engineering costs. Integrator and equipment manufacturing sales personnel usually pitch the concept that wireless is nearly self-deploying and self-healing. This marketing statement has an element of truth to it, and the simplest WLAN equipment setup *can and does* work well in certain environments such as small office spaces, but a simple setup can't cover all situations and opportunities.

While you can *often* get a WLAN to work well without much engineering (in small office environments, for example), large-scale deployments and deployments in complex settings such as hospitals and manufacturing *always* require careful design engineering, designs audits, monitoring, and maintenance. For this reason, it's not entirely helpful to the integrators when the equipment providers tout "seamless integration" and "plug-and-play" wireless technologies. Such statements rarely come from integrator engineering teams, because not only are they paid to design and install equipment, but they understand from experience that this technology is non-trivial to deploy reliably.

Mobility deployment costs to the customer are very significant, often in the range of 40 to 60 percent of the cost of the hardware. Mobility ranks among the most expensive IT technologies to deploy, largely because it has to perform with the same level of reliability as Ethernet or fiber-optics, but at the same time accommodate considerable distances over open air between the transmitter and receiver.

The open air, or "free space," element adds vast variations of what might happen to the wireless signal between the transmitter and receiver. Designing mobility systems to accommodate that risk is expensive, not broadly understood by many IT installation experts, and requires specialized techniques and tools to confirm reliability, the distance the signal will travel, and the speed at which the applications can reliably be transmitted and received. Laying fiber-optic or Ethernet cable is not the easiest deployment task either, but it involves far less potential for error.

Most integrators generate most of their money from engineering and maintenance. In general, most resellers resell equipment primarily as a bridge to sell services; in truth, they resell equipment to enable the sale of engineering services. Resellers gross about 10 percent on reselling equipment, though it costs considerably more than that for the very largest resellers. In general, and in contrast, they make something approaching 80 percent of their total revenue from engineering services.

Although integrators and technology vendors understand how integrators make most of their money, customers generally do not; hence the gap in customer expectation and budget. Customers often do not create budgets that include costs for vital engineering services, and financing can help with that as well.

Financing: The Path of Least Resistance

Every reputable CxO wants their company to "do more with less." It's a mantra used not only at struggling companies, but also at highly successful, well-run companies.

There's more to financing than the concept of dividing payments into manageable parts, however. Single lump sum payments are difficult if not impossible to increase. Lump sum payments usually require that the finance department calculate the impact of taking money from one project and giving it to another, a hardship for even the most successful business. On the other hand, adjusting the monthly payment and total financed amount from the technology vendor or integrator can often be completed with a single phone call or text message from the salesperson to a manager.

Finance providers generally seek to expand deals, while customer finance personnel carefully limit deal expansion. The former is looking to move as much capital as possible, with the latter seeking to conserve as much capital as possible. And, as you might expect, the former is generally far easier and faster to achieve than the latter.

Most mobility deployments end up costing more than what was initially anticipated. This is true of nearly all major projects; it's unusual for a large project to finish within, and especially under, budget. Large projects tend to experience "scope creep," which refers to a project expanding slowly as previously undiscovered elements are considered or customer requirements change.

While discovery can often mitigate scope creep, I believe that discovery and scope creep have different programmatic roots. Scope creep is closely associated with the balance between project discipline and flexibility required to accommodate elements that can be discovered only during the project. Discovery is one of the best tools now emerging in major project management and is often simulation based.

Adjusting a monthly payment to accommodate scope creep is generally far easier than proportionally increasing a single large payment from a single purchase order. Also, a modest expansion of the monthly payments has a disproportionately large impact on the scope of what is delivered. A 15 percent increase in monthly payments can increase wireless coverage to a whole new room or area, to include the engineering and maintenance services as well. It can also make the difference between a fairly reliable coverage design to a design coverage model that will readily accommodate voice, video, and other latency-sensitive applications, as well as accommodate significant increases in future data traffic and handheld device count. In other words, a modest expansion of the monthly payment can provide significant assurance that the system will work reliably now and in the future. It's far more cost effective to spend 15 percent up front than to spend a lot more two years later to amend a marginal design or deployment.

Benefit from Equipment, Not Ownership

Leasing mobility equipment enables the end user to benefit more from the *use* of equipment, as opposed to ownership of the equipment. While purchased equipment will show up on the asset side of the balance sheet, the higher value of the equipment is what it does versus how it shows up on the list of assets owned by the business. Most business mobility and IT investments are considered an *adjacency*. In other words, the business owns and uses the equipment, but the equipment is not part of its core competency.

For example, a shoe store is in the business of selling shoes; it's not in the IT or mobility business. Although it will use IT and mobility assets to manage inventory, improve customer satisfaction, increase the "wallet share" or amount derived from each customer, and so forth, mobility and IT assets are not part of the store's core business.

Of particular interest is that mobility and IT assets have become phenomenally complex in terms of design and maintenance. Enabling video traffic to a handheld device is a non-trivial mobility and IT objective. It is well beyond the competency range of all but a very few shoe store IT staff members. It's also beyond the competency range of IT staffs at mobility-intensive customers such as hospitals, education, and manufacturing—three of the largest users of mobility and IT infrastructure.

Fact is, these technologies have become vastly complex and fragmented. Long gone are the days when an average engineer understood every element of mobility—from RF propagation to client integration. These issues are now handled by subspecialist teams with ultra-specialized knowledge. The engineers and technicians on these teams know who to ask to apply what is needed to resolve a very specific type of problem. No single engineer in today's market understands all there is to know about mobility; the subject is simply far too vast and complex.

Not only are the pure technical capabilities of today's WLANs very complex, but the best business practices required to maximize the use and value of this technology are equally unknown to many end customers—hence the thriving businesses with leading companies such as Accenture and Perot Systems.

Leasing mobility allows the ownership and maintenance of these complex systems to reside with the technology provider, such as Cisco, Intermec, or Dell. This allows the end customer to enjoy the full benefits of the system without the many complications of ownership.

Financing and Technology Refresh

Those of us in the IT world tend to believe that investments in IT are among the best investments a business can make. While many in my industry believe this as universally true, it's apparent to me after 20 years in IT that this statement isn't always completely sound. There are times, circumstances, and opportunities that provide an end customer a much better return on its money than mobility and IT.

What that means for the purveyors of mobility and IT is that, on average, we need to provide *one* of the best financial returns, *and do so consistently*, year after year. The next best thing to a periodic spectacular return is consistent excellent returns. The best managers will generally choose excellent consistent returns, but few senior management teams will completely eliminate risk-taking. Financial windfalls generate a lot more excitement around the board room and water cooler than consistent excellent performance.

Financing mobility technology allows end customers to retain options and preserve capital to take advantage of excellent opportunities that often appear with little advance warning. Financing allows end customers to retain more capital over time, which is the optimal method top managers and analysts use to establish significant capital reserves. This is true at the individual level, and it's true at the large corporate level. Building significant capital reserves takes time, discipline, and the utilization of options that free up as much capital as possible while expanding the business.

Mobility Equipment Refresh

Like all technology, mobility assets have a limited "shelf life." IT technology evolves rapidly from state-of-the-art, to mass adoption, to next generation generally within periods of several years and not much more. This is generally the "amortization period," which is the amount of time the business is allowed to deduct the cost of the equipment as part of their income tax filings and balance sheet amendments. These "schedules" affect both how much income tax is paid and the approximate value of the business.

The equipment is designed to last much longer than that, of course, but there is a significant difference in how well a single piece of equipment works and how it performs as a network element inside a far larger array of equipment and applications. Network evolution results from two primary drivers: handheld devices and custom applications. Individual pieces of technology typically don't stop working within an ecosystem of network devices; they more often tend to be more difficult to integrate and more expensive to manage as the technology ages from the mass adoption phase to the release of the next generation. Older technologies also tend to carry, forward, and receive traffic less elegantly. What's relevant here is that in growth businesses, network traffic always increases, as does "latency sensitivity," which refers to how reliably the network needs to handle certain kinds of traffic such as voice and video.

The timing, therefore, of when to refresh the technology along with the purchase of the engineering to deploy it properly is an important consideration. Regardless of the marketing hype, technology is rarely easy to integrate; that is certainly true for enterprise-class deployments. "Plug-and-play" is an adopted sound bite that you won't hear used by experienced deployment engineers. You also want the network to "settle" for the right amount of time; in other words, it's optimal to allow the network to be in maintenance mode for two to three years versus a yearly integration of next-generation technology that is disruptive and expensive.

Around the three-year mark is a great time to begin earnest discussions, first with internal stakeholders and then with the integrator and technology provider, about refreshing the mobility equipment. If the equipment is leased, the negotiations are modest in duration and complexity, and a lease extension is often the norm. In practical terms, this means an addendum is added to the existing contract versus the negotiation of an entirely new contract.

A lease extension is simpler for the finance and legal teams at both the end customer and the integrator. Lease extensions are generally quick to approve, and as the engineering is wrapped into the new lease, the focus shifts more quickly to technical logistics deployment issues. Of course, the lease extension occurs after the customer internal stakeholder discussions with the integrator have occurred, the business objectives for the new technology have been settled, and other sequencing and preparation discussions have occurred, as outlined in Chapter 7.

Financing and Homogeneous Systems

Truly homogeneous networks exist far more often in home office networks than in large enterprise-class networks. A *homogeneous* network has equipment from only one very large technology provider, such as Cisco or Juniper. The opposite of a homogeneous network is a heterogeneous network; these are by far the norm in enterprise-class networks. Some technologies and products may not be available from even the largest technology providers, and some products available from their competitors may in fact work better than those offered by the large companies.

The prevailing concept, however, is that a homogeneous network offers significant advantages, including the following:

- Tends to function better as an ecosystem of components
- Is less expensive to manage
- Is easier to manage
- Has fewer types of network management systems

Financing allows the end customer to acquire and install larger blocks of updated mobility systems that are very tightly integrated into the wired portion of the network. The financing terms often allow for limited amounts of technology that aren't from the leasing source (assuming the leasing source is the same as the network technology provider). Even if the leasing source is independent of the technology provider, it's still a superior strategy to use equipment from as few technology providers as possible.

This is an excellent place and time to consider an expansion of the amount leased to ensure that the largest network module can be purchased. By networking module, I'm referring to a portion of the network that would cover a specific building, floor, or campus. This allows for less "piecemealing" of the network, which will result in a faster deployment, lower maintenance costs, and far better matching of technology to business requirements.

Financing vs. Leasing Mobility Equipment

Equipment purchase financing versus leasing is an important consideration. With the former, the end customer owns the equipment, the equipment is paid off at the end of a set term, and the customer disposes of or trades in the equipment as best it can several years down the road. It typically requires a fairly large down payment, and the monthly or quarterly payments are generally identical.

Leasing, on the other hand, is by far the more common approach to equipment purchases in the mobility networking world. The Equipment Leasing and Finance Association (ELFA; www.elfaonline.org/) recently published the following statistics:

- Four out of five U.S. companies use financing to acquire equipment.

- Almost one-third of all externally financed capital expenditures in the United States are financed through leasing.

- Equipment finance has grown at an average rate of 12.5 percent during the past ten years.

The leasing source is commonly referred to as the "lessor," and the party using the equipment is called the "lessee." A small up-front payment is usually required. The equipment is owned by the lessor throughout the life of the equipment, and it's theoretically returned to the lessor at the end of the term of the agreement. I use the term "theoretically" because what generally happens, at least where the lessor sales team is actively tracking the lease, is that the lease is offered for extension near the end of the term of the agreement.

Maintenance and deployment costs are included in the lease but the lessor will also provide the engineers and technicians to install and maintain the mobility and IT equipment—a boon to virtually every enterprise IT staff member. At the end of the lease, the lessor will not only arrive to pick up the old equipment, but will exchange the equipment with the latest versions of the hardware and software.

Leasing Mobility Gear and Security

When returning leased equipment, a couple issues should be considered: it's good business practice to have as much of the equipment either recycled or resold, and sensitive corporate data should be professionally wiped off the machine. Both the former and latter require special practices, tools, and other resources. The incorporation of the new equipment commonly includes password and other security updates, but it's surprising how often routers, switches, and wireless gear are simply tossed into a dumpster at the end of their useful existence.

It's pretty easy to take such equipment and remove passwords and other sensitive information, though it doesn't happen very often. For reference, the United Kingdom's largest mobile phone recycler, Regenersis, processes more than 2 million handsets per year. In a random sample test, it discovered that 99 percent of the recycled phones it handled contained personal data. A New York computer forensics firm, Kessler International, released a public statement in February 2009, indicating that 40 percent of the recycled hard drives on eBay contain personal, private, and sensitive information. Everything from banking data, to corporate financial data, to surfing histories and other private information has been found on these devices.

It's easy to believe that some significant portion of outbound mobility and IT gear leaves the customer's premises in full production format—that is, with all configurations and security settings in place. It's not that the professionals are careless; it's that most of them are focusing on tasks that are far more complex than wiping settings before disposing of the devices. To be clear, for those who are not professional technicians, mobility equipment doesn't typically contain sensitive information; it does, however, make up a portion of the virtual security wall around a business. If you can access the security information on the mobility equipment headed for the recycler, you can fairly easily gain penetration into the network the device just left, especially if the new equipment does not have updated passwords and user identification. Simply a thought here: use professionals to exchange the gear and verify that the outgoing equipment is properly wiped clean.

Leasing and Residuals

One of the many advantages of leasing is that, theoretically, you pay only for how much depreciation and maintenance occurred during the term of the lease. The value of the mobility equipment at the end of the lease is called the *residual* value. That's a fancy way of saying that after the lease term is completed, the equipment can be resold by the lessor. When you purchase equipment, you purchase the entire value of the equipment plus maintenance and other costs.

Of course, other factors are included in the lease payment, such as interest and various fees, such as documentation, which are little more than ways to pad the profit margin, but these are standard terms and most of this can be negotiated. The part of the deal that isn't generally negotiated is the residual value, because that's set according to tables generated and owned by the lessor or other financial institutions. Even with these factors calculated into the deal, it's usually a net-positive cash-flow strategy to lease equipment versus outright purchases of the equipment, if only because you're paying less to use the equipment. As mentioned earlier in the chapter, it's the use of the equipment, not the ownership, that generates more value for the end business.

The equipment is returned to the lessor at the end of the lease, and is then sold, reused, or recycled. The lessor disposes of the equipment at a fair market value and at the same time installs new equipment for the end customer to continue using. In slightly more technical terms, this means you're paying for the depreciation and not the equipment itself. This reduces the cost of ownership to the end customer who is paying only for the portion of the equipment life cycle that they actually use.

Plan Cash Flow as Carefully as the WLAN Itself

In Chapter 7, I wrote about the first step of a methodology for managing mobility and other IT projects—the assembly of the stakeholders. Notice that finance personnel are included in that group. There are two very good reasons for including individuals who seemingly know very little, if anything, about wireless mobility from a technical perspective. Certainly they will have experienced the benefits of wireless mobility and likely use a WLAN at home. Few of them could make much of a contribution to what appears to be a technology engagement among the end customer, the system integrator, and the technology provider.

Still, their presence at the stakeholder discussions could not be more important. My experience from deploying (and untangling deployments) for most of the last 20 years includes the observation that the very best managed deployments nearly always include financial people on the core stakeholder team. Two important things happen when financial reps are on the team:

- The scope of the project increases, largely due to leasing instead of purchasing the equipment outright.

- The discussions of cash-flow benefits of mobility allow the financial people to support the mobility investment.

This is in part why I have worked diligently to expand the mobility engagement from solely engineers to a full stakeholder team comprising many types of professional talents and perspectives. When these engagements are thus expanded, the deployments are generally larger, which is great for the system integrator and the technology provider such as Cisco. However, the primary winner in that scenario is the end customers, because of the operational improvements made to their business. When mobility is properly planned, deployed, and used to its potential, business improves.

The intent for mobility isn't to allow the business to recover from strategic corporate errors, though certainly it is a powerful asset for moving quickly and communicating well to correct errors or stay ahead of dynamic situations. The point is that to maximize the value of the mobility deployment, the cash-flow and profitability elements should be as carefully analyzed and planned as the deployment of the mobility technology itself.

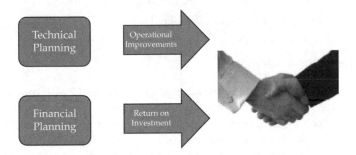

For this reason, two key tracks should be considered within the stakeholder team: One track focuses on the technical architecture that is built on the foundation of the functional requirements. The functional requirements are built on the foundation of the primary business objectives as set by either the end customer executive management team or by the stakeholder group itself.

The second and equally important track for the stakeholder team to consider is that of the cash-flow and profit model generated by the technology investment. Establishing financial objectives that are inclusive from the cost of the mobility investment to the operational enhancements brought by the mobility investment, and the projected date at which the investment will pay off, is at least as important as any technological considerations.

Financing as Strategy to Improve Business Operations

Few, if any, networks are in "perfect" operating condition. Enterprise-class networks are incredibly complex; they're not simply "systems" but more truly "ecosystems of systems." Few, if any, IT directors would declare "our network is finally finished," because they are never finished. By their nature, IT and mobility never reach a "final destination." The pursuit of not just performance improvements, but enhancements in capacity, security, pervasive coverage, ease of use, and much more, creates an endless pursuit of excellence.

Most businesses move through focused cycles of mobility investments, followed by dormant periods in which the mobility will move out of the top priority grouping for funding. The larger the network, the larger the continued flow of budget into it; however, most of cash flow into IT departments is used for maintenance.

The next generation of investment is often triggered by the following (in random order):

- Security breach
- Data loss
- Completion of new floor or building
- Business acquisition
- Response to personnel for increased or improved wireless coverage
- Release of new mobility technology such as 802.11n
- Next-generation wireless equipment
- Sales incentive programs

Every important business operational decision involves IT and mobility assets. By using financing instead of internal funding, the business can improve the mobility and other IT network elements and systems instead of waiting for optimal cash-flow timing or an event such as data loss or a security breach. It's generally much easier to make a more gradual, stepped improvement in a system versus a very large and infrequent upgrade.

Large and infrequent upgrades typically involve far more improvement to adjacent systems, such as midsized switches, routers, security, and handheld clients. A lot less training of internal personnel is generally required, and the upgrades are often less disruptive when they're smaller and more gradual in size. Certainly the incorporation of smaller improvements often features smoother deployment and planning cycles.

Financing is therefore an appropriate strategy for business operation improvement on a more scheduled basis rather than waiting for larger, more quantitative improvements every few years. There is, of course, a balance between working continually at upgrading systems and upgrading every five years: financing allows business operational improvements through upgrades on the two- to three-year basis. The final adjustment of the timing involves consideration of numerous operational, market, financial, and technological elements.

Mobility and IT: The Pathway of Finance

The technology, innovative uses of the network, and user demand for today's mobility-enhanced IT networks all continue to change. Each of these interactions has very different net outcomes, but the overarching premise is that a business cannot operate any better than how it handles its cash flow and profit.

Mobility and IT provide the pathways for vital information that significantly impacts cash flow and profitability. Financing those assets also directly affects cash flow and cash reserves in a very positive and immediate manner and allows these vital assets to be upgraded with far less regard to the ebb and flow of cash through a business. Financing as a strategy, versus outright purchase of the technology, ensures that these mission-critical assets are refreshed at times that allow the business to take maximum advantage of emerging technology, new business practices, and market opportunities with far less reliance on favorable cash-flow ebbs. Importantly, these technology and operational upgrades can be achieved through financing, thus leaving a much smaller initial demand for the cash and a much more predicable outlay of cash over time.

Financing mobility and IT assets plays a key role in ensuring that the business will retain a higher level of competition in their markets, respond in real time to market and business dynamics, and allow the business both to understand risks and take on new and appropriate risks when the opportunity calls for it. Risk and opportunity in business have always been closely coupled; having a real-time intelligence network that acts as a computational grid will allow far better targeting, timing, understanding of the opportunity, and highly granular insight into how external opportunities are managed internally.

The financing of mobility and IT should be as creative, carefully planned, and monitored for success metrics as the technology itself. It's one of the best mobility developments I've seen in the last few years because it directly contributes to the very objective of having mobility and IT assets in the first place—to improve cash flow and profitability.

CHAPTER 9 | System Integrator—Mobility Practice Resilience

The concept of resilience in business is important, because most enterprises, regardless of the industry in which they ply their trade, tend to be reactive as opposed to proactive regarding macroeconomic cycles. While reactivity is the norm, it is not the optimal path for corporate resilience and longevity; in fact, there is great risk in reacting to external forces or developments, unless the reaction is highly rehearsed. On the other hand, a proactive response necessarily includes a correct analysis of the forces applying change to a business. It also implies a certain degree of advance recognition for impending change.

Can a business foresee every impending change? Of course not, especially in the realm of IT and mobility technology. Practically every element of mobility is changing constantly, from the technology itself to how the technology is used. Much of what is experienced in the world of mobility has never before existed. But creating solid corporate, financial, and resource resilience and flexibility will ensure that not only will changes be endured, but they will be used to the best advantage for the purposes of business growth. Mobile practice resilience takes time and constant renewal and improvement based on correct observations.

Because change comes so fast and is so sweeping in the mobility and IT industry, nothing is more important than remaining adaptive and open to new opportunities. There is a greater demand now than ever before for high-performance managers and individual contributors. Perpetual self-improvement is one of the primary tools not only for surviving in the workplace, but for thriving in the modern market. In today's fast-paced world, greater change will occur in ever-decreasing amounts of time. Your resiliency depends on your ability to thrive in such dynamic circumstances.

On a macro level, while it's a hardship for a person to lose their job, it's an even greater loss for a business to fail. Above all else, businesses must survive and indeed thrive. Resilience should be fundamentally ethical as well as foundational, though oddly it's often far more incidental than foundational. Few businesses plan for resilience in a direct and proactive manner. The focus of most management teams is on pure profitability and growth, with excellent and vital business elements in place to ensure longevity.

But resilience is something more: business resilience is a state of corporate durability that goes well beyond the drive for excess profit. It requires a sequence of growth phases that, in combination, provide a level of fortitude, flexibility, and adaptability that mark a business as superior. You can sense this almost immediately if you visit the offices of successful corporations such as Cisco, Dell, Apple, and Accenture, to name a few. You'll detect an aura of calm and controlled assurance. These companies not only intend to do well, but actively discuss thriving for 100 years or more.

Corporate resilience requires significant reserves of capital, limited debt, and just the right amount of excess capacity in talent, physical resources such as office space, and an abundance of great ideas coupled with a corporate management willingness to take calculated risks. When companies run out of ideas, time, and capital, they almost certainly end up on the endangered corporate species list that eventually leads to extinction.

This isn't to say that great companies do not go through hard times, because they certainly do. The ability to triumph over major challenges is part of what makes some companies great. Cisco and Apple are two great examples of weather-tested corporations that have made it through hard periods with blazing brilliance. Apple may arguably be the all-time best example of resilience, having been reduced at one point to a nearly irrelevant status, and then returning to completely revamp the way people listen to music and use their cell phones and computers. Apple was the first ever company to dictate terms to AT&T and the entire music industry.

Apple, Cisco, and other top companies have a built-in resilience that enables them not only to endure challenges, but to emerge stronger after each challenge—and in some cases, change the way we consumers live, learn, work, and play. These companies know that more known and unknown challenges will be faced and harsher tests are ahead of them. But few would bet against these superb examples of resilience.

Weaving assets that yield resilience into the corporate fabric takes time, a long-range plan, executive sponsorship, and a culture that manages constant change with traditional tooling such as profit and loss. Because almost nothing is more important to business resilience than ideas, great companies take care of the most valuable corporate resource—talented people.

Resilience can be foundational but it's not easy, nor is it achieved quickly. Most great companies have always been great companies; they have the right combination of assets from their beginning. Great companies have resilience built into their corporate DNA.

Focus on What You Can Control

Many forces external to businesses often wield profound operational influence, including governmental regulation, supply chain issues, exposure to international economic and political developments, technology breakthroughs, and customer purchasing trends. While external forces and developments must be identified, and indeed harnessed, I have found that the number one cause of business success or failure is the quality of internal management and individual contributors.

More than any other single element, what happens inside the company has greater impact on corporate resilience than any external forces. The business world is replete with examples of major errors—think of the Canarsee natives who traded a few trinkets in 1626 for what became Manhattan Island, a piece of real estate now estimated at $1 trillion in value. The business world, however, is just as wondrously populated with spectacular successes, such as the router, the television, and, my favorite, wireless networks.

I've been allowed a close look into the inner clockworks of some of the best-performing mobility practices in the world. Some of these practices fare much better than others, yet they all have hard-working personnel, each business operates inside the same general economic environment, and each business offers reasonably similar technology. While a great deal of external and internal forces and developments can impact a mobility business, the two single largest factors of system integrator growth and stability are *macro-industry conditions* and *internal management practices and focal points*.

One of the most impactful lessons I've learned came from Cisco CEO John Chambers: We should focus on the things we can control as opposed to worrying about every possible negative potential. I've incorporated this lesson into my personal life as well as my professional obligations and opportunities. In my view, it's a healthy and eminently sensible approach to life.

Macro-industry conditions should be carefully monitored, because they represent the currents and tides of an economic voyage. Having a corporate culture in which as many people as possible are observing as many industry and economic aspects as possible creates a powerful intelligence network. In my view, it's physically impossible for one person to monitor all the key elements of an industry and the economy at large, to understand the implications of international developments, and to connect news items such as a collapsing credit industry and how it will affect their business.

Many of the implications of macro-industry and economic developments are learned by experience, because they have no broadly understood precedent. The credit industry collapse from credit default swaps is an example of this—we're learning as much about the linking and distant implications of events as we are about the actual events themselves. However, regardless of whether the implications of these incidents are understood, the broad-based gathering of good intelligence is vital for effective management practices; analyses will come after, and occasionally prior to, major events.

Internal Management Practices and Focal Points

As opposed to external forces on a business, internal management practices can be controlled with focus and flexible adherence to an optimal plan. Resilience is a state of operations that is steadily acquired over time. In my work with some of the best mobility practices in the industry, I have learned that four steps are necessary to set the stage for detailed mobility practice resilience:

1. Optimal project sequencing
2. Mobility and CIO insights
3. Mobility network assessments
4. Precision sales guidance

Optimal Project Sequencing

Optimal project sequencing is covered in detail in Chapter 7. I set this forth as the initial step in business resilience because optimal sequencing is essential in the planning process and ensures that IT investments resolve core business issues. In my experience, the largest projects always seem to be those that are not well planned.

The principle of optimal project sequencing is based on the principle of building wealth: it's essential to eliminate leaks in the bucket, so to speak, before a person or corporation can build wealth reserves. Put in another way, it's not how much a person or company earns, it's how much they spend against those earnings. Optimal project sequencing is largely about reducing resource leaks in large projects. Corporate wealth is more rapidly built after resource leakage is eliminated from large projects. (Note that I'm not advising companies to avoid large projects; my advice is that it's better *not* to win a large project if it's poorly managed.) There's a difference between resource *drains* and resource *leaks*: drains are about an organization's ability to scale; leaks are about a company managing large projects poorly.

In many cases, mobility project wins of more than $250,000 are so troubled by poor project management that these deployments are mostly paid for by the system integrator through losses in recovery and inefficiencies. On the other hand, in my experience, mobility projects of more than $1 million nearly always tend to be well managed—or at least they have far fewer project management problems. It's difficult to account for this, except to surmise that some sort of mental shift and special emphasis is placed on the project when the words "million dollars" are involved.

Mobility and CIO Insights

Discussed in Chapter 3, CIO insights are also included here as the second sequence element in mobility practice resilience because they are essential to shifting the project focus from cost of the hardware and engineering and the technical specifications of the wireless technology to focus on how mobility impacts business. Such considerations often mark a deep cultural shift for system integrators. Terabytes worth of technical sales information are supplied by the technology vendors, and millions of dollars are spent in training engineers. But, by comparison, very little is spent on the value side of the equation.

The CIO is the junction between business problems and technology. When the functional requirements of a customer are carefully understood by the stakeholders, it is relatively easy to assemble a WLAN design and audit that will meet those needs. Further, when the true value of mobility to a customer's organization is well relayed and understood, the scope of the mobility project nearly always increases.

This major cultural shift is important to make with regard to mobility practice resilience, because the expansion of integrator to customer discussions to include the "why" of mobility results in greater sales efficiency for the integrator, increased customer impact, and greater "wallet share" for the integrator for each sale.

Mobility Network Assessments

There has to be a compelling reason for a customer to invest, or expand investments, in mobility. Few reasons are more compelling than illuminating the delta between what a customer's CIO *wants* the network to do and what the network can *actually* do. In other words, there is nearly always a contrast between the top operational priorities as defined by a customer's C suite and the actual capabilities of the existing network.

This situation remains problematic because networks are never truly "completed." Further, operational aspirations are far easier to establish than the design, deployment, and payment for a network that will fully achieve those aspirations. Operational aspirations are also generally much more dynamic than the capabilities of an existing network.

In a typical scenario, a business consultant swoops in on a customer site, drops enough buzzwords, and demonstrates enough empathy so that the customer adopts a new mantra. Then the consultant speedily jumps on the next plane, leaving the customer in a tizzy about executing the new mantra, only to have the program dashed based on the realities of the current network capabilities.

Consultants that connect sequenced execution of ideas with the resource evolution necessary to fulfill the potential of the new mantra are indeed rare and very highly valued. This is where the truly elite mobility system integrator evolution is heading, however. System integrators are experts in matching the business process optimization and the IT technology and policy changes necessary to impact the customer in great and positive ways.

This is exactly why Cisco and Accenture are devoted by joint engagement to achieving the synthesis of business practice evolution that is correctly matched by next-generation IT technology. In the 2009 third-quarter earnings call, IBM stated that with the recent acquisition of SPSS, a well-known industry name in business analytics, IBM has invested $9 billion from 2005 to 2009 next-generation business analytics. Notably, this investment augments an existing analytics capability center in New York City with 450 consultants and researchers. It's of no small consequence that the next generation of IT technology is dependent on ensuring that applications can be accessed wirelessly by a multitude of varied handheld devices. No reputable business analytics team or business process improvement investment would sidestep the impact of mobility.

IBM's massive investment in analytics is hardly an isolated event; Dell purchased Perot Systems immediately after HP purchased EDS, and the two acquisitions weighed in at a staggering $14 billion. Talk on the street, according to *InformationWeek* and other reputable IT news sources, was that Dell might have purchased Accenture instead of Perot, but at a market cap price of $28 billion, it was considered prohibitively expensive. That Accenture retains that large of a valuation is indicative of the value it brings to business process analytics as well as outsourcing office systems and tasks such as financing and accounting.

Consider also where the mobility system integrator industry is heading—that is, the same general direction as the largest system integrator. What Sam Palmisano, CEO of IBM, said recently about IBM's overall strategy is very revealing. He stated to the media in September 2009 that IBM is looking "more towards outcome" and less toward assembly. Why? "Economic pressure. When you're under budget pressure, you cannot afford to do other people's work for them.... And buying at good prices in little pieces and then assembling them doesn't generate value for your enterprise.... We see that occurring today as more and more people want outcome, solutions, front-office transformational things versus just 'I'll assemble piece-parts better than somebody else.'"

This view will become pervasive through a majority of the mobility system integrator community, initially with the largest integrators such as IBM, but then filtering down to the midsized integrators that make up the bulk of the top mobility sellers.

What is *not* being said is that there will be a shortage of integrators. System integrators have evolved from pure box resellers to integrators of systems that feature elements from the handheld client to custom applications. From there, the next evolutionary milestone for mobility system integrators will be that of wrapping not just engineering and maintenance services around hardware sales, but also, and perhaps even more importantly, business practice optimization as a tightly integrated part of the deliverable package.

Palmisano's statement has to be understood in the context that IBM had a massive consulting practice prior to the latest major investment in a consulting center in one of the most expensive cities on the planet. Relatively few integrators share that capability; the vast majority remain focused on wrapping engineering services around third-party hardware. The most successful mobility integrators will evolve into delivery resources for something more expansive and indeed more impactful to the end customer.

The next phase of the relationship between network assessments and mobility practice resilience will be based on the concept that the integrator should not just sell mobility, but should clearly demonstrate the delta between C suite operational aspirations and the current state of the customer's IT investment, paying particular attention to mobility. Few customers can't or won't expand their investment in mobility when they are shown exactly how that investment will be paid for and how quickly it will be repaid. Properly deployed mobility investments commonly pay for themselves in a year or less. The primary point of operational aspiration is to improve corporate resilience through improved operations.

Precision Sales Guidance

After the operational improvements have occurred through optimal project sequencing and the expansion of customer engagements from purely technical to those of mobility operational benefits, there remains a long list of other methodologies for increasing the profit margin by reducing operational expenses. There is an art to this while expanding the business through new sales, calculated risks, and increased efficiencies. The faster path to corporate resilience begins with fixing the "leaky bucket"; after those leaks are repaired, the bucket can be filled much faster and more efficiently.

Next on the resilience improvement sequence is to accelerate the speed at which the bucket is filled. Few things will achieve this faster than increasing the amount of incoming water. And that's where precision sales guidance comes in. Precision sales guidance fills the bucket faster, largely because it does two things:

- Ensures that less water is wasted by missing the bucket
- Ensures that the hose is turned up much higher

Sending sales teams to the *right place* at the *right time* with the *right message* is what precision sales guidance is about. A four-year analysis of the majority of Cisco mobility equipment purchase orders from across the industry reveals some rather illuminating facts, including the following:

- Eighty percent of the equipment sales come from less than 15 percent of the purchase orders.
- Eighty-five percent of the sales bookings come from 6 percent of the salespersons.
- Ninety-four percent of the cost of sales generates 6 percent of the bookings.

What's astonishing about this analysis is that most integrators could reduce their sales forces by 90 percent with virtually no drop in sales, all the while enjoying an enormous reduction in sales cost, both in direct expenses and overhead costs from personnel and systems to track and report sales. I'm not suggesting every integrator should immediately lay off the majority of their sales force, but it's true that while sales people work very hard, most of their success is derived from a fraction of the entire team effort.

The even more eye-opening fact garnered from this analysis is that virtually every mobility sales force is inefficient because of a fundamental flaw in the strategy used by most salespeople. To use an analogy from World War II, nearly every salesperson uses a "carpet bombing" approach. In other words, salespeople do their very best to saturate their targeted areas of coverage. This approach requires hard work by the sales staff and sales management teams. And it requires significant expense on the part of the company. The result is highly expensive cost of sales, which drags down corporate profit, reduces the velocity at which the company closes sales, and, at the macro level for the company, decreases resilience by reducing the amount of sales generated.

On any sales team, a small handful of elite performers generate far more sales than any other salesperson, year after year. These top performers don't work proportionately harder than the rest of the sales force, they just know where to go, what to say, and when to say it. Top salespeople succeed because of their efficiency. The perennially most successful salespeople hunt in target-rich environments—every time. Their territorial coverage is similar to that of their peers who perform less well, but they have much better smarts regarding customer targeting within those geographies.

The Five Key Principles of Precision Sales Guidance

Five principles guide precision sales, as shown in the following list. The first four hinge on the premise of being in the right place, at the right time, and saying the right thing. The fifth principle resides in an essential element of business resilience, *adaptability*, and equally important, knowing *when* to adapt.

- Smart vertical targeting
- Smart account targeting
- The purpose of mobility: untether unified communications (UC)
- Technology is horizontal; knowledge is vertical
- Vertical agility: know when to shift

Smart Vertical Targeting   If you're going to hunt, it's imperative that you know *where* to hunt. About 70 percent of the mobility equipment sold between 2005 and 2009 has been a part of the same top verticals:

- Healthcare
- K-12 education
- Higher education

- Manufacturing
- Retail

The following other key industries are tracked universally in the business world:

- Federal government
- State and local government
- Energy
- Transportation
- Financial services
- Service providers
- Wholesale/distribution
- Technical services
- Media/entertainment
- Hospitality/hotels and leisure

The first rule of precision sales guidance is to *hunt where the most opportunities exist.* When I analyze the bookings performance of my company's mobility partners, I can see how scattered the bookings are across all 15 verticals. The bottom 11 verticals combined produce half as much sales as the top 4 verticals. Most of the money to be made in selling hardware, engineering services, and maintenance is in the top 4 verticals: healthcare, K-12 education, higher education, and manufacturing.

A correlation exists between tight vertical targeting and how well a top mobility integrator performs in terms of generating sales. Without question, when I'm asked to support a midlevel mobility integrator looking to grow its practice, the analysis quickly shows scattered sales across multiple verticals, most of which are well outside the top four for general sales volume. An enormous amount of time, energy, and expense is equally distributed across too many verticals. This random target selection dilutes focus from where the bulk of the money is initiated in the cash stream that flows from the end customer, through the integrator, and on to the technology equipment provider.

Salespersons prize business relationships that generate money for them. This is a good thing, except when midlevel performing customers garner more attention than top performing customers. Most well-intentioned salespeople believe they should retain existing sales relationships at all costs. Most live primarily on commission checks and rely heavily on "low-touch, high-velocity deals"—they want to sell as much as they can, with as little effort as possible, so they can cover as much geography as possible—in other words, a carpet bombing approach.

This approach has generated billions in WLAN sales over the last few years. It has worked very well when a considerable amount of money is involved. A billion-dollar business is enormous by any standard. However, when we evaluate the convergence of ever-tightening cost constraints to reduce operating expenses, we realize that the next evolution we'll see in sales forces is a tremendous drive for increased sales yields.

It's interesting to note the performance within the elite mobility system integrators. The following information is from a group of the top mobility system integrators, and their performance is revealing.

Considering that 70 percent of the equipment revenue generated across all sectors of U.S. business are centered in K-12 and higher education, manufacturing, government (which includes all government-operated facilities such as VA hospitals), and healthcare, it's informative to consider two elements: the percentage of purchase orders sourced from these verticals and the dollar value of the purchase orders. Both are important to note with regard to smart vertical targeting. Managing this element of smart targeting reduces a tremendous number of sales cycles, which result in nearly zero revenues for the mobility system integrator.

A significant group of the top mobility system integrators received purchase orders in the following percentages from the top-performing verticals:

- Government: 24 percent
- Manufacturing: 23 percent
- K-12: 20 percent
- Healthcare: 18 percent
- Higher education: 15 percent

It's tempting to analyze this information quickly and declare that a mobility system integrator should invest most of its time selling mobility to the government. As of this writing, according to the U.S. Office of Management and Budget, the U.S. government's budget is projected to be $3.5 trillion for 2010. Many analysts have declared the U.S. government as world's single largest customer. That's possible or likely, but it doesn't necessarily mean that the government is the best place to sell mobility. In fact, unless you're on a list of approved bidders, or on a preapproved equipment list, it can be very difficult, if not impossible, to sell to many government entities.

The list of prioritized verticals changes when we review the average amount per purchase order:

- Healthcare: $13K
- Higher education: $9K
- Government: $8K
- Manufacturing: $8K
- K-12: $8K

This information indicates the *average* amount of the purchase orders from the top five mobility verticals, and it places a different light on where the elite partners focus their sales efforts. You know that healthcare relies heavily on wireless networks for patient safety, increases in productivity, reduction in employee burnout, employee retention, and profitability.

What the information doesn't show are multiyear trends; the industry analysis shows two interesting phenomena. The first trend shows that K-12 is rapidly catching up with higher education in average purchase order value. Only a year prior to the time this information was gathered, higher education made up 80 percent of the mobility sales in education; it's now much closer to half. Given that the lion's share of government stimulus money is going toward the K-12 education market, I believe that we'll see the K-12 education subvertical significantly overtake the higher education subvertical for the first time in the history of WLAN sales. Given that higher education mobility sales often deal with covering a portion of acres of indoor and outdoor coverage, the shift to K-12 is important to understand.

The second trend is happening fairly quietly, and the summary data is a surprise even to most elite mobility partners. That quiet development is occurring in manufacturing, which easily outperformed retail in 2009 for mobility equipment sales. What many in the industry don't realize is that manufacturing has outperformed retail in mobility equipment sales since 2006. The only major mobility group of which I'm aware that focuses on manufacturing is the handheld equipment suppliers such as Intermec and their competitors. The handheld equipment providers and the small, but powerful, group of custom application providers exert considerable influence in the selection of the mobility equipment providers to support their handheld deployments.

Smart Vertical Targeting Alignment   A sales professional's sales goals don't normally reduce in a new year. I've seen only two periods in the last 20 years where this occurred—in 2001 after the technology industry crash, and in 2009 after the credit industry collapsed. When these reductions in sales goals occurred, it was primarily an effort to keep the sales force paid well enough to retain them. It's difficult to attract top sales talent and expensive to train them, and new sales personnel typically don't perform at the same level as more experienced personnel. It's a smart management move to retain a good sales force—that's the resource that brings in the money, after all.

I believe that we're going to see tremendous pressure placed on sales forces to improve their yield significantly. The improvements in business process analytics, which specifically includes sales yield performance, will illuminate on an industry-wide basis the point that approximately 85 percent of the cost of sales results in about 1 percent of the actual sales. It's probably one of the greatest areas for improvement for a mobility systems integrator.

Smart vertical targeting will shift approximately a third of the sales effort from low-yielding verticals to high-yielding verticals. It's theoretically easy enough to mandate no sales in nonperforming verticals, but in the real world, account managers have many relationships they'd be loath to abandon. My counsel to elite mobility partners is that a shift of a third of their time is a sufficiently large enough initial change that most of the sales force will generally adhere to the new executive mandate. It's also a methodology change.

Analyses I've performed for elite-level mobility system integrators show an increase of sales from 50 to 100 percent when vertical targeting is optimized from purely incidental sales (carpet bombing) to smart vertical targeting. This level of sales yield increase has no additional cost to the mobility integrator.

Smart vertical targeting increases mobility system integrator resilience by identifying the most target-rich areas for sales. Once the sales force is firmly planted in the best industries to hunt for the best deals that yield the best sales performance, the next step is to sharpen the focus via smart account targeting.

Smart Account Targeting   Every account and customer is valuable to a mobility system integrator, but they are not all of equal value. This is an important concept to realize if you're responsible for a sales force with limited resources in personnel and time—which is the case in nearly all businesses, from the smallest mobility integrator boutique to the very largest sales forces, such as those at IBM, Dell, and Cisco, with sales personnel in the 10,000-plus range.

Three prevailing principles apply to smart account targeting:

- Customer database analysis
- Improve sales yield
- Deep dive the top five

One of the most interesting and surprising illuminations I discovered during my work with top mobility integrators is in the analysis of existing versus prior mobility integrator customers. My research shows that mobility system integrators keep relatively loose records on where they've sold equipment in the past. It's not that they don't have the raw data, because they do. It's that, in general, it's very rarely harvested. This is largely due to existing budget constraints on accounting and sales management tools, but even more it's because there is so much demand to generate profit and sales *now* that most integrators focus more on what's at their feet than looking reasonably far ahead—and mining a treasure trove of accounts into which they already sold.

The logistics, cash flow, and profitability management are mind numbingly complex. Most integrators think a very great deal about profitability with granularity of 1 to 3 percentage points. Even so, the higher-performing mobility system integrators on average abandon at least one customer for every $15,000 in mobility equipment sales. Restated, for every million dollars in mobility hardware sales, there are approximately 66 customers that the integrator has not visited recently. What's even more surprising is that the data clearly shows these abandoned customers haven't purchased mobility hardware since 2005.

This is a significant period of abandonment given that two major generations of wireless technology have occurred since 2005—specifically, the controller-based technology and 802.11n. The shift in architecture from autonomous to centralized intelligence architectures is generally considered one of the single largest technology advancements in WLAN history. What we've learned about WLAN designs and deployments has equally increased since 2005: on the technical side, the industry has evolved by leaps and bounds. Consider also the enormous strides made in security, especially in the areas of regulation and compliance to Payment Card Industry (PCI) issues. Mobility integrators have learned an enormous amount about how to ensure error-free velocity with regard to deploying this mobility technology.

Further, most amortization cycles for mobility equipment are approximately three years in length, so the equipment is more than due for a refresh. By coupling third-party financing, along with technology equipment vendor incentives, the quality, performance, and timing for a WLAN refresh has never been better. There's a tremendous amount for a mobility integrator to present to an end customer—in fact, it would be hard to tee up an easier time to deploy and expand mobility sales. The original WLAN and network installed in 2005 has vastly changed and greatly improved since that time. If that isn't enough, more mobility integrators are much better versed in customer engagements with regard to focusing on operational problems versus the selling of pure technology.

Smart targeting, whether regarding military targeting or improving sales force performance, is largely about increasing the sales yield, or output, for a given amount of time and resources. In the case of smart account targeting, it's important to understand how money is changing hands between customers and integrators with regard to purchase orders for mobility equipment.

Approximately 250,000 equipment purchase orders are initiated across the entire IT industry for enterprise systems in the United States every year. In the analysis of this information, an astonishing discovery is that 93 percent of all mobility customers spend less than $25,000 per purchase order. There are some very good reasons for this, including of the fact that half of all purchase orders for equipment come directly from "click-and-ship" equipment provider giants such as CDW. Most mobility equipment orders are for something on the order of only five access points, bolstering the fact that the U.S. economy is largely based on the enormous number of small business owners.

However, the preceding information hardly tells the whole story about mobility equipment purchases. It turns out that 81 percent of all money that changes hands from mobility equipment sales is from purchase orders in excess of $50,000. In short, most purchase orders are small, but most of the equipment sourced money made from mobility equipment sales is from large purchase orders. The central premise of smart account targeting is to focus on WLAN opportunities in excess of $50,000. That's easier said than done when the mobility practice is largely based on incidental sales—well-intentioned, hard-working salespeople who close mobility opportunities as they become available.

Smart account targeting requires both intellectual rigor and precision intelligence. The precision intelligence is often already in the possession of the mobility integrator—in fact, it exists within its own customer database histories. Virtually every purchase order received from 2005 valued at $10,000 and above represent very specific targets for sales of $50,000 and up, for two reasons: the first being that the average size of a mobility purchase order has increased by a factor of two to three, and second, the demand for mobility in enterprise-class operations has evolved from "nice to have" in 2005 to "mission-critical" in 2010.

The primary sales targets for mobility sales forces would be, therefore, at the customer intersection of both mission-critical demand and the largest average purchase order. This makes an unmistakable case for the pursuit of healthcare customers. The risk/reward scenario in this case shows that those customers are sought after on a vigorous basis. The true opportunity is not in the largest hospitals, but in the "doc-in-a-box" and medical specialty outpatient clinics.

The second most target-rich environment resides in manufacturing. Every elite mobility practice I've worked with has declared it does not have a manufacturing practice. And, of course, they are quite correct; it is, after all, their business. Outside of the handheld devices vendors, no elite mobility integrator I'm aware of has a specialized focus or incentives to drive mobility sales in manufacturing. However, it comes as a pleasant surprise to them when they discover how much of their mobility sales actually does come from manufacturing, often ranking number three in their vertical stack ranking as determined by hardware bookings.

Deep dive the top five. The single most amazing discovery to me with regard to industry hardware bookings analysis is that on average, the top 5 percent of mobility customers generate approximately half of all the equipment bookings. Remember earlier in this chapter where I mentioned 90 percent plus of all mobility hardware bookings are derived from 5 percent of the sales force? The reason for this is that most of the bookings come from a very select customer base—a very *small* customer base.

One premise in most well-run companies, called "feed the strong," might sound a bit cold-hearted, but it's actually a smart business principle. You get the best return from the best-performing accounts, sales personnel, and programs. If you improve the best of what you have by 10 percent, you've moved the needle more than if you uplift the bottom 10 percent of a workforce, program, or investment.

The point here is that a mobility systems integrator would increase its resilience more quickly and build cash and resource reserves faster by focusing investments and personnel on the top 5 percent of their best customers—those who spend the most money in your business.

It's quite interesting that in business you often hear in glowing terms how a mobility partner received a visit or request for information from a very high-profile prospective customer. Those opportunities should be pursued, but at the same time it's important to remember that glamour won't keep the lights turned on. It's all well and good to have engagements with blue chip companies; it's far better to make good money. I repeat: Your best customers are those who spend the most money with your business. Focus, protect, and reinvest in your top customers. Analytically, no business strategy will deliver more operational resilience more quickly than this strategy.

The Purpose of Mobility: Untether UC   The more I closely observe mobility sales as a contributor to elite mobility system integrators, the better I realize the role of mobility and how it's shifting. Once solely the domain of network access, WLAN mobility now has the primary role of untethering UC. In other words, it's role is to ensure that UC applications are accessible by wireless handheld devices and their variants. This isn't just a good idea; in my view, the very relevance of mobility currently depends on it.

If you've been in mobility for a long time—as have this book's technical editors Mark Tyre and Bruce Alexander, as well as myself and others—you realize that we've had to battle for mindshare both inside and outside our companies for decades. That healthy competition has only just begun to be much more complex and interesting.

As part of my vigilance with regard to IT trends, I've been thinking recently about the relevance of mobility as the borderless network era has come upon the IT industry. These are the most exciting times ever for the IT industry in general. Currently, about $1 billion is spent annually in the United States in enterprise mobility hardware sales for enterprise-class networks. Yet, along with other mobility professionals, I've been reasonably concerned about mobility relevance as powerful incentive programs emerge for UC and data center equipment.

The power of those incentive programs became very clear to me as I recently sat in a meeting led by a colleague who is one of the top business development managers in the industry, Tami Murphy. Her presentation was brilliant for its combination of complexity and clarity on comparative technology program incentives. Her illustration was based on key analytics assembled by herself and a select group of her peers. This analysis illuminated the difference of approximately a dozen technology incentive programs in profit terms as offered by our mutual employer.

The meeting was catalytic for me because I'd been exposed to this type of data a number of times before, but it was never compiled in such a clear and comparative manner. It's a complex set of numbers and programs, and it's very difficult to make the data points clear and relevant. Bringing this array of information to a single defined landing point was part of what made the presentation one of the best analytical presentations I've seen in a long time.

The best presentations get us to think either differently or more clearly, and that's what this meeting achieved for me. Her presentation is why I realized for the first time that mobility in and of itself ranks about fourth, and occasionally third, on the list of top technology and sales priorities by mobility integrators. This is because the C suite at major integrators is very familiar with profit margins. Most of their time is spent either directly or indirectly managing profit margins.

To ensure maximum performance, the C suite and midlevel integrator managers are commissioned on the performance of profit contribution programs. These programs are very important: *they make or break the entire integrator business.*

The yang to the yin of integrator profit margins is that the C suite at my employer is also compensated on profit margin as the supplier of this technology. A natural and healthy tension exists between the sellers and resellers of IT technology; every point of benefit on one side is paid for by the other side. The fact that it all moves as smoothly and swiftly as it does is no small feat. For my employer, hardware sales aggregate to the tune of $150 million *each business day* of the year.

Tami's presentation provided pin-point program accuracy on the far larger map of seller and reseller relationships as managed by an array of incentive programs. In my view, incentive programs are easily the most efficient way to drive behavior with individual contributors, corporations, and entire industries.

The managers from both the technology seller and technology integrator are compensated from the same flow of money, typically measured in increments of a handful or less of margin percentage points. For this reason, the C suite at both the technology providers and the system integrators is intimately familiar with profit incentive programs.

Following are the top priorities for most IT systems integrators:

- Unified communications
- Data center
- Security
- WLAN

UC is typically a practice that is two to four times the size of an integrator's mobility practice. The data center is often similar in size but often twice the size of a mobility practice inside an integrator, and IT and physical security are now more or less the same size in terms of mobility equipment sales inside an integrator.

However, it's not just that UC and data center practices are much larger in terms of pure revenue streams to the general IT integrator. It's that the network is moving into a cloud-based architecture. Data center capitalizes on that very development, and UC ties it all together, both on the customer premises, but equally importantly, over the cloud.

Mobility risks losing stature with the integrators because it's generally viewed as no more than an access technology. In fact, the role of mobility is far greater than that of simply providing wireless access. Its role is to *untether the applications provided by UC*; it is foundational to the borderless network approach because it ensures connectivity to any device, by any person, in any place, at any time.

This ties very tightly into the messaging of smart account targeting, because precision sales guidance is not just about knowing which verticals and which customers to prioritize. It's about *knowing what to say* when the sales team arrives at the target site. It's not about enabling wireless handsets on the manufacturing or hospital floor. It's about connecting people and systems with little regard to their physical location on or off the worker premises because work is rapidly changing from a location to an activity.

Knowing what to say is how the business transaction gets completed. Saying the right things, at the right time, in the right place adds to business resilience because it increases the rate at which money flows into an integrator operation and decreases the rate at which money flows out of an integrator operation. Preservation of capital and resources is a fundamental doctrine of business resilience.

Technology Is Horizontal; Knowledge Is Vertical   There can be no doubt that IT and mobility have become so complex that an ever-widening army of specialists are dedicated to increasingly narrow, but vastly deeper, subspecialties. In mobility, the RF expert is usually one person and the security person is another individual. Of even greater interest to me are the new and highly innovative ways of using mobility in today's business, social, educational, and entertainment environments. The reason mobility is changing the way we live, work, learn, and play has as much to do with how we're adapting mobility technology as the technology developments themselves.

One of my primary points in guiding elite mobility partners is help them to narrow focus from a broad array of vertical sales. The reason for this is in part that the more broadly scattered the sales across verticals, the more incidental the sales tend to be. A key element of vertical scatter is that the greater the scatter, the smaller the purchase order tends to be. Also, the same sizing rule tends to apply to incidental sales. The greater the angle of the ricochet, the less impact on the element off which it's bounced.

The same holds true with sales engagements: the less carefully aimed and timed, the less impact. There's a quantum outcome difference between the questions, "Would you like wireless with that router order?" and, "If I could show you how an RFID system would virtually eliminate your loss of wheelchairs, and you would pay off the system in eight months with the savings, would you be interested?"

There's a practical reason for focusing sales forces on one to three industry verticals. It's nearly impossible for all but the very largest of sales forces to specialize in more than two or possibly three verticals. Even in the largest sales forces, specialist teams with vertical focus are put into motion. Selling into a 250-bed hospital is not at all the same sales engagement as a 250-bed hotel. This difference will become even more clear as mobility integrators are rightfully and firmly guided into outcome-based engagements. It's yet another reason to drive for discussion expansion from engineer to engineer to groups of stakeholders from the integrator and end customer.

Expertise is vertical, and technology is horizontal. What this means is that while each vertical requires very specific expertise, the technology sold into all verticals is essentially the same. With perhaps very limited exceptions, the wireless access point sold to a hospital is identical to the one sold to retail establishments and other verticals. There will probably be some differences in actual deployments—such as specialized enclosures for oil and gas refining plants versus those used in retail—but that's largely from unique industry requirements. The access point itself will not vary—the same unit used in a refinery can be used on a retail floor at a hardware store.

The horizontal nature of IT technology becomes even more apparent as you move up the OSI stack from the handheld client toward the application layer, and the access layer of the network to the core routers and switches. Note that I'm saying *toward* the application layer, as applications are very much industry-specific, and indeed customer-specific.

Mobility network design doesn't change that much from one industry to another either. There are as many variations in a retail floor design as retail floors themselves. If you took a grid of access point locations and configurations, you'd be hard pressed to tell whether the design was intended for a specific vertical. Unless the specific models of the access points were defined, it would be difficult to differentiate between an outdoor and an indoor design. Granted, point-to-point or point-to-multipoint bridges would not look the same as a WLAN; even in outdoor networks, the maximum distance used is generally based far more on handheld client performance than the access point. Those distances are surprisingly similar in both outdoor and indoor networks.

This is not to say that each vertical requires specific design expertise. In fact, each vertical requires unique considerations of elements such as dynamic environments, special heating or cooling, rough handling, physical client routes, and so forth. The actual device-level technology remains the essentially the same across the verticals.

Vertical Agility: Know When to Shift   The next evolutionary point of sales force strategy beyond smart targeting is vertical agility. At present, there's good reason to be satisfied at seeing mobility integrators tightening their focus from incidental sales in as many as nine or ten verticals to two or three verticals. Even if a sales force has reduced its vertical scatter by 30 percent, it could increase overall sales performance from 50 to 100 percent. Vertical scatter is measured by the percentage of sales outside the top five producing verticals. A commensurate overall reduction in sales performance results when the total mobility sales from the top five producing verticals drops below 70 percent.

The exception to this strategy is a windfall mobility purchase order in excess of $100,000. Close inspection of windfalls, however, shows that nearly all of them fall into the laps of mobility integrators and general IT technology providers. This is not to say these windfalls were unearned, however; far from it. Windfall mobility deals are usually granted to incumbent IT integrators with mobility specialists and who have well earned their incumbent status with the end customer. That status occurs neither quickly nor easily.

In some cases, mobility teams originate the sale and follow it through to a successful deployment. Those probably represent less than 10 percent of all windfall sales in mobility, however. In complete fairness to every mobility integrator and technology provider, every windfall deal that did not originate with the integrator or technology provider will surely be more than earned during the deployment. The larger the deal, the more difficult it is to design, manage, deploy, and maintain. Optimal project sequencing for large mobility projects is not for the faint of heart, or those new to mobility.

The next generation of sales evolution will incorporate vertical agility. This will require not only the ability to move swiftly and easily in two or perhaps three verticals, but equally importantly to know when to shift from one vertical to another while keeping track of windfall opportunities in verticals outside the primary focus.

And this is a key concept: Even though a vertical will necessarily expand and contract due to macro conditions such as economics, regulation, and technical breakthroughs, windfall opportunities will very likely remain. Major windfall deployments don't usually feature bleeding edge technology because the risk is too large.

Vertical agility requires both forward-looking intelligence systems that compile information on macro conditions such as economics, emerging opportunities, and markets, as well as shifts in policy and regulation. In the best-run practices, business analytics expand and evolve to include predictive analytics. Policy shifts are often tightly interwoven with macroeconomic conditions such as rapid spikes in oil prices that escalate travel costs. A rapid drop in oil prices can escalate spikes in hotel and auto rental expenses due to increased demand. Either swing in economics could initiate a travel restriction policy that would be offset in the end customer by an increase in IT investment such as telecommuting.

Another example of policy change is that of video meetings that drive a necessary increase in bandwidth and deployments of IP voice networks and voice-over-WLAN systems. My new iPhone has WebEx incorporated, which is a wonderful productivity application that allows me to attend meetings with far less regard to where I'm physically located.

A current example of vertical agility is the mobility sales increases into the K-12 market from the higher education market. As recently as 2008, it was estimated that about 80 percent of all education mobility sales came from higher education; today, mobility hardware sales are split nearly evenly between these two education subverticals. Even elite mobility integrators were not aware of this gradual shift until nearly a year after it had begun. Such a shift has to occur in amounts of tens of millions of hardware dollars—and that's challenging for any single mobility integrator. It's experienced first by the larger technology providers, because they see the greatest amount of market shift. (In fairness, nobody foresaw this until nearly a year after it occurred. It was, in my view, one of those market swings that has more to do with a tipping effect that occurs gradually, until enough momentum shifts that the trend becomes apparent to the technology providers and mobility integrators.)

Mobility integrators have now begun to shift toward this market, even as the higher education market struggles increasingly to manage limited cash flow for the greatest impact on its institutions. Tuitions in two- and four-year universities and technical institutions are increasing; this isn't because of profit demands, as these are obviously non-profit institutions. These increases are due to the rising expenses of running an education institution.

In parallel, much government stimulus money is destined for the K-12 market, thereby helping tip the mobility market from higher education to K-12. This shift is an example of where vertical agility will be important for mobility integrators and mobility technology providers to possess. The K-12 market largely propped up the education vertical in its entirety; it's noteworthy that it was the only vertical to escape a downturn initiated by the financial market collapse of 2009. Other examples include the shift from retail to manufacturing, which first began in 2006.

Being equally adept at diverse verticals will be increasingly important. The higher education market involves a customer engagement process that is significantly different from that of the K-12 market. Not only that, but relationships still count for a great deal even in today's business environment, where you are far more likely to have virtual meetings than those featuring rooms full of people.

The knowledge gap between markets is even more apparent when comparing healthcare to education. One thing seems certain, however, which is that for the next few years, the bulk of the money generated from mobility hardware sales will continue to be sourced largely from the top five leading verticals, which are, in random order, manufacturing, K-12 education, higher education, government sales, and healthcare. With such quantum leads in their mobility investments, these markets' demands for mobility will not only be sustained, but will increase as they deploy ever more expansive borderless networks.

Vertical agility will greatly ensure mobility integrator resilience as they move with correct timing from fading to expanding verticals.

Education and Manufacturing: Resilience par Excellence

Only two verticals have demonstrated resilience to every stock and economic market condition encountered in the United States: education and manufacturing. Education has proven to be especially resilient to macroeconomic conditions; it was the only vertical that held steady during one of the most challenging economic periods in recent times—the credit market freeze.

Most of the education market stability has resulted from strong growth in the K-12 sector, which offset the downturn in the higher education market. The education market in general, and the K-12 subvertical in particular, is propped up through government stimulus funding. The political and macroeconomic implications of funding sources are outside the scope of this book, but their effect on the mobility integrators and technology providers remains fundamentally the same, tax consequences aside.

The K-12 subvertical is currently predicted to be a growth industry for the next few years, and as the K-12 segment is far behind the higher education subvertical in terms of total deployments and technology deployments, the K-12 market today is far from approaching mobility deployment saturation. The higher education market has been the perennial early adopter of the 802.11 standard since its inception in the late 1990s.

The vertical most amazing to me is manufacturing. A careful review of the U.S. macroeconomic cycle versus the stock market cycle reveals a very interesting trend. When I first saw this data, it occurred to me that it would be interesting to lay the performance of stock purchases of manufacturing companies over the 11 indicated major verticals in terms of macroeconomic performance. Something rather interesting occurred upon overlaying this data. Various manufacturing subverticals, in particular consumer durable and nondurable products, basic industry, and precious metals, are positioned at nearly equal intervals in the macro cycles of the stock and economic markets.

This data is likely the single best example of market agility that combines relatively similar vertical expertise with varying macro market conditions. Market agility between education, healthcare, and the four main types of manufacturing will provide enormous resilience to system integrators and other enterprises selling into these verticals. Timing the entry and exit points of these verticals will assure maximum top-line growth and reduce swings between feast and famine cycles commonly found in most sales organizations.

While, of course, durable manufacturing goods such as dishwashers and automobiles are different from nondurable goods such as pizza boxes, the general design intent and mobility investment outcomes of both are quite similar. Inventory in motion, warehousing, and robotic and hand-assembly manufacturing lines are more or less the same no matter what goods are produced. Mobility integrator firms generally don't distinguish between manufacturing subverticals; they are, at least to mobility integrators, quite similar on a technical basis. The difference of course is vital in terms of how much revenue can be generated from these subverticals; they offer enormously variable differences in how much they can be harvested. And as with any other kind of harvesting, knowing when to advance and when to retreat is essential for business resilience.

From a tactical perspective, a program in pursuit of K-12 targets could involve customers that have not been contacted for five years. Consider those customers that have been assigned geographically or vertically to the top performing 10 percent of the sales force. The former SKUs sold and the delta to the current technology, plus the consulting outcome recommendations, such as network analysis and at least two elevator pitches on fast repayment scenarios per customer, should fully identify the target and fully arm the sales team to pursue it.

On the manufacturing side, gaining intelligence regarding a company's management priorities involves being able to weave those concerns into a vision of what is possible immediately through technology upgrades and how fast these investments will pay off for the customer. You'll find that such advance preparation will pay off handsomely when you're working with the customer on site. (A side tip: Avoid the "let me tell you about my company" sales line. All that due diligence will have been sorted by the customer in advance. Such an approach is rarely a good use of time unless the client asks for specifics about your company.)

As a mobility technology integrator, you can gain insight into the current political and economic climate inside the company by reviewing the company's public records. Cash-flow concerns could tip off the account team to arrive at the engagement armed with solid and attractive financing offers. Knowing the backgrounds of key players in the room by doing some research on LinkedIn or a similar site can help you in depressurizing certain points of the engagement if the talks are stalling or if transitions between topics aren't going as smoothly as they should be.

At least two cycles of priority transition should be examined on the manufacturing vertical: one cycle on the way out and another on the way in. It should be fairly easy to overlap the current economic and stock market conditions with the target manufacturer.

Select the top priority targets from the integrator's existing customer relationship management (CRM) database of past installs, ideally from the past five years. Acquire the product SKUs; the financing package, if any; the primary C suite–based operational priorities; and, if the customer is publicly traded, take a quick look at its last 10Qs and 10Ks financial statements for insight into its profit and cash flow. A combination offer that shores up the end customer's largest issues, as well as accelerating its most notable opportunity, will be well received and will show that you, the integrator, understand the business. Come fully armed with at least two elevator pitches that resolve top operational concerns.

Summary

Operational resilience is about the combination of reducing operating expenses while dramatically expanding sales force harvest rates. The combination of these two elements will allow a steady, and surprisingly fast, buildup of cash and other asset resources. Significant cash reserves with relatively little debt will afford many more options even during a business's most challenging periods. And those challenging times will surely come; every company is tested, and the great ones not only get through the challenge but are made more secure, more resourceful, more flexible, and more optimistic.

An indispensible asset regarding mobility practice resilience is a significant pool of cash reserves, sufficient time to make a plan, and brilliant management supported by brilliant individual contributors who are authorized to take calculated risks at every point of the macro and internal economic and other impactful condition sets.

The pool of cash is significantly augmented when the company experiences far fewer, and far less dramatic, reductions in sales. This is achieved primarily through smart targeting. Few strategies will bear more fruit than not only knowing where to find the maximum rates of deal closure, but, equally important, remaining agile in the sales targeting programs. A solid business analytics program will necessarily evolve into predictive analytics. Those predictions will clearly show when, where, and how to achieve maximum sales yields.

For this reason, the greatest single asset to build mobility practice resilience is great people who do the right things in the right places at the right time.

CHAPTER 10 | Next-Generation Mobility

Unlike Hernan Cortes and Francisco Pizarro, who both sailed to the New World in the 16th century, we don't need to leave home permanently to make progress, but just as surely as the Cortes's 11 beached ships weren't returning to water, or the mutineers to Spain, there's no going back in today's wireless networks. There's only forward, and what a forward it is. Although my employer, Cisco Systems, alone has shipped something on the order of 5 million access points (APs), easily ten times that number of devices has shipped from all providers, including wireless clients such as laptops, smartphones, laser scanners, and RFID tags. In spite of these staggering numbers, we remain in the earliest days of wireless devices. The next five years will see a proliferation of wireless devices in quantities dwarfing the total currently implemented in enterprise-class networks.

802.11 and Other Wireless Standards

Within the enterprise-class networking realm, the IEEE 802.11 standard is the undisputed king of broadband unlicensed wireless in terms of total chipsets deployed. *Broadband* in this context is a device capable of routinely delivering in excess of 1 megabit per second (Mbps). However, numerous other unlicensed wireless protocols are being deployed in today's networks, such as ZigBee, Bluetooth, HART, and others.

In the realm outside of enterprise-class networking, devices based on these protocols have shipped in much greater quantities than devices based on 802.11. It's noteworthy, then, that the two behemoths of wireless mobility, 802.11 and mobile cellular, are beginning to converge. Bluetooth and mobile cellular converged onto common platforms several years ago. If a "network device" is defined as anything that carries voice, video, or data, then mobile cellular, Bluetooth, and other wireless protocols have their rightful place in networking.

Networking is no longer the express unlicensed wireless domain for 802.11; and indeed it may never have been. For example, today's networks in healthcare facilities routinely have an enormous number of different wireless protocols and/or spectrums in use, including those in the following list, which should be considered only representative, because there are doubtless other spectrums and protocols transmitted and received at major healthcare facilities:

- 802.11
- ZigBee
- 802.15
- Mobile cellular in 850, 1700, 1900, 2100 MHz
- Bluetooth
- Medical telemetry
- Two-way walkie-talkie
- Licensed Mobile Radio (LMR)

- Microwave
- MRI equipment
- WiMax
- 700 MHz
- AM radio
- FM radio
- Broadcast television

However, being a broadly adopted protocol is by no means a guarantee of long-term survival. In fact, the larger and more pervasive unlicensed wireless becomes, the more challenging it is to ensure unlicensed wireless speed, range, and reliability. Most of today's unlicensed networks energize maximum amounts of electrons within their areas of coverage, and they have done so for years. Those of us in the industry who have been looking ahead some years have passionately urged equipment designers, systems integrators, resellers, and WLAN maintenance engineers to reduce power output and deploy designs with directional antennas rather than omnidirectional antennas.

As a quick aside, there is more than one view of how electrons actually propagate from and interact with antennas. Having discussed this in great depth with quantum physicists, RF component and antenna engineers, and seasoned professional wireless industry colleagues, I've carefully considered the various versions of what actually happens between a transmitting and receiving antenna. My view has evolved over the years, and it may change in the future as more information is derived from the quantum theorists.

After much thought, I believe that a transmitter does not add electrons into the air, nor does a receiver pull electrons out of the air. Rather, it's like a very large game of bumper cars. The electrons at the transmitting antenna "bump" the electrons adjacent to the antenna, and this bumper car game is played out between the transmitting and receiving antennas.

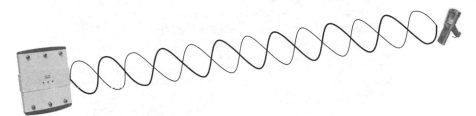

There is a whole lot more to this, and RF propagation theory gets very deep, very quickly. One enters the world of quantum mechanics fairly early in the discussion. While I've adopted my position on how RF propagates, I'm quite open to other arguments as to how it works. What is certain is that very smart people from varying professional and academic circles have widely divergent views on how RF propagation works. In the end, in my view it doesn't truly matter, outside of knowing how to harness this amazing phenomenon.

Without delving into a deep technical discussion, the practical implication of the preceding statements is that you should minimize the number of electrons set into motion in a room or area from wireless devices such as laptops, dual-mode phones, and access points. Electrons remain the theoretical medium transmitted from one end of a wireless link and received at the other end (or, in some cases, multiple endpoints) of a wireless link. One or both ends of the wireless link could be an AP, laptop, PDA, wireless handheld laser scanner, or some other device. The more electrons in motion in the air, the more challenging it can be to operate a wireless network effectively, such as 802.11, HART, 802.15, and so forth. Of course, it should be mentioned for the sake of the technical reader that a certain amount of noise is in fact necessary for these systems to work. The primary point is that the higher the noise floor (total number of electrons in the air) beyond a certain point, the shorter the range, reliability, and speed of most wireless deployments.

Above all is one very large impending change for the wireless networks, one that will likely dwarf all other issues related to next-generation networks: intelligent buildings.

Intelligent Buildings

An *intelligent building* is essentially the convergence of building automation systems (BASs) with the IT network. The following image is representative of the various systems that are being converged:

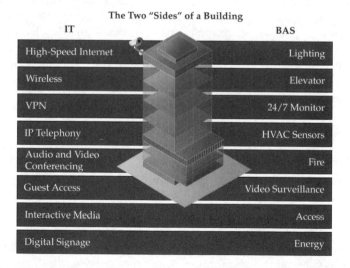

Intelligent buildings will add logarithmic increases in the number of both transmitters and receivers in a wireless network. The incoming age of smart electronics will see a shift from wireless links that feature an AP-type device mounted on a wall or ceiling and at the other endpoint a handheld device of some sort. The bulk of the links in a smart building will be used to manage the building systems, such as heating and lighting. Other systems will be used for security and communications. Devices that were once tethered for power will now be connected wirelessly. One or neither of the devices in a smart building may be handheld. These devices include, but are hardly limited to, the examples in the following list:

- Thermostats
- Lighting control systems
- Window shades
- Physical barrier management, such as doors
- Heating, ventilation, and air conditioning (HVAC)
- Video surveillance
- Emergency communications for first responders
- Fire sensors and fire suppression (such as sprinklers)
- Elevators

When you consider the dozens of variants of each of these devices, and the hundreds of locations available and appropriate within a building, it's easy to see how thousands, and even tens of thousands, of wireless devices can reside within a smart building.

This all said, I don't subscribe to the theory that the probability of RF interference is proportional to the sum of all wireless radiating devices within a building. Quite the contrary, it's my experience that business class wireless devices have fairly short ranges. It's only the devices within the radiating range of each other that may be compromised. Careful planning on a holistic, multifunctional system basis is what can mitigate many of the problems of wireless RF congestion.

Usage

With regard to the end user, first consider the various types of usage commonly in place today, as shown in Table 10-1. Most wireless communications to date have occurred between two human users. A very considerable amount of traffic, and arguably the fastest growing use of wireless mobility, is between humans and machines. A greater proportion of the communications in next-generation networks will include machine-to-machine communications as machines become smarter and appropriately independent.

Perhaps more correctly understood, the traffic between humans and machines is actually very much two-way. The data *from* machines is more often information for end user consumption, while traffic *to* machines is more instruction-based for the performance and guidance of the machine.

With an increasing shortage of experienced, credentialed workers, the wireless relationship between "things" and people will become a predominant driver in mobility. We have already found this to be true in healthcare and certain heavy

Usage Type	Current Uses	Future Capabilities
Communications	Worker to worker Supply chain Emergency Team assembly	Automated notification Sensor networks to humans Early warning Personnel ETA to work site
Inventory	Supply chain Asset control Safety Cost management Equipment status Tipping angle/condition Lot number	Automated supply chain management Smart asset destination advisory Condition granularity Suggested action for optimal cost reduction Real-time indication of excess/ extreme condition Stale dating, including ETA, time on shelf, and shelf life remaining Automated pricing based on remaining shelf life
Maintenance	Device history Time to next maintenance Extreme environments Critical conditions Fluid levels Mechanical shock Component failure	Wear indicators tied into automated supply chain management Environment controls based on inventory status/load Automated fluid level/type management based on load/ wear
Command/ control	Speed/direction/thermal control HVAC Emergency shutdown Physical positioning/ docking	Automated intelligence gathering Asset positioning based on environmental or threat conditions Smart building automation systems that respond to environmental loads, energy cost, energy sources, and automated shading devices for buildings

Table 10-1.   Types of Usage

industries such as nuclear power generation, where the facilities are vast and the areas covered by workers and supervisors are large enough that spanning them has clear productivity implications. The more critical the shortage of talent, the smaller the physical area necessary to cover before it becomes a productivity issue. The concept of "distance made irrelevant" by mobility will become mission-critical. Time and productivity are not luxuries when assets are limited.

Wireless communication between humans and machines is being driven primarily by managers looking to increase the granularity (amount of management visibility) in flow-based control systems. In the early days of business class wireless mobility, generally considered to be the mid- to late 1980s, knowing the location of an item was quite satisfactory. The story of how I first entered the wireless industry is illustrative.

Prior to my career of about 19 years in the wireless industry, I was an automotive aerodynamicist with a focus on racing cars. It was great fun working on some of the world's fastest racing equipment in the United States, but also for the America's Cup racing yachts (as a hydrodynamicist and aerodynamicist), the National Hot Rod Association (NHRA), and even a bit of Formula One consulting. In the early spring of 1991 while en route to some testing for Patrick Racing in Phoenix, Arizona, I stopped at a major auto rental company to rent a car large enough to carry my equipment and some personnel. I was told there were no cars available of the description I was seeking. I indicated that, in fact, I passed about three of them in the customer area on my way to the rental counter. The person at the counter refused to believe me, but assured me that if they had one of those cars they would be happy to rent it to me. I decided to take my business to another rental agency, but while leaving this auto rental company, I passed yet at least half a dozen more identical cars of the type I was seeking. I called the rental agency from my very large Motorola cell phone (referred to affectionately by those who've been around for a while as the "flying bricks").

"Hi," I said, "I know you said you don't have any of the cars I requested but I'm standing right next to six of them in your parking lot." The reply: "I'm sorry, sir, but we can't possibly have any—there are absolutely none showing on my computer screen." At that point, I decided there had to be a better way to resolve this. My vision was to put on each rental car a wireless box that would instantly update the rental agency computer system as to the lot on which each car resided. The car would interact with a gate-mounted receiver at the auto rental return lots. No more customers would have to make the same call I just did if I my idea was implemented. Inventory would be exact and updated in real time from any of the agency's lots to any of its customer service personnel.

So, I ventured into the wireless industry, and a long road involved equipment demonstrations, negotiations for very large contracts, and the near acquisition of the company I founded. It all eventually led to my position with my current employer, Cisco Systems. It's been a marvelous experience. The point of the story is that it would have been a significant advantage to the rental agency simply to know how many cars it had available for rent. At least nine were available in the situation I experienced. For all I know, those cars are still sitting in the exact same spots. Although that's not likely, you can bet there are thousands of rental cars that could be placed in service that are idle and not generating revenue for the company.

Location-Based Services

One of the most interesting changes I foresee in the next five years for wireless mobility is the increased reliance on location-based services (LBS), which currently are being considered or deployed at virtually every major healthcare institution in the United States. It was estimated at the 2009 Healthcare Information and Management Systems conference that only 2 to 5 percent of all healthcare facilities have deployed LBS. The reasons for this are varied but are likely a combination of untried technology on a scaled basis, lack of experience by end users, cost, and poor financial return modeling portrayed by the vendors and integrators.

Those offering LBS components and services will possibly be mildly incensed at my claim that LBS technology remains somewhat untried. There have been many good LBS deployments, but most of them are what we call "choke point" deployments. In other words, the LBS technology can determine whether or not an object or person is in a certain room, but it generally cannot provide high-definition location granularity.

There are "lab queens," very highly tuned LBS deployments that do indeed offer excellent location granularity, even down to a few meters. These systems are not ready, however, for deployment by an average network or WLAN engineer, given that they require an uncommon depth of technical knowledge, specific to tags or elements provided by a specific manufacturer. This isn't to say that the average WLAN engineer is incapable of obtaining highly granular positioning; the issue is that of error-free velocity—how fast it can be completed at the highest levels of performance.

Providers of LBS components and services must be able to offer to the average WLAN deployment team relative ease of deployment on a repeatable and cost-effective basis. Currently, LBS can be delivered on a high-definition basis, but not without using some of the best location, networking, application, and RF engineers in the industry. There isn't now, nor has there ever been, enough of this talent to scale across even the healthcare industry, much less manufacturing, education, retail, and other key industries that in combination purchase billions of dollars' worth of wireless equipment each year. It remains to be perhaps the single hardest WLAN service to deploy reliably on an error-free and high-speed basis.

That all stated, there is rapidly growing pressure on vendors and system integrators to provide LBS. Currently, LBS is a good networking practice with a profitable future. Few top integrators can provide it at scale, but the number is slowly increasing, and considerable effort by the vendors and integrators, pulled by a large market demand, will eventually move this from the cutting edge to something much more routinely deployed by most reputable systems integrators.

Next-generation mobility will be driven by use more than by cost or complexity. Usage drives value more than virtually any other element. If something is used a lot in business, it's seen as valuable. Usage, when carefully analyzed, is what drives the evolution of devices, systems, and indeed how a device itself is used. The standards protocol itself is constantly evaluated and driven by usage and the belief that usage will be high in the future.

As we consider the element of usage in next-generation wireless networks, it is appropriate to consider the two main groups of individuals exposed to WLANs and the primary uses within those groups. The primary personnel exposed to WLANs can be partitioned in a number of different ways, but I suggest that the two primary users are those who deploy the technology and the end users.

Designers, Deployment, and Maintenance Engineers

If you ever get an opportunity, speak with some of the people who were very close to the design and delivery of the original 802.11 equipment for enterprise networks, such as my manager, Mark Tyre, and my colleague Bruce Alexander (both of whom, not incidentally, are the technical editors of this work). You'll soon discover that today's wireless equipment usage is way beyond what was originally imagined by the designers and teams who defined and drove protocols such as 802.11. When the protocol originated in the mid-1990s, voice, video, smart buildings, IPv6, and similar issues were breathtakingly complex and far beyond the intent of the IEEE standards body and designers. Yet most, if not all, of those elements are now routinely a part of current WLAN systems.

Today's WLAN complexities were also well beyond what we were doing in the field in terms of our knowledge of how to respond to design requirements. We knew some things about the importance of RF design, but not so much with regard to site surveys. Site surveys were used for many years to ensure that nothing within the radiating range of the transmitter or receiver would cause interference or other problems.

The measurement tools at the time were complex and crude. You had to be pretty good at using an expensive spectrum analyzer to have a decent chance of eliminating or managing interference problems. The output of these devices was not easy to interpret. The best of the spectrum analyzers were backpack-sized and required an electrical plug-in. In later years, battery-powered analyzers became available, though their power didn't last long before a recharge was required.

Site surveys were used later to verify design coverage on a multinode design basis, and then the tools quickly became used for WLAN designs. This occurred because no tools were generally available for RF coverage. RF design tools cost around $100,000, required extensive training, and didn't actually cover all that much for the 802.11 and other radio spectrums. Tools with far more attractive pricing came much later in the industry's evolution.

We knew so little about truly effective coverage in the late 1980s and early 1990s. Nearly all the early design work was custom crafted by degreed engineers or RF technicians with many years in the industry. While careful measurements were made, the bulk of what was completed had a lot more to do with art than science. Little design documentation or formal training existed at the onset of today's WLANs. More often than not, both ends of the wireless links were stationary. Today, it's rare for that to occur; one link end is nearly always in motion. Originally, wireless was more of a bridge in many applications, whereas today it's far more generally about enabling motion.

Wireless Training: The Early Days

I was the founder of wireless training for engineering and sales teams at Cisco. The first worldwide session was held in early 2000 on the San Jose campus. I wouldn't claim it was the first one in the industry, but it was the first major training event at Cisco. Discussions ensued between the design and field engineers prior to this meeting, but no open and scaled forum was planned for design and auditing.

The early years of this training were contentious, highly polarized, and often quite funny. The design engineers felt "everything is the field engineers' fault, because they don't understand the equipment." The field engineers retorted that the designers knew nothing about real-world RF and what happens at customer sites. Virtually none of the political correctness of today's training sessions happened there; it was much more like something from the Wild West. Indeed, in a real sense, it was frontier work. The level of engineering talent from every participant was exceptionally high, and we were all passionate and very much engaged in work that had never previously been attempted on a large-scale, indeed global, basis.

Most of us in those early meetings knew a few things from our hands-on experience in deploying the equipment, and we had enough confidence to make grand statements that often included the words "always" and "never." Looking back on what we really knew then, compared to what we know now, I'm amazed at what we achieved and how well the deployments truly worked. Some of the gear we deployed in those days remains operational at this writing.

A good portion of the original discussions centered on features and next-generation devices. Today's design and site survey discussions are far more centered on design and audit practices than on features. There is a necessary relationship among technological features, design, and site surveys, of course, but training sessions today are more about the technology and primary design elements, principles, and site survey tooling than the technology in the wireless devices themselves. This is partly because the tooling available today is quite excellent for predictability, granularity of performance insight, ease of use, documentation, and value, as discussed next.

RF Design and Site Survey Tooling

RF design and site survey tooling have evolved and gone down a number of different specialization paths. Today, four kinds of RF analyzers are commonly used in the design and site survey phase of deployments:

- Protocol
- Spectrum
- Site survey
- Performance/security

Excellent tools are available from at least eight different companies:

- BVS
- Cisco

- Network General
- Wild Packets
- AirMagnet
- Ekahau
- Fluke
- Wireless Valley (now part of Motorola)

These tools greatly improve the quality of today's wireless networks. They also reduce the time invested in design as well as auditing.

Wireless Design Work

Wireless unlicensed designs originally began with virtually no concept that the entire room would be shared among multiple APs and a large number of heterogeneous (unique) wireless clients. In fact, in the earliest days of 802.11, we simply hung an AP where we thought it might work best, took some measurements in the area adjacent to the AP, and pretty much declared it good to go unless we found some significant anomaly nearby. At that time, the engineering community knew little about how various RF devices would work together or interfere with one another when deployed en masse.

Most of what the early deployment gurus knew was learned strictly from trial and error. I have to chuckle a bit when looking at the term "early deployment gurus" because I was one of the most experienced people from the earliest days of the industry and I certainly didn't feel like a guru. I knew some things that worked and a lot of things that didn't work. Most of my colleagues felt the same way.

Few folks were working on systems like those we were working on, and there were no rooms full of eager, younger engineers looking to learn from us. It wasn't a secret society by any means; those of us who knew what to do more or less simply kept to ourselves—kind of like bears out in the wilderness, each to his own, each one on its own territory. Except for 802.15, there were no forums, no open standard around which we could rally until 802.11, but the 802.11 forums were much smaller and less supported than 802.15 for some years. Many of us knew about 802.11 and liked the equipment based on it, but it was by no means something most of us thought would become a multibillion-dollar-per-year industry.

Eventually for each of us "bears," sales became large enough that we needed help, and that's when we began breaking in new engineers and telling them what needed to be done in the field. The passing of information from one to another was more like an artisan's apprenticeship compared to now, where we train well-schooled folks in highly structured symposiums with well-prepared slide decks and multiyear technology roadmaps. Today, by the time we train them, many budding RF engineers have had significant networking experience, have credentials, and often have genuine electrical or computer science degrees. In the late 1980s, a few engineers had a ham radio license, but not much else in terms of practical experience.

Today's designs are first approximated by the software incorporated into cutting-edge wireless controllers, which is more or less the central computer of the WLAN.

Those designs are generally used for budgetary purposes with the customer. The budget, if approved, is then rendered into a highly detailed design with very sophisticated software from top-shelf companies such as AirMagnet. Most complex RF designs today remain largely similar regardless of the industry in which the network is ultimately deployed. The commonalities across most WLAN designs today include the following:

- Mostly omnidirectional antennas
- Fairly low power, something on average approximating 30 mW in output power
- About 2000 to 3000 square feet of coverage per AP
- A maximum of about 25 wireless clients per AP
- Predominantly ceiling-mounted APs versus wall-mounted
- About 80 percent of the APs are pillar or wall-mounted (manufacturing, outdoor)

Next-generation designs will incorporate the following elements and their associated pros, cons, and hurdles to mass market adoption.

Smart Antennas

Smart antennas allow much faster and more reliable AP-to-client links without flooding the general area with RF noise. They place energy where it needs to be and not where it doesn't need to be. The concept of a smart antenna is more correctly an architecture of the antenna, sophisticated processing hardware, and software for both transmitting and receiving signals. It's quite arguable that the 802.11 protocol uses smart antennas in that they can alter certain transmitting characteristics, the result of which is an improved RF link between the transmitter and receiver. The following illustration shows a Cisco 1250 series AP that features smart antenna capability.

As client domains (areas in which clients travel) continue to increase in size, applications will increase in latency sensitivity. Ever-increasing market demand for "set and forget" reliability will motivate wireless providers to use the spectrum more intelligently by sending information specifically where it's needed and avoiding sending it where excessive noise exists. Challenges to achieving this include increased cost of goods sold and miniaturization of devices, as well as a current lack of demand for this technology.

Further, installing smart antennas, like most other kinds of antennas, reliably and in a highly durable manner on clients is more challenging than installing them on APs.

Cell Sizes

Whereas in the past cells were designed to be static in size and shape, next-generation RF cells (the area covered by a single transmitter) will migrate from a single preset size, some "large" and some "small," to become dynamic in size. In next-generation WLANs, cell sizes will be more commonly based on load, quality of service needs, local RF and environmental dynamics, and application latency sensitivity.

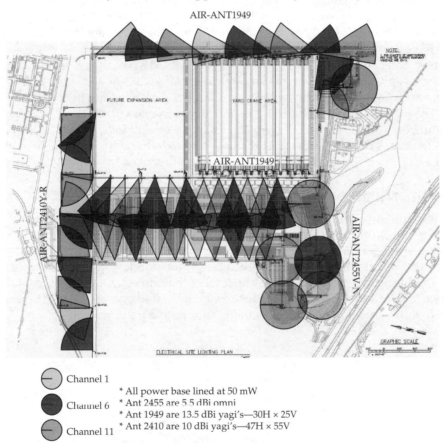

Channel 1

Channel 6

Channel 11

* All power base lined at 50 mW
* Ant 2455 are 5.5 dBi omni
* Ant 1949 are 13.5 dBi yagi's—30H × 25V
* Ant 2410 are 10 dBi yagi's—47H × 55V

Consequently, wireless designs and deployments will evolve to resemble more closely licensed mobile radio, which has used this technique for years. Maintaining a static cell size regardless of traffic, latency requirements, RF, and environmental dynamics has necessarily forced engineers to compromise on optimal cell size without being able to see into the future adequately as to how the cell might be used. Dynamic cell size is an adaptable and appropriate response to changes in RF environments, traffic load, client count, and latency sensitivity.

Dynamic cell sizing allows optimization of a radiating environment on a dynamic basis. This has significant implications for range, speed, and reliability. While it can be argued that the controllers currently available achieve that, I'd point out that today's controllers from all manufacturers achieve this in a fairly rudimentary format—the cell size is throttled purely by output power. There is much more to consider in this technical objective.

The dynamic cell sizing I'm envisioning for the future includes the proper synthesizing of not just output power, but also modulation complexity, dynamic Fresnel control, and cell shape through smart antennas that could deliver an array of coverage from omni- to highly directional. The downside of this development is that it would require smarter clients, meaning more CPU capacity, which engenders greater amounts of power, heat, and size—none of which is welcomed in the realm of handheld clients. There is, of course, increased cost for both the AP and the client, and the clients would need to have more or less the same level of cell size adaptability as the AP.

Feature and capability parity between clients and APs has always been a challenge, with clients typically having far less smarts, antenna capability, and other technical features requiring power. Parity will likely remain a challenge into the foreseeable future. The prime directive for a client in an enterprise-class network is to last at least eight hours on a single battery charge. The total investment in handheld clients is often three to ten times the cost of the APs. Better sales modeling for returns on investment will have to be derived for this to be financed and amortized by end customers.

Multispectrum, Multiprotocol Devices

Multispectrum, multiprotocol devices will combine both licensed and wireless spectrums and protocols at the silicon level. This will reduce deployment and redundant engineering costs and will free the customer to pursue a broader range of more capable clients. We have already seen this in the wireless industry in what are called "mobile access routers," which are devices that are essentially routers and radios combined into a single device. These devices are mounted onto mobile platforms such as buses, trains, trucks, forklifts, and similar automotive platforms.

Multispectrum, multiprotocol technology is particularly effective when long distances are covered, often outdoors, although many indoor buildings are so vast they are treated by engineers and network technicians as outdoor sites (minus the heavy weather, of course). Radios are less expensive on a per-transmission basis because they are what we call "toll bypass" radios. In other words, there is no charge for their time in the air, as we see commonly in mobile cellular. The general architectural approach is that IP traffic uses lower-powered RF at fairly close ranges on a toll bypass (no charge for transmission or reception) and high-powered, licensed links for when distances are outside the range of radios.

More than just in outdoor networks and very large indoor networks, multispectrum, multiprotocol radios are being used more and more in healthcare and manufacturing. Today, numerous spectrums and protocols are in play from various clients such as tablets, medical carts, MRI machines, smart buildings, and more. We have been in the healthcare, rail car, and other industries where the AP-to-client physical range can vary from a few feet to miles. Clients at these extreme ranges are devices such as mobile routers, which feature very high performance radios. Bluetooth, mobile cellular, and 802.11 are commonly integrated into a single handheld unit, and they have been since around 2007.

Importantly, the advantage of this architecture also extends to the ability to send various applications selectively across various spectrums and protocols. Not all applications are the same for value. Not all wireless connections are equal in capacity, range, and *ubuity* (a term of art indicating coverage in all user areas).

The challenge for this development is, again, to overcome the cost versus value discussion. Like any good tool, this architecture is great where it should be used and expensive or inappropriate where it's not ideal. These kinds of radios are as much about accommodating numerous types of endpoint devices as they are about accommodating wildly varying transmission and reception ranges.

Also important, of course, are the implications for the power, nimbleness, and reliability of the management system to stream and recombine applications autonomously over various wireless spectrums and protocols. IP processors have done this for years as they slice and recombine IP packets over various routes, and some are massive in their capacity. This makes it easy to believe that streaming applications over various spectrums and protocols is imminently achievable.

Designs and Increasingly Complex Services

The wireless industry originally delivered data only, and discussions about deploying voice-capable RF networks were more theoretical than practical. It worked in the labs, but we were not at all confident it would work on a mass-production basis. It wasn't long, however (in fact, only a few years), before we experimented and learned enough to show thousands of engineers and hundreds of system integrators how to replicate what we had done not only in carpeted office space, but also in very challenging environments.

Services such as voice and applications such as video have brought tremendous increases in latency-sensitive capabilities to the networks. This was no small problem to resolve in a network where the signals were originally tightly and carefully limited to well-shielded and highly predictive copper and fiber cabling systems. Taking these same signals and tossing them over the air with the same commitment to similar degrees of latency and reliability was, and still is, a breathtaking feat by comparison. It is, however, done, and done rather well in most cases. This is mostly because today's radio and bit-recovery systems are highly sophisticated devices that can overcome many engineering oversights. It should *not* be construed that an RF, WLAN, or other networking system will routinely replace solid engineering practices.

There is no "engineer in a box," despite the considerable sums of money spent by vendor marketing teams to convince end customers that there is. It never was true, and it's becoming even less likely going forward. The one exception to this may be simple coverage in a carpeted office environment. However, the majority of future growth of WLANs isn't so much in the simple carpeted, small office space as in the complex RF environments found in healthcare, education, manufacturing, retail, and outdoors for municipalities. Further, as the industry evolves from voice to video, LBS, and smart buildings, the days of "hang and hope" will likely eventually end for the carpeted office space as well.

Even great equipment can make up for only so much engineering error, and often less than the customer is led to believe by vendor marketing teams.

The equipment is vastly superior to what we used in the late 1980s, and the deployment design and audit engineering have become far more sophisticated. Today's wireless networks that carry latency-sensitive broadband traffic in complex radiating environments require levels of engineering similar to those used in most licensed wireless networks.

We are beginning to see the best system integrators move their top WLAN designers into pure design roles from combined design, deployment, and auditing assignments. In addition, today's WLAN RF engineering is becoming so industry-specific that not many wireless network engineers who deploy networks in the education industry could demonstrate error-free velocity in a nuclear power plant, heavy manufacturing facility, or most healthcare environments.

It's not difficult for complex-design engineers to design coverage for carpeted office spaces, but it's a steep curve with high levels of visibility to move from simple to complex RF coverage designs. Few engineers will attempt it willingly, and I've bailed out more than a few engineers who've attempted this transition. It's much more difficult to do at a high rate of speed than it looks given the uncertainty of environmental dynamics. (I mention speed here because error-free velocity is a key differentiator between amateurs and pros.)

Clients and AP Pairings

In today's WLANs, and to a large degree in those of the past, the concept of homogeneous (same) clients was nearly always more of a theoretical issue than a realistic one. While homogeneous client sets are the norm in small enterprise networks, they're greatly the exception in major enterprise wireless networks (a network with more than 100 APs and/or transmitters).

In virtually every major enterprise wireless deployment I've been involved in, the bulk of the deployment challenge was to get the clients to work seamlessly with the APs. The challenge initiates with simply getting the APs to associate reliably with the clients. From there, security is layered and resolved, and then the application layer is applied and resolved, and, finally, roaming tests are conducted and completed. This is very demanding work that typically requires custom code on either or both the AP and the client.

Only a small handful of major client manufacturers in the United States routinely deploy at major enterprise networks. The number of major manufacturers who supply APs and controllers for the same wireless enterprise networks is also limited to a handful.

These parties provide a stunning array of unique models, with an even wider array of software code releases. Combine that with 802.11a/b/g/n, an equally diverse set of application software releases, with various levels of security protocol on top of that, and you get a sense of how many combinations and permutations exist and how challenging it is to get client and AP pairs simply to associate at an RF level. When the software among security, applications, and firmware begins interacting at the processor and memory layers inside the clients and APs, the complexity is vast.

A movement is already afoot at the vendors to offer precertified sets ("precerts") of APs and clients. This is a great idea, but it's harder in practice than in theory and marketing because it's virtually impossible to keep up with the never-ending changes of software codes that arrive in "maintenance" and "new release" trains of code. These precerts already cover a considerable amount of the integration of clients to APs.

In next-generation networks, pairings from specific AP and client vendors will be more rigorously tested, the applications will be better integrated, and well-defined "packages" of APs, clients, and applications will be offered to the market. It's likely that the true scope of what can be precertified will be considerably less than what the customers deploy in a production network. These pairings will still require extensive testing and integration but will reduce deployment time, improve engineering margins for system integrators, and improve reliability and stability for end customers.

The final integration and maintenance of these bundles should not be oversimplified in terms of ease of deployment, but it will become much better over time as automated testing systems work in conjunction with very tight code development across the suppliers of APs, clients, security, and applications.

Link Role Flexibility in Clients

"Link role flexibility" is an industry term coined initially by my colleague Jon Leary and myself. It refers to the various roles one or both of the devices can play in an RF link, and the assumption is that, over time, certain clients could be variably configured to act as a bridge, workgroup bridge, or something similar. As this industry continues to mature, the infrastructure side of the WLAN link (the AP in most cases) may be less flexible in its roles while the clients take on a much wider set of roles. Examples of link role flexibility could include a smartphone reconfigured as a handheld RFID scanner, barcode reader, phone, PDA, and LBS client. The concept in full execution would be that the client could be reconfigured either by the person holding the client or a remote user.

Client-Centric Networks

From the inception of the wireless network era in the mid-1980s, the design work has been virtually all infrastructure oriented. This is to say that increasing amounts of care, planning, auditing, and documentation have been focused on the AP side of the WLAN links. The design assumption was, and often still is, that if the APs lay down a pervasive set of overlapping cells, the clients can roam freely. This isn't a bad or deficient assumption.

However, that mode of thinking has increasingly evolved toward more of a client-centric wireless network design. This is an entirely appropriate and exciting development that will better ensure client performance and more robust RF links. As the engineering community progressed in its sophistication and understanding of WLAN RF links, it became apparent that the client side of the link is nearly always the weaker side of the link where the preponderance of troubleshooting occurs. As our understanding of network design continues to mature, one of the next elements we'll see is a shift from infrastructure-centric to client-centric designs.

Client-centric designs begin primarily with physical client routes. In other words, the infrastructure will be placed with regard to client needs and coverage versus the current approach of having clients adapt to AP physical locations. Client-centric designs will then place APs inside client RF cells, instead of placing clients inside AP cells. In the short run, this will considerably reduce the average AP cell size. Over the long run, cell sizes will be dynamic and *set by the clients, not the APs*.

The challenge to client-centric designs as part of next-generation networks is that these designs will be manyfold greater in number and type than infrastructure-based designs, because infrastructure designs are primarily based on industry type—healthcare, education, manufacturing, and so forth. While of course subcategories exist within each of these industries, from a client-centric perspective, far more categories exist because there are far more types of radiating environments.

As an example, while several types of manufacturing designs are created, such as light manufacturing, heavy manufacturing, and robotic- or conveyor-based manufacturing, five or more fundamental types of radiating environments may reside within a single client cell. Put another way, clients are much more susceptible to environmental dynamics than APs because of the smaller client antennas, lower power rates, and the fact that clients are oriented in a large number of physical directions as they are carried about by their users.

Dynamic cell sizes and other smart adaptations will enable more nimble and resilient clients that perform closer to their maximum for the triumvirate of speed, range, and reliability.

So when we consider next-generation usage, it's important to expand the discussion to the engineers, designers, and system integrators. How those elements of the industry engage and enhance their understanding of the technology has a great deal to do with how the end users engage the technology. A tight relationship among the groups is necessary.

Clients, of course, should not have to be very technically oriented to use wireless technology properly and fully. The best of the technical group are literate in the mindset and actual usage of the technology by the end users. Though less technical, it is indeed the end user who arguably propels the greatest changes in the evolution of the technology.

Future Wildcards

In looking five to ten years ahead, there are of course wildcard elements, any of which could easily change the technology roadmaps, how networks are used, how network security is implemented, and how engineering design is practiced. These wildcards might propel further technology and usage evolution even beyond to the next generation. And, as surely as past and current generations of technology, markets, and users exist, there will be a generation after the next one soon upon us. Three of the more obvious wildcards I see are

- High-speed picocell networks
- The future of audits (site surveys)
- Self-defending and self-healing networks

High-Speed Picocell Networks

Serious consideration is being given to the concept of *picocell networks*. While certain mobile cellular phone companies use this term, the "picocell" they refer to typically means a building-size cell. In the enterprise-class world of low-power wireless, the term refers to something far smaller in size.

Picocells are wireless cells as small as an office cube and serviced by an AP that resides within the cube itself. Some of the original concepts included building the AP into a desk phone, a wall socket outlet, or desk light. Perhaps one or more of these designs may become available on a mass-produced basis, but not until the controller and network-edge architectures have evolved enough to support a tremendous increase in the number of cells, which would essentially be allocated on a one-per-user basis.

This generally is not a bad or even necessarily difficult-to-implement concept. Picocells would have the advantage of possibly not requiring a discrete audit (a site survey performed by a technician) once the system was deployed. The audits might be built into the remote and automated maintenance and monitoring regime of each cell. However, you should realize that not having a discrete audit is not the same as deploying without a design.

Picocells would probably not be the standard cell size common to current-generation designs, but would more realistically be one of three to five different cell sizes afforded in next-generation networks. In a next-generation network of dynamic cell sizes, picocells would probably be the one cell size that would change the least, if at all, as it would necessarily need to service only one user in one office or cube. Variants of this, of course, are possible, but as cell sizes are reduced, they tend to include dramatically fewer dynamic elements. Certain RF dynamics such as split cells (a cell split into two or more subsections because of a door closing or another large object being introduced into the cell) would not likely occur at all.

RF interference is a phenomenon that nearly always takes place near the receiving antenna versus the transmitting antenna. In part this is because the signal drop is enormous between the two antennas, even if they are at fairly close range. The signal near the receiving antenna is always far weaker than that the one at the transmitter.

Therefore, the farther the RF dynamic (the source of interference) is from the receiving antenna, the less effect the dynamic tends to have on the cell. At very close distances, such as 2 meters of range between transmitters and receivers, it is difficult (though not impossible) to introduce enough interference to be relevant at all. Possible, yes, but likely something extraordinary and not typical for an office cube or small office. (Of course, some smart executive will doubtless find a way to break this rule. It's all part of what keeps the industry new—you never know what you'll see next. Unintended outcomes are very normal to unlicensed, and licensed, wireless networks.)

Picocell deployments, though small in individual size, would in the aggregate require the same or more total engineering than a WLAN with more traditional cell sizes, which are currently approximately 2000 to 3000 square feet per AP, whereas a picocell may average something closer to 100 square feet. These cells would feature very low output power; small, hidden antennas; and very complex modulation schemes to accommodate the high speeds that would be one of the more interesting elements of a picocell design.

Another interesting question of a picocell design would be that of replacing ether ports, one of the more cherished and most aggressively defended, elements of sales teams and vendors who sell switches. Whether or not picocells would replace ether ports is difficult to assess, though possibly the resolution may lie in redefining the term "ether port" to that of a port as found on a controller, virtual though that may be in the future. The pushback by ether port sales personnel could be mitigated if sales teams would be compensated according to the new definition.

How much speed to the desktop is provided would be another interesting element of picocell networks. Current speeds and configurations can be amended such that 600 Mbps per user is possible with current 802.11n technology. While no standard exists in a deployable form at this writing for much higher speeds in 802.11, few doubt that we'll see much higher speeds yet.

High-end modulation schemes, which are one of the primary speed elements of wireless, are well understood and have been routinely used in the cable television and fiber-optics industries for years. Smaller, smart antenna technology has existed since the mid-1990s and even earlier. Miniaturization has also for some time allowed the current industry to build very attractive desktop devices such as IP phones with an AP built in.

The one area lacking for gigabit Ethernet to the desktop? Clients. Endpoint devices have lagged the infrastructure side of a link by several development years for some time now. While the largest vendors have been selling pallet loads of 802.11n APs and clients, the industry is just now seeing 11n clients. 802.11n design and audit software has been available only from the best commercial providers since around 2008, though 802.11n has been available, in a prestandard format, since around 2007.

Providing client performance at the same levels as infrastructure is very challenging, because clients have severe limitations on power consumption, antenna size, heat dissipation, and ruggedness. It's difficult to arrive at the right set of engineering and user compromises that at the same time will ensure the mass market adoption of the units at prices that will allow huge levels of performance.

Audits (Site Surveys)

I prefer to use the term "audits" when referring to RF site surveys, because a site survey is an audit mechanism, not a design tool. This distinction is important now and will become even more essential in the future.

In every healthy business, network traffic loads always increase in complexity and size over time. Untethering applications will require more detailed deployment engineering, more detailed auditing (site surveys), recurring audits, and more sophisticated client integration. One of the most important changes we'll see with regard to next-generation networks is the concept of recurring audits versus today's approach, which is generally to perform a single audit to test the design in its real-world setting. The best system integrators also perform one final audit after the WLAN is completely installed, and they do so prior to turning over the network to the customer. In the future, post-deployment audits will be integrated into routine remote management operations.

If it's good to catch a problem before it becomes major, it's even better to catch it in its earliest phases. This of course extends to the concept of intrusion detection and prevention. However, increases in traffic, latency sensitivity, clients, and proliferation of wireless devices will require that audits occur as part of the normal observation of a healthy network. This is yet another reason why enterprise-class networks are shifting from in-house management to that of third parties that already possess far more sophisticated monitoring and response tools.

Fewer and fewer enterprise-class companies have enough IT talent to plan, deploy, and maintain their own enterprise-class networks. The scope, task complexity, and tooling for monitoring and maintaining major WLANs are now well out of the range of all but very few companies.

RF auditing on a post-deployment basis will make a critical shift from APs to clients. What few customers, and even relatively few system integrators, understand is that controllers measure and monitor what occurs just outside the AP itself. However, the vast majority of RF problems occur at the client side of the link. However, no major integrations of auditing software take measurements inside the actual clients in production use at enterprise networks. Of course, system integrators measure the areas where clients reside. That much is given and is highly appropriate and necessary.

However, if you measured the total amount of time spent at a particular point in space where a particular client physically resides, it's infinitesimally small compared to the time the client spends in that exact or adjacent space over its total life. This is why audits will eventually reside on clients and will be embedded in the same silicon. Expensive, yes. It will require more power and generate more heat, but the cost of a client not working is much higher. It's far greater than simply replacing the client—the value is measured in productivity lost by the end customer. Even in small factories, this runs quickly into the hundreds and thousands of dollars per hour. Catching problems near the time and place they begin to occur is a highly cost-effective way to manage WLANs.

What isn't well understood is that most RF problems, if not intermittent, tend to start small and get worse over time. This can result from a combination of cables and connectors wearing, or wiring shielding eroding or abrading to allow electron leakage, but it can also be caused by certain environmental dynamics such as increases of inventory or significant reductions of inventory that once shielded sources of interference. In other words, as cables and connectors wear and physical environments change, a common outcome is that RF reception is compromised. On some occasions, it's actually enhanced from changes in physical environments, but this is far less common than a degradation of RF performance.

Remote network management that includes audit data as a routine part of the management and observation traffic, as seen by the client, will greatly help reduce the cost of WLANs and also improve their reliability and average performance.

Auditing in general is one of my favorite subjects, but the topic of the future of auditing appeals to me even more. Over the years, since first designing my own chipsets, devices, and WLANs, developed with my own small team, I've worked diligently to share with others what I've learned via hands-on experience preparing site surveys. It's been my good fortune to have as close colleagues two of the godfathers of site surveys, Mark Tyre and Bruce Alexander. We've discussed the past, current, and future states of audits for many years.

My colleagues and I agree that the concept of "engineer in a box," as mentioned earlier in this chapter, was vastly overhyped by very well-intentioned marketing departments. We strongly agree that wireless engineers who can not only design but audit WLANs with high-speed velocity have a pretty solid future ahead of them, because wireless networks are becoming far more complex.

That post-deployment audits will be completely automated in the future seems certain to me. I remain equally convinced that deployment-phase audits will not be automated. At present I do not see how a design can be properly audited without physically walking around the site to verify the cell edges, cell edge stability, and cell overlap. Even if the client has audit software embedded, a designer would need to walk around its domain area. For dynamic cell size and performance audits, one would set the cells to maximum size to verify the appropriate cell edge for signal strength and quality, and then reduce the cells to minimum size to ensure appropriate overlap for effective client coverage. It's not realistic in the near future to see that kind of test performed automatically during a WLAN deployment phase.

Again, once the original design audit is completed to verify and adjust the WLAN RF design, a second audit should be performed once the entire WLAN is up and operational. The former audit will be completed on a spot basis, the latter with the entire WLAN up and running. This approach adds significant margins of assurance to the customer. It also helps protect the system integrator's profit margin because they do not have to return to patch and amend the system.

Once the WLAN has been turned over to the customer, next-generation WLANs will benefit from recurring audits performed automatically by a remote management team.

Remote monitoring will require that audit software to be embedded into production clients, something that does not usually occur today. Until that point in our industry, audits will need to be performed by live technicians.

The wildcard, then, is how soon the industry will see embedded into most clients top-notch software such as that from AirMagnet and its competitors.

Self-Defending and Self-Healing Networks

Self-defending networks have been an interesting concept for some time, especially as they pertain to wireless networks. The wildcard issue here is how to build enough intelligence into a client and the wireless infrastructure to remain one step ahead of the bad guys, who invariably and occasionally get ahead of the good guys. Bad guys routinely concoct methodologies to perform an end run around the technology, policies, or procedures in use by the good guys.

There is perhaps no grander element to unauthorized intrusion than stealth. Hackers, programs, and intrusion attempts are cleverly disguised to appear as normal and authorized. It's possible that in the future, authorized IP packets will be encoded in such a manner that the system will easily recognize them as "good" and yet the encoding will be so complex that the bad guys won't be able to replicate it.

The interesting element about wireless is that it can be detected from great distances outside buildings and even campuses. Wireless signals are routinely tracked and monitored from satellites 30,000 miles into space. That renders most kinds of perimeters at the campus edge ineffective. Better to invest in barriers as decoration, because in general putting distance between a bad guy and an open wireless signal doesn't afford much security.

However—and it's a very large however—it's one thing to be able to detect a signal, and quite another to be able to *use* a signal, *read* a signal, or *inject* a signal into the system. Injecting a signal past the AP or client is quite difficult. Using layers of security barriers, beginning at the clients, APs, and controllers and extending inward toward the network core, is a well-regarded approach, along with continual monitoring to detect and prevent intrusion.

Security has long been routinely sold with wireless. It's common for major vendors to sell both security and wireless as a joint technology; this is of course appropriate and prudent for system integrators and customers.

My personal bet is that the bad guys will always, eventually, find a way into or around a system. Security is an illusion because it's temporary at best. A dynamic security system is better. I don't see the bad guys having to work too hard for a living just yet, because there are far too many open systems or systems with well-known security deficiencies. Simply take a look at how often security updates are provided by Microsoft and you get the picture.

Wireless security can be very good; it has to be, because it's used by every federal government, banking, and financial system on the planet. Wireless systems now routinely use some of that technology. Security is an essential element of a network, and one of the key factors to robust security is the rate at which it evolves to respond to threats, which most certainly evolve rapidly. However, the ultimate wildcard here is the possibility that security can be so good in wireless (and it is when properly applied) that the bad guy simply moves to a softer target, of which there is no current shortage.

Markets

Next-generation markets will feature an interesting dichotomy. The technology will remain horizontally oriented but the value proposition will become increasingly vertically oriented. This is to say that no major vendor will provide much in the way of specialized wireless systems for specific verticals (industries) such as healthcare, manufacturing, and so forth. The development programs become too expensive and complicated for even the largest vendors, such as Cisco.

Where specialization comes into play on a vertically specific basis is at the system integrator (SI). The SI's primary task is to glue together all the various systems such as hardware, software, applications, security, and services such as video and voice. It's a daunting task that requires specific insights into the verticals.

One place where we'll see market changes as pertain to next-generation networks won't be so much on the technology side, but rather on the great expansion of knowledge on the value proposition side of the equation. We are already seeing the larger and better SIs narrow down the number of verticals from which they harvest revenue. The larger SIs now commonly have expertise in three to five verticals, but there's a clear shift toward the lower end of that spectrum. The reason, in part, is that selling into the healthcare market, for example, is not at all like selling into the energy market. While this seems painfully apparent from the onset, we see smaller companies trying to do exactly that. This does not do much for scaling a small operation. Training, deal specifics, and upper-management support become quickly tapped out when a lone salesperson, crack though they may be in an obscure market, requests support for a large and complex deal.

Large deals are rarely, if ever, done in isolation; you need a team composed of finance, marketing, technology, engineering, support, and maintenance not just to close but also retain large deals over time. These same teams are also required for what is called "run rate business," or, in other words, the many smaller deals that are essential to the cash flow of a systems integrator or other technology specialist entity.

Deals begin and end with the concept of value proposition and success metrics. The faster and clearer the return on investment is illuminated, the faster the deal is closed. This type of illumination takes time and experience. This illumination is far more valuable to the customer than simply being able to declare upward through a management stack that a certain technology will pay off more quickly than others. In the credit market available at the time of this writing, many companies have gone way out on a ledge for cash flow. Those most affected by the current credit crunch are those with the weakest cash flow and balance sheets.

It's not realistic to expect the U.S. and global economies to shift rapidly from credit-based operations to a cash-surplus basis. Most companies and customers will continue to rely on credit for most of their transactions and other corporate investments such as those in IT. Therefore, how the cash flows on a return basis from a technology will be increasingly important. Those technologies, such as wireless, that offer the largest and earliest return *and* resolve the largest operational problems will receive a priority ranking for deployment.

Hence, SIs and vendors who most carefully and clearly illuminate *exactly* how and when a wireless technology will pay off will retain a priority position in receiving revenues from their customers. There is no more important shift for SIs and technology vendors than to elevate the wireless network discussions from engineers to include the various stakeholders.

IT assets are at the center of every major corporate policy, program, and objective. It's not about radios, and it's not about "solutions." It's about solving business problems. Those who connect the resolution of business problems with specific applications of the correct technology—not too much and not too little—will prevail in the market of the next-generation networks. Here's why: At the heart of the matter, *business is about information dominance*. It's not about having assets; it's about *knowing what to do with assets*. All businesses are competitors. Competitors that acquire and retain information dominance have a much clearer view into exactly how and where to place salespersons, customer incentives, and demand generation assets.

Businesses with information dominance know better how to neutralize the competition. There's only one better competitive technique than to take the money off the customer's table before the competitor arrives, and that's to take the money off the table for future deals. Hence the concept that the market will become increasingly specialized. This should hardly come as a surprise; the next-generation prediction here is that the technology will evolve on feature tracks relatively independent of sales in specific verticals. The probability of a technology feature making it into the marketplace is directly proportional to how many verticals that enhancement would affect in a positive manner. This leads us to the next element of next-generation networks: technology development.

Technology Development

What is interesting about next-generation technology development isn't necessarily the technology development itself but rather *how* it will be developed. We're beginning to see a relevant shift in how technology is developed in the wireless industry.

The shift is that decision making is moving from closed-loop teams to decision by consensus. Teams and entities once outside these closed loops are now being inserted into the middle of decision-making processes. This is being achieved by assembling testing teams comprising customers, system integrators, experienced internal sales engineers, and sales personnel. New teams are focusing more on setting up the right feedback mechanisms such as polls, early access to restricted release, and prototype product sets for evaluation much closer to the real-world conditions.

Relatively few development engineers spend time in the real world of production deployments, and few production workers spend time in the engineering realm. Observing these engagements has been rewarding, because both sides are eager to learn from each other. This engagement has extended beyond exposure to the next generation of product release to include deep discussions about the trajectory from the current generation of technology to products far over the development horizon (more than three years out).

This will result in technology features and right-sized generational steps for products. This will in turn result in increased sales for the vendors and increased profitability for system integrators. More work remains to be done regarding the evaluation mechanism required to determine accurately which features will impact the greatest number of verticals and correctly prioritize them. This is key given that much more than half of the revenue generated by vendors and system integrators is from the top third or so of industry verticals.

The Future Is Bright

Next-generation networks will be significantly different from what we see today. How we design, audit, and maintain wireless networks today will have a significant impact on how smooth or challenging the transition will be to the next generation of wireless networks.

Intelligent buildings will have numbers of clients and infrastructure devices vastly in excess of today's networks as building automation systems such as HVAC, fire control, energy systems, and physical security converge with IP networks.

How networks will be designed, audited, and maintained will include considerations for human-to-machine communications versus strictly e-mail, voice, and video. Smart antennas, picocells, dynamically sized cells, and multispectrum, multiprotocol devices will collectively, and singularly, change the way businesses are operated and how we interact with each other.

What Cortes and Pizarro achieved was controversial. Not all versions of the stories align. However, once Cortes and Pizarro saw the New World, their lives were never the same. I like to think these intrepid explorers saw that the future is brighter than the past. More complex, certainly. But better in nearly every way.

CHAPTER 11 | Mobility and Intelligent Buildings

The future of IT is an exciting prospect; we have only just begun to understand the true impact of a connected society. And there is no single more significant change to information and mobility technology than *intelligent buildings,* structures and systems with highly integrated IT and building management systems.

About eight different kinds of building automation systems are in use today, with a similar number of major IT systems. Of course, dozens of corresponding subsystems are also in use in most buildings. The following illustration highlights the two "sides" of a building: IT and building management. What is of interest from the wireless mobility perspective is that all the systems shown in the illustration require or include wireless variants. Only the virtual private network (VPN), an encryption mechanism, has no wireless variant.

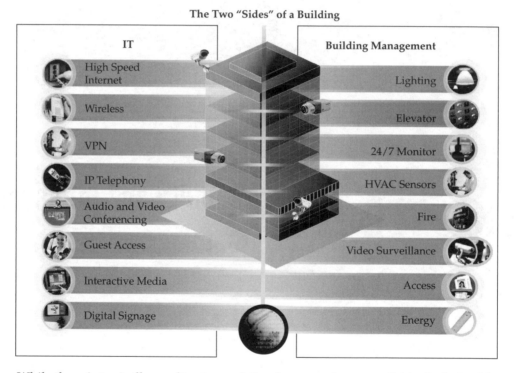

The Two "Sides" of a Building

While there is typically no direct correlation between these two "sides" of a building (for example, no building management system directly corresponds to IT mobility), commonalities certainly exist between IT systems and building automation systems. One very good example is wireless—wireless IT assets and wireless building control systems such as handheld PDAs for managing temperature, lighting, physical security, and so forth. When most of us walk into a large commercial building, we rarely stop to think of how very complex the building truly is. We see lighting systems in the ceilings above, we feel the cool air from the air conditioning system when we enter from a sweltering summer day, or we feel warm and comforting air when entering the building from cold outdoor weather. Most of us enjoy the ease of an elevator to rise or descend multiple floors in a building. Many systems are in place to manage all this, of course—indeed, far more is behind the scenes than what we actually see as we enter a building.

Driving Forces for Intelligent Buildings

By the time your children are grown, the concept of a "nonintelligent building" will seem as quaint as a log cabin by today's standards. These enormous and sweeping sets of changes to commercial and residential buildings in our surroundings were created as a result of six compelling factors:

- Urbanization
- Technology advances
- Transformation of business organizations
- Asset utilization
- Building productivity
- Energy consumption

Urbanization

The world's population growth is largely concentrated in ten city or area centers, according to the publicly available information from the U.S. Central Intelligence Agency (www.cia.gov/library/publications/the-world-factbook/rankorder/rankorderguide.html). Of interest, the site also indicates that for every worldwide death, 2.5 births occur. About 60 percent of the world's population live in urban areas, and the general shift for the human population is toward metropolitan areas from rural areas. Reasons for this are complicated and generally outside the scope of this book, but it suffices to recognize this general trend. The significant part of the trend is that about 2 percent of the population shifts from rural to urban areas each year. At the current rates of population shift, nearly 70 percent of the world's population will live within cities by the year 2015.

This places tremendous strain on urban infrastructure to house, feed, and otherwise support an enormous number of people. The rate at which buildings are added to population centers is not projected to grow at similar rates, so they must become far more efficient and much more efficiently utilized to accommodate requirements. Automating and managing building systems through existing IT assets offers a tremendous return on investment, and perhaps equally important, it allows the buildings to serve a population that will place higher demands on every building system, from heating and cooling, to lighting and physical security.

Technology Advances

Every IT technology, without exception, has advanced and evolved rapidly in the last few years (and each continues to do so). Speeds, capacity, reliability, and cost reductions through advanced management have been achieved with such rapidity and scope that technology specialists are constantly driven to narrower and deeper specialization.

In parallel with the technical evolution, equally enormous changes have also occurred in technology, protocols, standards, and compliance. This is important to realize, because technology hardly advances in a vacuum; protocols, standards, and compliance are vital adjacencies. One other key element has come to pass with IT technology, and that is pervasiveness.

Pervasiveness is an important element of IT, because the more broadly it exists, the more systems it can touch, and the more elements can be measured, monitored, and maintained. An appropriate analogy may be the U.S. highway system: people can travel farther now with higher rates of comfort, safety, and speed than ever before. It has taken decades to achieve this, and it's a welcome level of societal maturity. Relatively few people travel on dirt and gravel roads routinely within the borders of industrialized countries; many more are found on multi-lane freeways. Consider the rush hour jams in every city as prime evidence.

Technology system design is also far more advanced now; much more is understood about wireless network design than ever before. Although deploying a voice-over-WLAN system requires considerable technical expertise and experience, deploying voice-quality WLANs is now pretty routine. These systems were fairly painful to deliver on a scaled basis only five years ago. The tooling today to design, audit, and maintain systems is more advanced than ever.

In 1999, we used a simple dashboard with one of three levels of RF signal: Excellent, Good, and Poor. While certainly the brilliant folks at Aironet were training engineers on advanced site survey best practices that included complex RF measurements, few unlicensed wireless industry people outside of the technical editors and myself were even using rudimentary signal strength measurements in decibels. In my view, this was because only a few network engineers considered sophisticated forms of design and measurement of the RF signal. Remember that in enterprise networking, there weren't any "wireless engineers"; they were simply "network guys" who also installed a new wireless network technology. In the late 1990s and early 2000s, there were very few network specialists: the same person deployed wireless, security, and data transport. Today, the technology has grown almost immeasurably more complex, thus requiring specialists. In fact, I'm unaware of any engineer who is an expert in more than two network technologies.

Of course, a much more sophisticated level of engineering, and tooling, existed in the licensed RF space; we were decades behind those developments in the unlicensed WLAN industry. Today's WLAN system tooling, however, is enormously complex and comprehensive and covers not just pure RF signal, but various levels of health and status across much of the OSI stack, as well as security analysis, applications, and much more. In the late 1990s, the tooling was typically included in the WLAN package; investments in WLAN tooling today quickly reach into the thousands and, not uncommonly, tens of thousands of dollars.

Technical advances have also been made in processor power, memory capacity and speed, and battery life. We only have to look at an iPhone or Blackberry to be awestruck at the level of technology we can easily acquire.

Technical developments on the building management side have been equally breathtaking. Companies such as Gridlogix were able to place automated systems inside nearly every government building in the state of Missouri within the last several years. Fortune 500 company Johnson Controls was impressed enough that it purchased Gridlogix, and in my view, that was a very shrewd and well-timed investment. Gridlogix technology allows the marriage of IT assets such as routers and switches to interface with building management systems such as heating, lighting, and physical security.

The marriage of building management systems and IT assets expands the value of both the IT and building automation systems because it allows for the evolution of a single building-wide system instead of dozens of disparate systems, each with their own operating code, bug types, and unique user interfaces. The development of technologies that allow a "middleware" layer to enable communications between IT and building management systems is a brilliant development and an important milestone toward the existence of full building management systems that are designed and deployed for the express purpose of creating smart buildings.

Asset Utilization

The high demand for increased asset utilization will continue to increase as executives and building managers look for ways to maximize the investment of every dollar into the management of a building. Finding completely new uses for IT assets so that they can manage a building is a wonderful development for the IT industry. This development drives the evolution of the IT network from a series of boxes connected by wires and antennas to a computational grid, not just within a single building, but within a campus, a business park, a city, and a region.

Some networks, such as the electrical grid, have operated on this premise for more than 100 years. The additive effect of a single residence, commercial building floor, or business park has enormous implications in power management and generation. The same is now also true for mobile cellular and IT assets. We sometimes forget how, even at the turn of the millennium, it was nearly impossible to make a cell phone call around 5:00 P.M. on a weekday in a major metropolitan area because of voice traffic load. We hardly ever see that now that capacity and reliability have been tremendously built out, although getting data off the cellular network and onto the WLAN network is a priority for the major cell providers, due to the impact of exceptional smartphones such as the current Blackberry, Android, and iPhone.

Asset utilization within the smart building is also important to advance because maintenance and longevity are greatly affected by duty cycles, or the amount of time a device runs. Air conditioning units run less than they used to, for example, thanks to improved building insulation, ducting, and design and increased efficiency of the air conditioning units themselves.

As an example, smart building management allows lighting in stairwells to be turned off when no one is using the stairs. Stairwells are used less than 1 percent of the time, yet the lighting is left on 100 percent of the time in most of these building areas. With a minimum of smart sensor technology and management, a five-year light bulb could last decades, greatly reducing the cost of lighting and maintenance for that area of the building. The concept of asset utilization therefore is not simply about using an asset more; it's about getting the best return on the asset. Longevity is clearly an element affecting operating expenses; a smart building will decrease operating expenses as one of its primary value propositions.

Building Productivity

Building productivity is an interesting concept because it largely entails not just filling a space to capacity for as many hours as possible, but using the right size and type of facilities for employees, guests, partners, and customers.

For office workers now, especially in companies with mobile workforces, having a single type of office space no longer adequately fulfills their professional needs. In my work, I use a number of different facilities in my employer's office about 25 minutes from my house. When meeting with partners and associates, I need a conference room that seats ten people. On another visit, I may need only a small, quiet room to participate in a conference call. At other times, I may be visiting a corporate executive in their office, so we need a small, comfortable room where we can meet with privacy. At other times, I've been at our corporate office site with 100 or so other colleagues; we need a large conference room with suitable audio, visual, and wireless network connectivity.

Much of my time is spent working out of a home office; this enables my employer to outfit my home office with excellent telecommuting equipment, which saves Cisco from reserving an office or cubicle for me. It's not just the 100 square feet of carpeted space required to ensure a suitable workspace, but also lighting, air conditioning, physical security, water, and waste facilities.

By using "flexible" assets, mobile workers ensure that any employer can use the right size of building instead of a large building. The savings are significant in this scenario; if an employer reduced a 100,000 square foot facility by 40 percent by setting up a mobility workforce that operated out of their home offices (as I do), the employer would save 1500 tons of concrete and 280 tons of steel, not to mention hundreds of thousands of dollars of labor costs to assemble it all. It would also be the equivalent of taking 560 cars off the road for a year. Fewer miles driven also means fewer automobile accidents, fewer traffic jams, fewer repairs to roads and cars, less pollution into the air, and so on; the cascading effects from increased building production are impressive and vast in scope.

Energy Consumption

Perhaps no single aspect of smart buildings is as impressive as energy savings. These savings are direct, occur immediately upon deployment, and are far-reaching in terms of reduced cost for the building owner, lessors, and users.

The number one complaint in most buildings is temperature setting. Given a large enough group, some people will be too warm and some people too cold. This problem led to the production of dual climate controls in modern vehicles, in which the passenger can enjoy one heating or cooling setting and the driver another.

While even in smart buildings getting the temperature right for every occupant remains an elusive task, individual offices are routinely set for individual comfort levels. Air conditioning remains the single largest use of power in a commercial building as well as residential areas. However, significant operating expense implications result from lighting and other building costs such as water, waste, and total energy consumption. The following illustration highlights the typical cost reduction by a smart building.

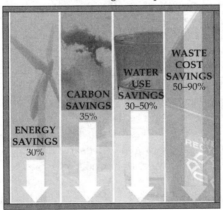

Smart Building Cost Impact

With carbon trading becoming more common throughout the industrialized world, mid-sized companies with as few as 100 employees will become more focused on their carbon footprints. Larger companies have been considering how to reduce their carbon footprints for years, since there is a correlation between carbon footprint and employee satisfaction and retention when factors such as commuting, parking, and gasoline consumption are considered.

The Fourth Utility: Network Access

We hardly give a thought these days to the three fundamental elements that are standard in our homes and commercial buildings: gas, electricity, and water. No commercial or private residence would be considered comfortable and usable without these utilities. A fourth element in the information age is network access.

In an industrialized society, connectivity exists nearly pervasively. Farmers out in the field commonly carry cell phones. GPS connectivity is routinely used to guide farm implements for seeding, watering, fertilizing, and pest control. And in the cities, taxi drivers often carry on conversations with someone through their cell phones, and commuters on trains, in cars, and in airplanes, on the ground and in the air, are in constant contact with other people and networks.

Connectivity and productivity are tightly coupled; they are entirely reliant on each other in the era of connectivity and collaboration. In smart buildings, connectivity is now offered as part of the tenant package. Even the lowest-end motels offered cable TV as part of their roadside advertising in the 1970s; it was an early form of connectivity, later eclipsed by the modern-day variant: wireless Internet access.

Very few, if any, major commercial property developers don't offer connectivity as part of their leasing packages. It's interesting to note that the ownership of IT networks and mobile connectivity is shifting from the individual business in multi-tenant office buildings to the owners and operators of the commercial buildings. This not only reduces a small business's operating expense, but also allows the small business to focus on its core business: selling its products or services instead of dedicating time, resources, and capital to maintain a small network.

Adding the fourth utility not only benefits most tenants, but it also expands the revenue stream for the building owners. Commercial real estate owners will tell you that commercial properties have economic cycles like any other industry; the interesting element about commercial real estate is the cycle of excess supply is nearly always longer than the cycle of excess demand. This maintains downward pressure on pricing and leasing terms; additional services are nearly always welcomed. The offering of a vital service such as Internet connectivity is rare and very welcomed by the commercial real estate industry.

Leases offered by commercial property managers and owners in which connectivity is included in the package now have a simple checklist of what kinds of connectivity the lessee desires and how much Internet speed and reliability are required. Entire voice, and now video security systems, are available. A example of this menu is found in the following illustration, from one of the premier shopping malls in the United States, which has become renowned for not just being a smart building, but for being a smart mall.

1 Sign up	
✓ **Basic Digital Access** (Full package detailed on reverse of card)	$299
2 Enter number of telecom upgrades	
# **Additional Cisco display phone** (First 1-3 $59 ea., next 4-7 $49 ea., next 7+$39 ea.)	$39–$59
# **Cisco color display phone**	$9
# **Cisco wireless, all-campus phone**	$9
# **Additional voice mail box w/auto-attend**	$9
# **Additional outlet activation**	$9
3 Check premium services desired	
✓ **Muzak™**	$59
✓ **Muzak™ On-Hold**	$9
✓ **Satellite Television**	$59
✓ **ScentAir™ Environment**	$99
✓ **Premium Internet & Data** (Firewall, 4mbps Bidirectional Internet, Remote Access)	$129
✓ **Digital Signage Advertising** (Ad Placement on: Digital Signs, Hot Spot, Way-Finding, Web Site)	$199

Examples of Connectivity Solutions

Some of the finest connectivity solutions are to be found in smart buildings. Given the enormous physical size of these structures compared to most businesses, these connectivity solutions are especially worth considering. The scale of the return on investments of capital, time, and other assets affords significant increases in profit margin even if the productivity of the spaces increases a fraction of a dollar per square foot. With energy reduction, increased traffic, decreased vacancies, and increased revenue per square foot converge, these solutions ensure that building owners, investors, and managers endow a "must-have" status on this technology.

Ballantyne Village Shopping Mall, Charlotte, North Carolina

Ballantyne Village shopping mall had a tremendous amount of smart building intelligence and systems built into the structure from the onset of construction. One of the most beautiful and elegant malls in the United States, it is a local destination and hotspot of social, shopping, and recreational opportunities. It provides not only retail businesses a premier address and reputation, but it also rents office space. Upscale and pleasing to the eye, the mall has one of the best operating margins in the industry and one of the lowest tenant vacancies.

Ballantyne was the first smart building structure I saw that had a simple checklist menu for tenants moving into its facilities. It offers both wired and wireless connectivity as well as IP voice systems. The Ballantyne management team has been very public and proud of their operational achievements, which include the following:

- Cost avoidance of $1 to $2 per square foot by minimizing maintenance issues from early detection and resolution, reduction in losses from vandalism through IP video surveillance, and operating expense reduction through remote monitoring and management. Ballantyne requires fewer onsite staff, yet enjoys faster turnaround time for facility problem and maintenance resolution. Advertising and marketing expenditures have also been avoided because local and regionally located businesses are more aware of the mall's reputation.

- Operational savings of 50 cents per square foot by using smart power and heating/cooling methodologies coupled with smart sensor and remote management packages. These major systems are turned off or turned down when not populated; this includes power usage decrease during the approximately 80 to 90 hours per week when the mall is closed.

- New hard dollar revenue of $3 per square foot. Ballantyne charges a premium for tenants, which makes sense given the prestige of the address and cash flow directed to the tenants from the mall itself. Tenants have realized this leasing premium is a high-value option for them as their sales have proportionally increased due to high levels of foot traffic into the mall, which leads to increased traffic and market share into each mall tenant store.

- Faster move-in by tenants is achieved in part because each store location is already pre-wired for Internet connectivity as well as wireless coverage. As the lessor in this case delivers the IT infrastructure, the tenant can focus on moving in inventory and personnel and in completing custom remodeling.

One America Plaza, San Diego, California

One of the most prestigious businesses addresses on the West Coast is One America Plaza in San Diego. This 570,000 square foot facility has been valued at approximately $300 per square foot. Many elements of this high-visibility superstructure are impressive; however, one of the items I found most noteworthy was during a presentation on the facility by the building managers. They were quick to state that the value of the building itself was growing faster than normal on an annual basis because it was considered a smart building.

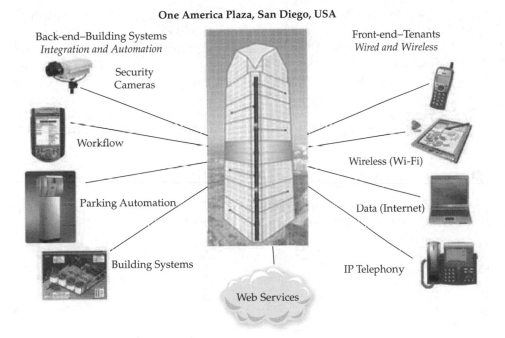

One America Plaza, San Diego, USA

Back-end–Building Systems
Integration and Automation

Security Cameras

Workflow

Parking Automation

Building Systems

Front-end–Tenants
Wired and Wireless

Wireless (Wi-Fi)

Data (Internet)

IP Telephony

Web Services

The element of enhancing the overall property value is significant among high-end commercial real estate developments. The concept of disproportionate increases in building value is called "leveraging"; it is challenging to succeed at, but important because buying, enhancing, and then reselling commercial real estate is a key strategy by property owners. The ultimate trajectory is about buying at a lower cost, enhancing the site, and selling at a profit. This is followed by reinvestment at increasingly larger and diverse properties with the end goal of amassing as much wealth as possible. Much easier said than done, it is nonetheless the path that many financially successful individuals and corporations have taken.

The owners of the One America building have estimated their investments in smart building technology have increased the building's value by approximately $8 million. My experience in wireless deployments is such that it costs approximately $1.85 per square foot to provide wireless coverage in a typical office environment; this would work out to approximately $1 million to cover the entire building. The actual coverage model would be less than half of that; it's rare that one provided RF coverage wall to wall on all floors, in all areas.

If you therefore used a cost of $500,000 to cover the building, and considered the standard proportion of wireless to wired IT infrastructure, which is about 15 percent, you'd have about $3.5 million in total IT equipment costs. Add another $2 million for building automation systems (approximate cost), and the total smart building investment would be approximately $5.5 million. The $8 million increase in building value would allow something approaching a 40 percent return on the smart building investment—a very attractive return.

Further discounting of this calculation may be appropriate, and it is for capital expenditure only, but the key point is that the smart building investment is compelling to the commercial property owner. From cash-flow and profitability perspectives, not only does an intelligent building increase profit margins because it reduces electrical power consumption by 30 percent, among other operating expense reductions, but it also adds to the value of the overall building. The owners and investors therefore reside in the best of both commercial property worlds: they get a reduction of operating expenses and are further rewarded at the exit phase of the investment with an enhanced return.

Value Proposition Summary for Intelligent Buildings

Numerous value propositions are apparent for intelligent buildings, but it is generally agreed that these value propositions are found in four key areas:

- Financial
- Process and policy
- People
- Community

Financial Propositions

Whenever financial value propositions are considered, the elements of capital expenditures (CAPEX) and operating expenditures (OPEX) are generally foremost in discussions, planning, and executive consideration. Of interest, executive compensation is commonly closely tied to profitability, which is inextricably coupled with OPEX. Accordingly, OPEX reduction investments generally receive the lion's share of resource allocation, measurement, and visibility. An appropriate balance nearly always exists between simply reducing costs and doing so while enabling the business to expand. The link is in productivity; a closer examination reveals that it's not just enough to do more with less, but you must invest in better tooling, policies, and technologies that allow people to do more good without asking them to spend more hours at work or requiring them to work harder and faster.

With intelligent buildings, mobility means that building systems can be monitored remotely by wireless handheld devices from virtually any place where people commonly reside or travel. In speaking with building automation engineers at top companies such as Johnson Controls, I've learned that a third to a half of all system alarms are false or non-urgent. Remote analysis greatly increases building engineer productivity and allows them to focus on significant building maintenance and other events.

Another area of financial value proposition for intelligent buildings is in the simplified design and construction of smart buildings versus traditional, "non-smart" buildings. Buildings today have dozens and dozens of unique systems, each with its own operating language, conductors (wire, fiber, or wireless), sensors, and unique user interface. One of the strongest value propositions here is in the use of a common master system, and the best option from my view is clearly the Internet Protocol (IP), one of the most broadly adopted standards in the world today.

OPEX Reduction

By using IP networks to manage, monitor, and maintain building automation systems, users can remotely engage and manage the building with common and well-understood commands and user interfaces. IP interfaces are understood by hundreds of thousands of technicians in every industrialize country on the planet. Even better now are the graphic user interfaces for systems; technicians and managers commonly use touch screens with simple panels that are color coded and easy to view and understand.

Not only does this reduce the OPEX through simplified and remote management, but it also requires fewer people who can monitor more systems and buildings. From a maintenance perspective, it is far less expensive to use one common protocol, such as IP, throughout a building, instead of dozens of unique systems. Instead of training people on a wide array of systems, a business or organization can train more people to understand much more of the overall system. In today's world, where systems are actually "systems of systems" or "networks of networks," the premise of broadly understanding macro systems is important to reduce costs, improve reaction time, and resolve complex problems before they become more expensive.

One of the more compelling OPEX reduction elements is in remote monitoring. When an intelligent building is monitored, it is now primarily monitored with what is called a Building Operations Center (BOC). This is the networking equivalent of what is called a Network Operations Center (NOC). Building operations centers are generally far more complex than NOCs primarily because they have far more diverse systems to track and manage. NOCs, by comparison, are complex, but they generally have far fewer technology types and interfaces than BOCs.

Of significant interest is the trend for BOCs being replaced by NOCs because the modern intelligent building is IP-based. Managing both the network of communications devices along with the direct management of the building at a single facility has significant OPEX reduction implications. This is why leading network managing companies such as Insight Networking are taking an active role in managing and servicing the intelligent building market.

Perhaps the easiest OPEX reduction value proposition is energy management. It doesn't take much imagination to realize how much power is wasted in a commercial building. In total, the electrical power consumed by commercial buildings is vast and amounts to about 40 percent of *all* the energy used in an industrialized country.

It takes 966 pounds of coal to run a 100 watt light bulb for a year; multiply that by all the power sources in a commercial building and it's easy to envision very long lines of coal cars rolling endlessly into power plants to generate electricity. It costs about 1 cent per hour to power this same bulb; that aggregates to about $88 per year. A smart building could reduce that cost by a third quite easily by turning on the bulb only when people are present. Multiply that by hundreds of light bulbs, and the energy equivalent of tens of thousands of light bulbs, and the energy savings become readily apparent.

Office buildings are somewhere near the middle of all types of commercial buildings in terms of consumption. The following chart shows the average use of electrical and gas power in commercial buildings from both gas and electricity, as measured in tens of thousands of BTUs (British Thermal Units). (Assembled from data provided by the U.S. Energy Information Administration, www.eia.doe.gov/emeu/cbecs/cbecs2003/detailed_tables2003/2003set19/2003html/e01a.html.)

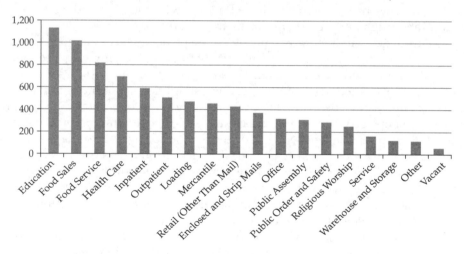

It's interesting to note that even vacant buildings use electrical power, and often gas, as it's less expensive to maintain a building by generally preserving its internal environment than by simply leaving the building cold and unlit. There are obvious physical security and blight issues (abandoned real estate properties are referred to as "blight" properties by communities and city managers) that are mitigated with modest amounts of power and light even in unused buildings.

CAPEX Reduction

CAPEX reduction is clear when building automation systems are reduced in numbers. CAPEX reduction in smart buildings is achieved primarily through vastly simplified inventories of spare parts. Reduction in spare parts also means a smaller support network of parts dealers. While it may seem contrary to the standard economic rules of supply and demand, a smaller parts supplier network results in deeper discounts from each supplier, because the providers of components will bid more competitively if the potential sales from the customer is higher.

The more homogeneous the system, the fewer interface parts are required, because systems tend to "fit" together much better when fewer elements are included. The more heterogeneous the system, the more complex the spares inventory necessarily tends to be. Much troubleshooting tends to occur at junctions between systems. This has not only a CAPEX implication, but also an OPEX implication for additional time spent troubleshooting.

Intelligent buildings with homogeneous systems tend to feature less complicated interfaces to the buildings in which they reside. This results in a simpler building design, partly from the use of combination sensors that include power, physical security, and emergency response. You might be surprised by how many places use video cameras; they used to be inside ominous-looking smoked plastic domes attached to a ceiling, but modern video cameras now routinely reside in smoke detectors, fire sprinkler systems, motion detectors, and ceiling lights. Installing a single module instead of two or three reduces the cost of a building design, equipment, and construction.

Process and Policy Improvement

Technology always affects process and policy; the very purpose of technology is to affect outcome. Processes and policies are rule sets that manage outcome; they rely on both processed intelligence and accurate data points. An intelligent building is superbly crafted for providing both the data points and the processed intelligence. This allows managers to make the best decisions for the well-being and protection of the building. These decisions can be made while in the building, near the building, and at any distance from the building wherever network connectivity is available.

Data that can be generated, processed, and distilled continuously into a set of conditions that are acted upon, largely without human intervention, are of considerable value to building owners and managers. The more the intervention is preset by policy and condition, the more productive the management staff. This in turn allows management to provide recommendations to the building owners, which, by extension, allows for optimal profit margins and returns on investment.

Integrating maintenance and physical security elements into building management are effective and appropriate in today's connected world. Integrating building information, the tenants, visitors, and support personnel such as couriers and package delivery services takes the productivity and value of the site to another level. For example, when a worker enters a building, an RFID tag integrated into the worker's identification tag tells the building that the worker has arrived. While in the elevator, the worker's office can be heated or cooled to the preferred setting, lights are turned on, and the computer boot sequence is initiated. The building's physical security staff can know in real time which people are in the building and their locations—and this is less about "big brother" knowing about your whereabouts and more about being able to find and contact you in the event of an emergency or catastrophic event.

Maintenance personnel often mention that it's generally far less expensive to repair an item during an early stage of failure than a late stage of failure. Consider, for example, vibration sensors that are attached to the shafts of major cooling, ventilation, and heating equipment. Mechanical devices called bearings enable shafts to turn while being held in place. These shafts produce a constant vibration. When the bearings begin to fail, and they all eventually fail, a corresponding increase appears in the amount and type of vibration produced by the shaft and bearing assembly. When these bearings are properly monitored, maintenance personnel can replace them at the right time of day and at the exact right time in their wear cycle. Repairing a major bearing assembly can cost several hundred dollars if repaired at the right time, versus thousands of dollars or more if the bearing completely fails and damages the shaft and motor assembly to which it is attached.

People

Employee turnover and job satisfaction are key criteria in the best-managed companies in the world, and I'd offer Cisco as one of the leading-edge examples of this. Cisco's annual awards and industry recognition for being one of the best places to work are well earned. The integration of communications technology, management by objective versus punching a clock, and converting work from a location to an experience have had enormous implications in my personal and professional life. Having an optimal physical environment in which to work has a lot to do with worker satisfaction.

Work Place Resources is a group within Cisco that has primary responsibility for the environmental conditions in which we operate the business of our company. Cisco conducted an interesting worker satisfaction survey in 2007 in connection with an effort to understand the implications of a smart building and employee satisfaction.

It showed that intelligent building systems investments have paid off: 82 percent of Cisco workers polled indicated they have a high level of worker satisfaction, in part due to the quality of the physical environment. Often cited in the details, workers feel safe that the environment is stimulating without being distracting, and the physical environment—such as desks, chairs, lighting, work room choices, and access to productivity enablers such as projector systems, collaboration areas, and work spaces—enable a high degree of productivity.

Another 82 percent of Cisco workers indicated that the communications systems built into the physical facilities have improved communications. Not only has 802.11 wireless been pervasively deployed in every Cisco building for several years, but gigabit-speed Ethernet ports for laptops are ubiquitous, reliable, and provide some of the fastest network speeds available, which is very handy for moving large files or for complex presentations.

The physical access to the interiors of the buildings is another element of this satisfaction. The majority of Cisco workers believe a balance between security and ease of access has been achieved. A single badge entry gets an employee into nearly every internal room within a Cisco building. Additional badge entry points can be found for labs, executive briefing centers, and certain freight-handling facilities.

In addition, 77 percent of Cisco workers see the corporate environment as the preferred work site. This is an interesting statistic and is complimentary to the smart building strategy, because a June 2009 internal study by Cisco's Internet Business Services Group, the company's global strategic consulting arm, showed that employees spend 63 percent of their time communicating and collaborating; 40 percent say they are not located in the same city as their manager. The average Cisco employee telecommutes two days per week; 60 percent of the time saved by telecommuting is spent working, and 40 percent is spent on personal time. The fact that around 75 percent of the employee population indicate that the corporate site is the preferred working location even though they telecommute from home or other places 40 percent of the time is a testament to the quality of the Cisco workplace environment.

This combination of internal mobility that allows people to remain easily connected heightens the degree of productivity within a building; it's an outstanding example of network connectivity as the fourth utility afforded by smart buildings. The advent of consumer-based productivity devices such as the Blackberry and iPhone is well integrated into Cisco's intelligent building program. It's quite interesting to me that an increasing number of people are attending meetings without laptops; they bring notepads and their smartphone. It's a lighter, faster, more comfortable way to move around both inside and outside the corporate offices, allowing workers to do the right things at the right time with little regard to their physical location.

Virtually every Cisco building I've visited is a smart building, whether it is a standalone, dedicated Cisco building or office space rented in multi-tenant facilities across the United States and the world.

The Local Community

Smart buildings have a tremendous impact on businesses, corporate process and policy, and the workforce. The impact of this type of building also extends to the local community in which it resides.

Communities vigorously compete for businesses because they improve the local economy. More workers mean more people are buying more things locally— from meals at local restaurants, to dry cleaning, to the purchase of automobiles and homes. While the job market is clearly showing signs of stress with high rates of unemployment, a strong demand still exists for the best employees who have the right skill sets. Common threads exist in nearly every business, including a shortage of good workers.

Communities want these people to work, shop, and live in their neighborhoods and towns because these workers elevate the quality of local life with not just their money, but also their ideas and demands for pleasant living, working, and shopping spaces. This is why, in part, communities are studied for average income, age of workers, number of university degrees, and other key measurements that allow and attract people who improve communities. There are far fewer communities than people, and communities are carefully marketed on a regional and occasionally national basis to attract the best and brightest of workers and residents.

Intelligent buildings play a role in allowing communities to differentiate themselves, because the best work environments attract the best people. Intelligent buildings also reduce the ecological footprint of businesses because they allow workers to remain connected to the building and corporation with little regard for the worker's location. This reduces local automobile traffic, improves the air quality, and allows for more grass, trees, and parks.

Networked energy management ensures that not just the least amount of water, electricity, and gas energy is used, but that the *right* amount of these vital energies is used. This means fewer overhead electrical wiring systems and fewer trenches. Given that all power infrastructures, including electricity, water, and gas, require maintenance, smart buildings also reduce the maintenance required on these infrastructure items because the demand is reduced by a third or more.

Ultimately, intelligent buildings are about more than operating and capital expenditure reduction; they are closely linked to improvements in the quality of both our personal and professional lives. The best businesses have an obligation to contribute to the well-being of the communities in which they reside. High-quality employees are commonly found giving back to the communities in which they reside through fun and charitable events and the donation of their personal and professional time to improve the lives of others. Intelligent buildings are an excellent way for a company to exercise social responsibility through improving the community in which these structures reside for decades. Smart buildings house smart people. And that's good for everyone.

CHAPTER 12 | Summary and Future Trends

This book has covered a considerable amount of ground; it's helpful now, in this last chapter, to take a half step back and view the big picture to see how it all fits together. This book is intended to help you expand discussions on mobility from its purely technical aspects to its ability to resolve business problems. Today's mobility networks, and especially tomorrow's mobility networks, will find competition more intense for CAPEX and OPEX funding within the end customers. Because mobility has a disproportionately high value compared to vital investments made in unified communications, data centers, and other technologies, mobility must retain a usable share of CAPEX and OPEX resources. All of those various investments are important; getting the balance correct will become increasingly more challenging for end customer management, integrators, and technology providers.

Mobility Challenge Within System Integrators

An interesting and little-known challenge exists within the mobility industry—in particular, the portion of the industry that deals in 802.11 mobility. Mobility system integrators are under increasing scrutiny to maximize the return on their investments of time and capital. The challenge for mobility technology providers, and end users, is that system integrators are increasingly moving mobility into a "nice to have" status within their organizations, for several reasons, including the following:

- Profitability
- Zero sum talent pool
- Bigger bet, more sales

Profitability

Unified communications (UC) and data center programs are huge at every level, from the technology providers such as Cisco, Juniper, and Brocade, within the ranks of the system integrators, and on to the end customers. These programs and technologies, not coincidentally, make up the vast majority of the CAPEX and OPEX within a customer network.

The incentives offered by the OEM equipment providers such as Cisco and Juniper to sell, deploy, and maintain UC and data centers are commonly anywhere from three to five times the incentives afforded by mobility technology providers. Major technology vendors that remain successful in this industry offer a steady stream of incentives to sell their technology. Some technology providers offer as many as a dozen or more incentive programs from various customer demand generation and loyalty program teams.

Tracking such an array of programs often requires dedicated specialists who are masters of spreadsheets and relationships, and who gather large amounts of information on these programs. The intent is to maximize the profitability of the system integrator, which ensures loyalty to the technology provider, and this is the prize for any provider. The competition is fierce for system integrators, and so is the continual stream of incentive programs. Such competitive fierceness exists not only between technology providers, but often from within the same technology provider.

Incentive programs are stack ranked at the better system integrators, and the management teams at these integrators can rapidly and quickly determine on which technology they should base their business plans and goals. While mobility incentives are quite good, these incentives are rarely as broad in scope or total profit dollars as those of the unified communications and data center profit incentive programs.

The challenge is that, programmatically, mobility is becoming "nice to have" at the incentive program level within the system integrators. However, at the customer end of the cash-flow stream, mobility remains a mission-critical element. What gets caught falls in the middle—engineering talent at the system integrator.

Zero Sum Talent Pool

Incentive parity is less of an issue for smaller integrators, which tend to be specialists in a specific technology such as voice or wireless mobility. The larger the integrator, the more likely it will have three to five different kinds of services and technology offerings. Smaller integrators simply don't have the breadth of talent to sustain too many service offerings. Each type of talent required to deploy and maintain wireless mobility, voice, unified communications, security, and so forth is considerable in each of the respective fields. It is largely for this reason that talent diversity is proportional to the number of personnel in an operation.

Even mid-sized integrators (with $50 million to $250 million in product sales) are reducing their primary focuses to two main, and perhaps a third, technologies: typically unified communications and data centers, with a third technology typically being mobility. This brings us to talent pool management; top management within many system integrators believe that a smart engineer can be moved from technology to technology and needs little time to get up to speed with a new assignment. This is where the concept of zero sum applies, however: a limited and set amount of engineering talent is actually available within an organization.

It's certainly true that engineers, like other professionals, are increasing their productivity out of necessity, but this is a generally an organic increase given the general maturity of the IT industry. Organic productivity growth is not the same net increase for an organization, such as gaining new personnel. The art in managing productivity to increase the maximum benefits to the integrator, customer, and technology provider demands that you proportion this talent well.

Engineers are indeed bright, hard-working people with enormous appetites for constant training, priority changes, and productivity pressures when deployments don't work properly. And nearly every deployment goes wrong at some point before it achieves expectations. The integration of core elements, which include the largest routers and switches, to clients that are the far distant endpoints of a network such as handheld devices is far more difficult than most end users and well-intentioned marketing teams understand; it's very challenging work.

The more well-intentioned marketing teams provide "plug-and-play" messaging to end customers, the more substantial disconnect with actual deployments. True to the marketing and sales pitches, each specific technology is becoming far more automated to configure and easier to manage remotely, and the tooling to deploy these technologies has vastly improved over what we used even five years ago. However, I tip my hat to engineers, who carry the industry on their backs and in their tool kits, and whose motto is, "Never confuse selling with deploying technology."

This is exactly why even the best engineers can't merely be shifted from unified communications to mobility or from mobility to data center, for example. Each of these technologies demands intricate knowledge, and very few engineers thoroughly understand the problems of any two of the top three leading network technologies: unified communications, data center, and mobility. It's rare to find an engineer with more than one high-end industry certification such as a CCIE (Cisco Certified Internetworking Expert).

Another challenge for mobility is that, as with the competing technologies of unified communications and data center, good engineers are both born and made over time. It takes at least three years of intense hands-on experience for an engineer to become a good mobility engineer, and that's assuming they intuitively understand free space propagation, which may be the single most notable wild card that separates mobility from any other primary network technology.

Free space propagation concerns how data moves through the air between a transmitter and a receiver. It is a complex concept and unique to every environment; no "cookie cutter design" is repeatable from one location to another. Even when a reliable, high-speed, long-range, unlicensed wireless link is established, it takes surprisingly little to degrade that wireless link to the point at which an engineer must be sent out to resolve the matter.

The biggest challenges come in complex environments such as healthcare, manufacturing, and mega-deployments as in sports stadiums. Healthcare and manufacturing make up two of the top three industries in which today's mobility is most commonly deployed. What I call error-free velocity (the ability to design, deploy, verify, and maintain complex wireless links) is a skill not broadly held in the engineering community. When we see a choice mobility engineer transferred to data center or unified communications, it's a genuine loss to the wireless team and indeed the wireless industry, and it's a loss from which recovery takes three to five years, because that's how long it takes to become a journeyman mobility engineer.

Bigger Bet, More Sales

If I were running a major system integrator, I would be tempted to do exactly what I'm seeing: place my biggest bets on the largest opportunities. Every business, from the smallest startups to mega companies such as Cisco and GE, have resource limits. It makes the most sense to harvest the maximum amount of sales for a given time and resource set, and that takes commitment of personnel, funding, and programs. Given that unified communications sales are around three to five times as large as mobility product sales, it's justifiable to place the bulk of the sales, marketing, and engineering forces on that opportunity.

Data center is much closer in size in terms of product sales to mobility, though the incentive programs are generally more profitable to the system integrator than those offered by mobility. Combining the power, server, and storage capabilities of an enterprise network into a single facility is eminently sensible and cost effective; there can be little argument that data centers are a highly appropriate investment.

Given that every company has resource limits, proportioning talent according to the size of the cash-flow stream is simply good management. The artful part comes in managing disproportionately valuable technologies such as mobility. In my 20 years in this field, I have never seen an excess of talent; there has always been a perpetual shortage of qualified engineers, marketing, and sales personnel. The view from inside the industry is that we're always grateful to see new talent added to our teams; we can use the additional intellectual capital and commitment to a technology we believe is amazing, highly relevant, and mission critical. Ask a doctor, nurse, soldier, FedEx driver, or retail floor manager if wireless technology is important, and their answer is always a resounding "yes!"

This doesn't make unified communications or data center less relevant; the doctor, nurse, and other professional generally sees very little of what goes on behind the scenes to make wireless work. You need a wide array of interlocked systems to enable productivity and usefulness for the end user. Networks have evolved to their current state with many dozens of subsystems, because that's what it takes for a network to operate reliably, at speed, and ubiquitously.

The siren call to allocate as many resources as possible in unified communications and data center is absolutely justified, because these technical disciplines are the center of mass for IT networks. As an industry of technology providers and system integrators, we would do well to ensure that what works best from a business perspective within the system integrators is well matched to what customers are demanding. Customers need unified communications and data centers, no doubt about that. Maximizing productivity by deploying borderless networks and by changing work from an activity to a location is the role of mobility.

Looking Forward: Four Key Industry Elements

If any one thing is important to understand in today's enterprise wireless market, it's the context among these four primary elements:

- Customers
- System integrators
- Technology
- Usage

The purpose of this chapter is to weave these elements together as tightly as possible such that a mosaic emerges. By viewing this mosaic, you should be able to make the most informed decisions for the present and the few years ahead. The latter part of this chapter will focus on where I see the matrix of these four items heading.

In the briefest of terms and review, it's possible to distill the single most important concept to consider with regard to these elements:

- *Customers* will demand financial and benefit modeling for their mobility investments.

- *System integrators* will need to evolve from simply gluing third-party technology to business consultants, including the key deliverable of smart targeting on a vertical and account basis. They will also need to prioritize their internal incentives, training, and reliance on the top 10 percent of their own sales staffs to provide maximum return on their own efforts and maximum return on for the investments made by the system integrator customers.

- *Technology* will evolve on two key fronts: the proliferation of clients within smart buildings and the proliferation of consumer-based smartphones. The former will grow IT networks by orders of magnitude and, accordingly, will afford some of the largest reductions in operating expenses. Smartphones such as the Blackberry and the iPhone will provide a rich combination of lifestyle and professional work tools.

- *Usage* with handheld devices will become the modern-day oracle of information on not just data points, but predictive modeling and services provided to the end user, and they will further allow work to change from a location to an event.

Future Trends

Perhaps the single largest difference between where we are now and where we were in the mid-1960s when DARPA first funded the precursor for the Internet is that we're looking farther ahead now. There is much more discussion now about not only the Internet and its future, but how connectivity affects us in powerful ways, both for the good and the not so good.

I've had the privilege of looking forward into the mobility future on an annual basis since 2004 because I've spent most of my time in this industry with the most incredible and relevant customers, with the largest and most relevant provider of unlicensed wireless technology, and with some of the best engineers and thinkers in the IT industry.

I've enjoyed casting a look a few years down the road to see what may become of the technology, the market, and mobility usage. This is truly the most exciting time ever in the IT industry; the capabilities, usages, and benefits from IT and mobility are earthshaking. Without mobility, we'd be taking major steps backward in productivity, quality of life, and lifestyle.

By bringing various landscapes to us instead of the other way around, we can sample much more life with much greater speed and reduced expense and effort. It's quite wonderful, and quite important. If you believe as I do that we've never seen a more exciting time in mobility and IT, you will enjoy a peek into the potential of this technology for the next three to five years. That's about as far forward a view as can be reliably offered.

Reliable predictions are fairly easy for most of us in terms of what we'll see in mobility by the year 2013. Predictions much beyond that enter aggressively into the realm of speculation. There is simply no way to foresee what lies that far ahead. In terms of a physical lifetime, it's not that long. In terms of technology, however, five years is a long time—not because any single element of the future will change that much, but because the convergence of various trends makes it virtually impossible to know our future with even moderate degrees of assurance.

Policies May Become More Important than Technology

Ultimately, the *policies* of technology might affect us more than the actual technology itself. In particular, I'm thinking of the implications of pervasive technology. The more pervasive the number of network endpoints, the more you can do with a network. Conversely, the more pervasive the number of network endpoints, the more privacy and constitutional issues arise—privacy versus ubiquitous information access will create tension across technical and nontechnical stakeholders.

In polarized matters such as privacy and ubiquitous networks, I'm presently reserving my own opinion as to which side may offer the most benefit to individuals and society at large. The purpose of offering a view into the future is to foster a contemplation of this in your own mind, and hopefully raise your awareness of both sides of the matter. There remain more good people than bad in society; I'm confident that the pendulum will sway more or less near the center and thereby provide benefits at both ends of the idea spectrum.

The larger the policy source, the more broadly impactful the policy. Privacy matters are perhaps more a matter of federal and state governments than a matter of business, though a mishandling of confidential data from end customers can easily become major issues.

The absence of policy can, however, be as damaging as the presence of a broad policy. Events such as the theft of millions of credit card numbers result in losses of billions of dollars for businesses after legal fees, call center costs, and regulatory fines are considered. Even while the nation and world were focused on the inauguration of a new U.S. president in January 2009, Heartland Payment Systems revealed that more than 100 million credit card numbers were stolen by hackers.

No technology, system, or safe is truly and completely secure. Total security is an illusion in part because people need to access goods and information. Complete security is incompatible with ease of use, and ease of use is a measure of productivity. Doctors, nurses, financial industry personnel, and others cannot afford to wend their way through complex security mazes every time they need to access people or information; neither their jobs nor the national economy would scale or operate with any appreciable efficiency. Policies are what balance opposing requirements such as security and access.

Impactful policies abound in areas such as the integration of Blackberries and iPhones into enterprise-class networks. What's remarkable about this development is that smartphones are so compelling and powerful that employees are paying for them out of their own pockets versus using smartphones assigned by their employer.

This is the second time we've seen this trend in the wireless world. Employees began bringing wireless access points into offices around 2001 and attaching 802.11 cards into their laptops so they could roam around small offices instead of being attached to a cubicle. This sidestepped the security policies of many companies. One of the largest motivators for 802.11 enterprise-class networks between 2002 and 2005 was the ability to find unauthorized wireless equipment through mobility network tooling and to bring those elements into compliance. Companies such as Cisco changed policies to include stiff sanctions for employees who brought unauthorized wireless equipment into the workspace. Those sanctions included the forfeiture of the equipment and termination of employment.

While those issues have been largely resolved today, what has not been forgotten is the impact of technology brought in by users from home for personal use, and then migrated into office use. The 802.11 wireless access point and the smartphone are two prominent examples of how policy needed to catch up with end user preference. The consumerization of network endpoints is a major development for network managers, especially along the lines of network security, expensing of device use, and integration of the devices to allow access to business applications. In some companies, the adoption rate of these devices has been so fast that the best the company and IT managers can do is allow employees to set up their own user groups to incorporate the devices onto the company network.

In general, this works surprisingly well, especially given that the majority of the new adopters of the technology are not especially technically minded. The benefits for these devices are compelling when we see early mass adoption, such as that of the iPhone, into corporate networks by nontechnical personnel. It's also a testament to the quality and usability of these devices, which can be incorporated into the network through informal user groups.

System Integrator: From Box Integrator to Business Practice Partner

One of the key trends I see emerging over the next few years with mobility system integrators will be the transition from "box integrator" to business practice partner. We're already seeing this trend in the largest of integrators such as HP and IBM. I believe this trend will cascade into the bulk of the integrator community with system integrators who generate $25 to $500 million in annual product sales. Integrators from boutiques, which typically employ one to five people, to those with up to $25 million in annual product sales will likely remain focused more on the design and installation of network elements including mobility. The larger integrators will almost certainly offer varying degrees of business partner deliverables such as business intelligence, analytics, and smart targeting data for customers.

Partners who can provide equal amounts of operational consulting with engineering will emerge as "super partners" who will enjoy privileged relationships with not just the largest end customers, but perhaps more importantly the most profitable customers. These privileged engagements will be part of a larger trend in which stakeholder teams will comprise personnel from both inside and outside the company.

This is not a shift to more bureaucracy for bureaucracy's sake; instead, there will be less tolerance of nonessential personnel in meetings and programs. This will be driven by the need for increasingly greater levels of productivity and to gain the maximum benefit for employees on a pure cost basis. In other words, employees will come under increasing scrutiny in terms of the value they add to an organization. It may sound cold-hearted and somewhat ruthless, but this trend will also drive more employees to find ways in which they can add value. It will cause improvements in collaboration skills, knowledge of communication tools, and the innate ability to work from any location with a deft incorporation of personal and professional obligations.

This will also drive systems integrators, end customers, and technology providers to understand several key verticals—most likely healthcare, K-12 education, and manufacturing. Where most businesses now sell in a primarily opportunistic manner, the deep integration of the three primary cash stream participants—technology providers, integrators, and end customers—will require a far better understanding of far fewer verticals. The term "cash stream participant" is used here because the cash flow involves one continual stream that originates with the end customer, flows through the integrator, and then moves to the technology provider. Many adjacencies occur for each of these participants, but for our purposes, the cash-flow stream exists from end to end along these three constituents.

Knowing the differences in how the cash stream operates from one vertical to another will be increasingly important and will be a key attribute in how well each of the constituents can operate within the common cash-flow stream. For example, a hospital is quite different from a hotel though both have many beds, require large buildings, and depend on customer traffic for their existence. A manufacturer is quite a different business from a warehouse, though both reside in large buildings with conveyor belts, shelves, and multiple docks for the arrival and departure of inventory.

Knowing not just the primary vertical in which each of the three primary cash stream constituents reside but, even more so, the specific business within each vertical will be key to synergistic and profitable relationships. Each business within a specific vertical has unique priorities, financial and management systems, and many other unique attributes that will require an increased dedication and focus by the other cash stream constituents.

The rewards for managing these key relationships will be worth the effort in part because each constituent will commit to long-term services and goods on a noncompetitive basis. This reduces the cost for the other constituents, thereby freeing resources and capital for increased profitability and increased quality of service and products to the other constituents. Customer lists will therefore become shorter, but much more valuable.

Mobility Becomes a Vital Ad Hoc Technology

I see the role of mobility changing within two of the primary cash-flow constituents: the mobility technology providers such as Cisco and Aruba, and the system integrators such as NEC America and INX. In short, it seems clear that mobility technology is only as relevant as that which it untethers.

Put another way, allowing personnel and machines to access information while in motion is important, but the information itself is the most important part. I enjoy my iPhone: I like how it looks, its user interface, and the approving looks from other iPhone users, but the applications, voice capabilities, e-mail, browsing, and the 50 or so applications made available on my iPhone make it valuable. The ability to access each of these applications and uses is of course valuable to me. The experience would be diminished if I had to plug the device into an Ethernet port each time I used the phone.

While I'm not at all concerned for the future of wireless mobility, I see it becoming increasingly coupled to unified communications over the next few years. It will not be absorbed entirely into unified communications, though, because it's too unique. Attempts were made previously to combine wireless LANs to security; that worked on a cursory basis only, because, while inextricably coupled because wireless is always deployed in enterprise-class networks in a secure manner, the two technologies were never going to be understood as being similar.

The same will be found true in the convergence of unified communications and wireless mobility. They will be tightly coupled because 74 percent of all unified communication applications are optimized for value by using wireless handheld clients. There will always be a clear delineation between wireless mobility and unified communications, but these technologies will be sold, maintained, and used much more in combination, rather than as separate and stand-alone technologies.

IT Outsourcing

A great deal is being written about outsourcing IT, and for good reason. The trend in business is quite clear, and most technology pundits believe passionately that the near future will see even more of this. I'm in agreement, but for reasons not generally illuminated by the analysts and IT media.

The part they may not see quite clearly is what is happening deep inside the customers, the integrators, and the technology providers. I see three primary elements in play that will drive outsourcing at the end customer:

- Increasing complexity per technology
- Shortage of experienced personnel
- Outmoded talent management techniques

As stated previously in this work, when I'm asked by college students what it's like to work in IT, I tell them it's generally like coming home and finding your family has moved somewhere else—and there's no forwarding address. To add to the intensity of the situation, this scenario recurs every three to six months. The technology changes so much during that short time that it's challenging not just to maintain my current workload, but to keep up with where and how the technology is changing.

The changes are now occurring more from a convergence of other issues such as policy, scale of deployments, the incorporation of consumer sourced clients, and integration complexity of clients, to name a few. As a result, fewer deeply experienced personnel exist relative to the size of an IT staff. Having taught wireless and mobility to engineers for 20 years, including the last 10 in the 802.11 industry, I have seen pretty much the same group of professionals in the training rooms year after year. When we break the groups into two subgroups—those with more than five years of experience and those with less than five years—I see very few changes in the faces we see every six months or so. The greater concern is that, if anything, we're seeing a slight shrinkage of true experts with more than five years of experience in mobility. This isn't occurring just at Cisco; it's happening across the mobility industry.

This issue is even more pervasive than that, however: when I work on networks with nuclear power companies, the one single statistic that gets every stakeholder into the conversation is that 40 percent of the current technical personnel in that industry will be retiring by the year 2013. You can imagine how interesting and passionate the discussions on productivity and employee satisfaction are.

The shortage of highly experienced IT personnel is also well recognized in education, manufacturing, retail, healthcare, and every major industry vertical.

One of the key elements of outsourcing IT is that companies that own network operations centers (NOCs) such as NEC, INX, Perot Systems, and others have incredibly efficient mechanisms, tools, and experienced personnel to monitor, maintain, and repair networks that are more complex than ever. The efficiency of NOCs is increasing noticeably; the efficiency of even some of the best IT teams in the world is much less noticeable.

This in part is due to the practice of deploying the most seasoned engineers into situations of greatly varying complexity. A good model for the IT industry to consider is that of law firms, where senior partners oversee detailed cases and mid-level and junior attorneys handle the block and tackling of basic work. If you visit the deployment site today at most major and minor customers, you'll see some of the most experienced engineers pulling cable and assembling and testing cable connectors, and you'll see these same top engineers at the peak of a ladder or scissors lift bolting an access point to a pole or side of a structure or wall.

Where that methodology is truly impactful is on the future trend outlined next: practice choke points.

Mobility Practice Choke Point: RF Designs

When I perform an analysis of a mobility system integrator, I look at a number of key elements quite closely. One of them is the number of personnel who can perform complex wireless network designs without error. It's not very difficult to assemble a design for a wireless network with less than ten access points for a small office, but it's quite another matter not only to design a wireless network for a manufacturing or healthcare facility, but to know how to audit the design for maximum reliability, speed, range, and integration of clients. Although I've worked with some of the top mobility integrators on the planet, I've never experienced a situation in which enough personnel were available to perform all the design work required to generate sufficient revenues to make the mobility practice a worthwhile investment for the integrator.

This isn't to say the mobility practices at the better integrators are going to be wound up anytime soon; what happens is that the few engineers who can do designs are pulling double duty as deployment engineers as well, and, more to the point, they end up not only designing the WLANs, but also hanging access points, pulling cables, and configuring controllers and switches. This is simply an enormous load for one or two people at a mobility practice.

I see another trend as well: mid-level engineers are being sent to a site to perform a site survey. A mid-level engineer can take this data and assemble a quite good design, as long as the radiating environment is not too dynamic, the scope of the project is not too large, or the access point density is such that the RF requires special tuning through either the controller or manual intervention by the engineer.

An increasing amount of the latter is becoming more common: a fairly quick site survey followed by a design to fill in most of the coverage. There may be no suitable alternative for this situation in the next few years, although I think a solid business opportunity could be to establish and maintain a premium RF design house that would quickly turn around complex designs from the establishment of functional requirements from the customer to the design, deployment, and all other steps as outlined in Chapter 7.

Personal and Business Device Convergence

One of the most intriguing and impactful developments in the wireless mobility world is the convergence of personal and business devices—in particular, the incorporation of smartphones such as the iPhone, the Blackberry, and the Droid.

What's particularly relevant is not so much the technical sides of ensuring secure access to business applications, but the integration of work and personal life. For many, work will remain location-based far into the future. At some point, human hands have to touch products and services; not even the most Orwellian vision would preclude the economy from extensively relying on the physical presence of people. We know of no robotic system that can work as consistently with the precision of a human hand—though some may argue that robotic surgery and some manufacturing assembly is better than that which human hands can provide.

My prevailing point, however, is that even for those who work with their hands carry cell phones. It's completely common to see taxi drivers, landscapers, waitresses, steel workers, and others contact their families, friends, banks, and other important—and not so important—individuals and institutions from their cell phones. This saves them time from traveling to see people and businesses.

In the not-too-distant future, we'll migrate from carrying phones and other communication devices to communicating through devices that are embedded into buildings, furniture, and clothing. These devices have long since been built into our automobiles; we can now order a wireless router with a new 2010 model GM car. In fact, my current car has Bluetooth and power outlets for my smartphone as well as spare power outlets for other devices such as laptops.

In the future, we'll be able to authorize professionals to manipulate entire electrical power grids, attend meetings with 3-D images of our counterparts, and so much more. The images, content, and remote participation will become so real that it may become the dominant method by which we relate, communicate, and achieve our professional and personal objectives. Truly, in this regard, the best is yet to come.

Smart Targeting

Customer relationship management software granularity will become mission critical as smart targeting for verticals, geographies, and customers becomes the differentiator among competitors. Those who possess the best understanding through intelligence gathering and processing will have enormous advantages over competitors who "wing it" in terms of customer engagements.

Integrators, like other businesses, can be romanced by the glamour of a well-known end customer. There is clearly value in having a blue chip list of clients because there is an implied sense of trust and achievement in servicing the most well-known customers. In the future, the shift may move from purely blue chip to most profitable customers.

Relatively few businesses now rely on sales analytics, but my prediction is that this will change as sales forces come under considerable pressure to produce far more in sales than ever before. I use the term "sales yield" when I work with my business partners; this term refers to a specific set of measurements that demonstrate the amount of money sales forces generate over specific periods of time, in specific geographies, and in other key metrics.

The sales yield of an average sales force is largely dependent on how well a smart targeting model is used versus the more common territorial coverage. The good news is that there is now tremendous room for expanded sales, primarily because many sales teams focus on territory coverage versus smart targeting of the most likely accounts that will produce sales. Territories yield exactly zero sales. Customers yield sales; knowing which customers are the most likely to purchase and knowing exactly what to offer, with what discounts, and for which value propositions can enormously impact the performance of a sales team.

Smart targeting of the most optimal customers through intelligence gathering and processing will also enable companies to reduce their cost of sales. Instead of simply hiring enough people to cover a territory, businesses can focus on the top 20 percent of their customers, which, incidentally, generally provide something approaching 90 percent of their sales.

Consolidation

The largest will become larger. Many mid-sized partners will either become acquired or consolidate. Boutique partners will become scarce due to cash flow and market reach. Exceptions will be boutiques with solid, long-term contracts with major customers.

Consolidation will be primarily driven by the need to incorporate specialist teams with deep knowledge and experience of various networking elements such as mobility, video, and applications expertise in workplace productivity and application acceleration, which is the technology of ensuring that applications work at their fastest and most reliable rates of speed.

We're already seeing this with major acquisitions such as that of Perot Systems by Dell. Perot will be a separate and stand-alone division within Dell, as the acquired team will focus on providing IT services and remote network operations support. I've attended meetings with integrators who are reviewing or have reviewed a similar strategy, especially as it concerns mobility. Boutique integrators are often, but not always, somewhat cash-constrained. The purchase of this talent by larger companies smoothes out the cash flow to the acquired company's employees and shareholders and provides the benefit of essential and highly specialized services to the larger firm.

It's my further prediction that we'll see companies returning to focus on a very short list of three or four priorities. This represents a return to "core businesses." A tremendous amount of institutional memory and expertise resides in the core businesses of many IT operations. The last few years have seen experimentation and expansion into areas that at times have not been profitable enough. With an increased focus on corporate performance, a return to core businesses such as servicing the K-12 education industry, healthcare, and so forth will allow businesses to apply native and longstanding expertise. Equally important, it will allow them to harvest their own databases on former and abandoned customers, which is an essential element in smart targeting. A focus on partner profitability incentive programs, additionally fueled by smart targeting, will enable a higher level of corporate performance in terms of top-line sales and bottom-line profitability.

Smart Buildings

Perhaps only the integration of smartphones into enterprise networks rivals the excitement I feel and the bright hope I have for smart buildings. Smart buildings will not only enable an explosive growth in IP-centric networking, but they are likely our best opportunity to reduce the enormous amount of energy we use on the planet. I am not offering any opinion on global warming or other macro issues outside those that are traditionally associated with business operations, in this case profit and loss. Reducing the amount of energy wasted in a building will provide enormous improvements in operating margins.

Providing granularity in terms of how much energy is used, and for what reason, will enable management teams better to monitor, allocate, and provide compensation-based incentives for energy consumption to employees and shareholders. Energy will then be much closer to its potential value by being used in the same careful manner as any other critical resource in a business, including people, inventory, and information.

Given that approximately 40 percent of all energy consumed in the United States goes into commercial buildings, the reduction of energy will reduce the stress on an aging electrical grid, thus giving us time to consider and deploy alternative forms of energy. The smart use of energy will allow us to consider options such as self-contained buildings (structures that generate and recycle their water, heat, waste, and electricity). This will have a cascading effect on local environments, making our neighborhoods better places to live, and attracting productive, happy people to our local businesses and therefore our communities.

One of the brightest hopes we have in the near future of business is the integration of our massive IT assets into another massive investment we've made: our buildings. The concept of smartly managing our energy, along with making our buildings more productive places to work, will create places that are more pleasurable to work in. The convergence of IT and building management systems will create wonderful opportunities for all three constituents in the current cash-flow stream that begins with IT end customers, flows through the integrator community, and moves on into the technology providers. New, high-value careers will emerge, further enhancing our economy on a local and national basis.

Outcome-based Engagements

And so we land at the end of this work. And like all endings, it's good to look at the beginning. The primary purpose of this book has been to elevate and expand mobility discussions from the technical to those of the "why" of mobility.

Outcome-based engagements will be the future at every level of those involved in mobility: the end customer, the systems integrator, and the technology provider. I'm already seeing this in our industry. Value propositions are driving the "why" of mobility far more than they ever have. I know because I'm spending time each workday on this very issue; my colleagues and business partners are easily among the most capable professionals I've ever met, and they are enthusiastic in the support of this concept. It's gratifying to see the best and brightest in our industry working diligently to connect the best reasoning possible for investing in mobility and IT in general.

Outcome-based engagements are the future of mobility, borderless networks, and IT, because the better the job we all do of connecting business priorities with IT investments, in particular that of mobility, the better we'll all live, work, worship, and play.

It's that simple, and it's that challenging.

APPENDIX A | Mobility Glossary

Although the intended audience of this book is primarily nontechnical, such as IT managers, directors, and program managers, all mobility workers can benefit from knowledge of technical terms and issues. I believed that a person can make more effective contributions if they first understand the basic technical terms and the context in which these items are used. For this reason, an extensive glossary of technical terms is included in this book.

It's my hope that you'll keep this glossary handy and use it in preparation for technical meetings where WLANs are being planned and discussed. This list is not intended to be comprehensive; an exhaustive list of IT terms could easily be a dictionary-length work. You won't see or hear most this language commonly in project management and business operational discussions, but you may hear some of these terms mentioned by engineers in those meetings.

Many of these terms are more often associated with network elements such as routers, switches, and so forth, and many terms pertain to the issue of network security. These terms are intentionally included in this glossary because 802.11 elements, when properly deployed, configured, and managed, are no longer simply "radios," but rather essential network elements that operate in a secure manner while retaining a high degree of performance. You'll also see some terms that aren't necessarily part of either the 802.11 or network lexicons, but are included because they are associated with closely related subjects.

802.1X   An IEEE standard that defines the operation of a Medium Access Control (MAC) bridge to provide port-based network access control capability. This standard uses the Extensible Authentication Protocol (EAP) and ties it to the physical medium, be it Ethernet, Token Ring, or wireless LAN. EAP messages are encapsulated in 802.1X messages and referred to as EAP over LAN (EAPOL).

802.11   An IEEE standard for unlicensed wireless connectivity originally entitled "802.11-1999," reaffirmed in 2003, and now formally referred to as "802.11-2007." The *.11* part of the broader *802* IEEE standard focuses primarily on two levels of the OSI stack called the MAC and physical layers. Of interest, and not well known, is that the standard is enormously comprehensive, with 1184 pages of description and guidance including the appendices and bibliographies. As of early 2010, this standard includes the following subparts:

- 802.11a
- 802.11b
- 802.11d
- 802.11e
- 802.11g
- 802.11h
- 802.11i
- 802.11j
- 802.11n

An exhaustive list of definitions of 802.11 are not included in this glossary but can be found at www.standards.ieee.org and in Appendix B.

802.11i   An IEEE standard that focuses on enhancing the current 802.11 MAC to improve security.

802.11n   An IEEE standard that focuses on a high-speed and a more reliable version of 802.11. This amendment to the broader 802.11 standard was ratified by the IEEE in September 2009 after seven years of negotiating the standard across a working group of 400 individuals from 20 countries comprised predominantly of wireless industry professionals. This enhancement is intended to address the greatly increased demand on networks for wireless speed, range, and reliability to support next-generation multimedia applications such as voice and video. It also defines wireless equipment interoperability, data rates, quality of service, device link options, management, and security.

access method   Generally, the way in which network devices access the network at large; in other words, the medium that connects LANs. Examples include broadband fixed wireless, DSL, and cable modems.

adjacent channel   A channel or frequency that is directly above or below a specific channel or frequency.

AES   Acronym for Advanced Encryption Standard. AES is a U.S. Federal Information Processing Standards (FIPS) standard and specifically refers to FIPS Publication 197, which specifies a cryptographic algorithm for use by U.S. government organizations to protect sensitive, unclassified information. Security experts generally agree that this standard will rapidly be adopted on a voluntary basis by many commercial entities and network development companies such as Cisco and others.

algorithm   A well-defined rule or process for arriving at a solution to a problem.

amplitude   The magnitude or strength of a varying waveform; refers to radio frequency (RF) "waves" of energy. Amplitude is understood in mathematical terms and demonstrated visually as a graphic representation of an RF signal.

analog signal   The representation of information with a continuously variable physical quantity, such as voltage. Because of this constant changing of the wave shape with regard to its passing a given point in time or space, an analog signal may have an infinite number of states or values. This contrasts with a digital signal, which has, by comparison, a limited number of discrete states.

ANSI   Acronym for American National Standards Institute. This voluntary organization composed of corporate, governmental, and other members coordinates standards-related activities, approves U.S. national standards, and develops positions for the United States in international standards organizations. ANSI helps develop international and U.S. standards relating to, among other things, communications and networking. ANSI is a member of IEC and ISO.

antenna   A device for transmitting or receiving a radio frequency (RF). Antennas are usually designed for specific and relatively tightly defined frequencies and are quite varied in design. As an example, an antenna for a 2.4 GHz (802.11) system will generally not perform for a 28 GHz (LMDS) design. Antennas radiate and receive signals over a very wide range, but specific design characteristics enable the antenna to perform at optimum levels for the spectrum in which it is intended.

antenna gain   The measure of an antenna *assembly's* performance relative to a theoretically perfect antenna called an isotropic radiator (*radiator* is another term for antenna). Certain antenna designs feature higher performance relative to radiating a specific area or with regard to frequencies.

AP   Acronym for access point, a device used to connect client devices, such as handheld devices such as laser scanners, to the Ethernet portion of a LAN. An AP generally has an Ethernet port and a power port on its backside and two or more antennas that transmit and receive RF signals from client devices, other APs, or workgroup bridges.

application layer   Layer 7 of the OSI reference model that provides services to application processes such as e-mail, video, and custom applications for industries such as healthcare, manufacturing, and so forth. Applications generally do not adhere to the OSI standard, but may adhere to industry-specific standards and are therefore considered as outside the OSI model.

The application layer identifies and establishes the availability of intended communication partners (and the resources required to connect with them), synchronizes cooperating applications, and establishes agreement on procedures for error recovery and control of data integrity. This layer corresponds roughly with the transaction services layer in the Systems Network Architecture (SNA) model. Other associated terms include *physical layer*, *data-link layer*, *network layer*, *transport layer*, *session layer*, and *physical layer*.

ARP   Acronym for Address Resolution Protocol, an OSI Layer 3 protocol used to map IP network addresses to the hardware addresses used by a Layer 2 data-link protocol. The protocol is used when IP is carried over Ethernet.

ARQ   Acronym for automatic repeat request. Communication technique in which the receiving device detects errors and requests retransmissions.

ASCII   Acronym for American Standard Code for Information Interchange. Specifies 8-bit code for character representation (7 bits plus parity).

ATM   Acronym for Asynchronous Transfer Mode. International standard for cell relay in which multiple service types (such as voice, video, or data) are conveyed in fixed-length (53-byte) cells. Fixed-length cells allow cell processing to occur in hardware, thereby reducing transit delays. ATM is designed to take advantage of high-speed transmission media such as E3, SONET, and T3.

attenuation   Loss of communication signal energy, whether by equipment design, operator manipulation, or transmission through a medium such as the atmosphere, copper, or fiber.

authentication   In security, the verification of the identity of a person or process.

autonomous WLAN architecture   An architecture predominantly found in deployments of fewer than ten access points; is an architecture were most of the wireless control and management resides within the access point itself. There are no wireless access point controllers in this kind of architecture. See also centralized WLAN architecture.

backbone   Part of a network that acts as the primary path for traffic that is most often sourced from, and destined for, other networks.

backplane   Physical connection between an interface processor or card and the data buses and power distribution buses inside a chassis. A backplane typically resides inside major network components such as switches and routers.

bandwidth   The frequency range necessary to convey a signal, typically measured in units of hertz (Hz). For example, voice signals typically require approximately 7 kHz of bandwidth, and data traffic typically requires approximately 50 kHz of bandwidth, but this depends greatly on modulation scheme, data rates, and how many channels of a radio spectrum are used.

baseband   Characteristic of a network technology where only one carrier frequency is used. Ethernet is an example of a baseband network. Also called *narrowband*.

baud   Unit of signaling speed equal to the number of discrete signal elements transmitted per second. Baud is synonymous with bits per second (bps) if each signal element represents exactly 1 bit.

BBFW   Acronym for broadband fixed wireless and one of the most commonly used terms in the fixed wireless industry. In general, it implies data transfers in excess of 1.5 Mbps. This term is becoming, or has become, somewhat dated.

beamwidth   Refers to the "directiveness" of an antenna, more specifically used in regard to a patch, parabola, or yagi antenna and is defined as the angle between two half-power (-3dB) points on either side of the main lobe of radiation.

BER   Acronym for bit error ratio. Ratio of received bits that contain errors compared to bits received without error.

best effort   The type of traffic that has the lowest priority between two or more devices. Best effort traffic is commonly data that is not sensitive to delay. E-mail is generally the best example of this.

bit   A contraction of *binary digit*, which is the smallest possible unit of information a computer can handle. An alphabetic character or number is generally made up of 8 bits, which comprise 1 *byte* of information. Therefore, a single character, such as the letter *b*, requires a combination of eight 1's and 0's.

block   A *block* of information is information of a certain number of bits that is treated as a single unit. For example, 256 DES is a common encryption method used on the Internet and is termed *256* DES because it encrypts 64 bits at a time. While even a single bit can be encrypted, it would be easy to decode; the solution would likely be the opposite of that which is shown. In other words, if the encrypted bit is a 0, the decoded value would be a 1.

BootPC   Short for Bootstrap Protocol-Client. A boot protocol used to acquire a number identifying a server or other platform. Other information is also acquired by this protocol such as IP number and DNS setup. To boot over the network, the computer must usually acquire three things: an identity, an operating system image, and (usually) a working file system.

BootPS   Short for Bootstrap Protocol-Server. Before a device can communicate on a network, it first must have an IP address. A bootstrap server provides this information, because some network devices don't have sufficient or existing memory to perform this function. The *Bootstrap Protocol (BOOTP)* was created to enable this function between the new device and the device that assists in getting the new device onto a network.

BPSK   Acronym for binary phase shift keying, a digital frequency modulation technique used for transmitting information. This type of modulation is less efficient but more robust than similar modulation techniques, such as QPSK and 64QAM.

bridge   A device that connects and passes packets between two network segments that use the same communications protocol. Bridges operate at the data-link layer (Layer 2) of the OSI reference model. In general, a bridge will filter, forward, or flood an incoming frame based on the MAC address of that frame.

broadband   A data system that has a constant data rate at or in excess of 1.5 Mbps. Its corresponding opposite is *narrowband,* though with today's speeds, the term is somewhat dated except with regard to low-powered radios that adhere to standards such as Bluetooth.

Historically, it refers to a transmission system that multiplexes multiple independent signals onto one cable—or, in telecommunications terminology, it refers to any channel having a bandwidth greater than a voice-grade channel (4 kHz). In LAN terms, it can refer to a coaxial cable on which analog signaling is used. Also called *wideband* (by LAN definition).

broadcast   Infers that a signal is sent to many points at the same time and/or is transmitted to cover a fairly wide physical area. In general, the opposite of *narrowcast.* In the radio world, "broadcast" is a term of art, which means it has a special meaning relative to a specific technology. A broadcast signal is intended for reception by the general public. This should not be confused with the term "multicast," in which a single originating point connects with multiple sites; in the networking world, "multicast" and "broadcast" are synonymous.

BTA   Acronym for basic trading area, the geographical area frequently used by the FCC for assigning licensed frequencies. BTAs are typically contiguous counties or trading areas and were first described by the Rand McNally mapping company. Rand McNally eventually licensed these area descriptions to the FCC.

buffer Storage area used for handling data in transit. Buffers are used in internetworking to compensate for differences in processing speed between network devices. Bursts of data can be stored in buffers until they can be handled by slower-processing devices. Sometimes referred to as a *packet buffer*.

byte A series of consecutive binary digits that are operated upon as a unit (for example, an 8-bit byte).

caching Form of replication in which information learned during a previous transaction is used to process later transactions.

CALEA Acronym for Communications Assistance for Law Enforcement Act, a set of federal laws enacted within the United States that requires that all commercially available Internet devices such as routers, switches, and so forth, that can carry voice or data traffic over their networks be able to deliver to law enforcement agencies detailed information on voice calls and data traffic.

CAPWAP Control And Provisioning of Wireless Access Points. A protocol referring to an approach on how an AP may use Layer 2 of the OSI stack.

carrier frequency The frequency of a transmitted signal that would be transmitted if it were not modulated. Some RF systems also have intermediate frequencies, which reside between the indoor equipment and the outdoor equipment. Carrier "frequency" can be either a single frequency or a range of frequencies carried at one time between the transmitter and receiver.

Category 5 cable One of five grades of UTP cabling described in the EIA/TIA-586 standard. Category 5 cable can transmit data at speeds up to 100 Mbps.

CBR Acronym for committed bit rate, a prioritization of information that is higher than BE (best effort) type traffic, but lower than unsolicited grant service (UGS). In ATM networks, CBR refers to constant bit rate and is used for connections that depend on precise clocking to ensure undistorted delivery.

CDMA Acronym for Code Division Multiple Access, a transmission scheme that allows multiple users to share the same RF range of frequencies. In effect, the system divides a small range of frequencies out of a larger set and divides the data transmission among them. The transmitting device divides the data among a preselected set of nonsequential frequencies. The receiver then collates the various data "pieces" from the disparate frequencies and into a coherent data stream. As part of the RF system setup, the receiver components are "advised" of the scrambled order of the incoming frequencies. An important aspect of this scheme is that the receiver system filters out any signals other than those specified for a given transmission.

centralized WLAN architecture A WLAN architecture which features a wireless controller, either as a standalone device or imbedded into a router or switch that controls the wireless management and intelligence of a group of access points. Please see autonomous WLAN architecture in contrast.

certificate A digitally signed statement from an entity saying that the public key of some other entity has some particular value. Certificates are a common concept in modern society. We use them for driver's licenses, for club memberships, and as identification. In an electronic sense, these items bind a public key to an individual, position, or organization.

channel A communications path. Multiple channels can be multiplexed over a single contiguous amount of spectrum. It also refers to a specific frequency allocation and bandwidth. As an example, downstream channels used for television in the United States are 6 MHz wide.

channel reuse A methodology in which certain frequencies are allocated for certain physical areas, devices, or types of network traffic to reduce RF interference. Because a limited number of channels are available in a typical RF system, they are used in parallel (typically) across different physical areas, devices, or types of network traffic such as voice, data, and video.

checksum An integer value computed from a sequence of octets taken through a series of arithmetic operations. The value is recomputed at the receiving end and compared for verification. Checksums are used as a method for checking the integrity of transmitted data.

cipher A key that converts plaintext to ciphertext.

ciphertext Text that has been *ciphered*, or encrypted. While ciphertext contains the same information as plaintext, it may or may not be the same number of bits. Certain lower end systems may have difficulty accommodating encryption, the technical term being *data expansion ciphering*. Ciphertext always requires a key to determine the plaintext.

CTS Acronym for Clear to Send. The EIA/TIA-232 control signal allows a data transmission on a communications line. This is granted after an "RTS" command is sent from a client such as a handheld device to a device such as an access point. CTS commands are given when airborne data traffic is low enough to allow additional traffic between devices such as handheld clients and accesss points. Compare to RTS, Request to Send.

CLI Acronym for command-line interface, which is where network technicians control the radio and network element settings on devices such as access points, switches, routers, and so forth. A CLI resides on the routers or switches at each point of a communications link. CLI access is commonly and appropriately protected by a username and password.

coaxial cable The type of cable used to connect Internet equipment to antennas and indoor/outdoor gear. Coaxial cable, or *coax*, usually consists of a center wire surrounded by a metal shield with an insulator separating the two. The "axis" of the cable is located down the center of the cable. "Coaxial" indicates that more than one conductor is oriented around a common axis for the length of the cable. Coaxial cable is one of the primary means of transporting cable TV and radio signals.

collision domain   In Ethernet, the network area within which frames that have collided are propagated. Repeaters and hubs propagate collisions; LAN switches, bridges, and routers do not.

convergence   Speed and ability of a group of internetworking devices running a specific routing protocol to agree on the topology of an internetwork after a change in that topology. A topology is a group of network elements such as APs, switches, and routers. Topologies can be virtual, physical, or logical in their arrangements. Is also a reference to a number of different applications or network usage combined over a single network.

converter   A device that converts the intermediate frequency to and from the carrier frequency; generally a technical concept reserved for high-performance outdoor systems. Some RF systems have two fundamental frequencies: one that is sent over the air (carrier frequency) and another that is sent back and forth between the indoor equipment and the outdoor equipment (intermediate frequency). Also referred to as *up/down converter* or *transverter.*

cookies   A group of information that users provide to a web server when accessing specific or types of websites. Each time a website is accessed, a trail about the user is left behind. This could include the user's computer name and IP address, operating system, and the URL of the last page visited. While cookies themselves are not gathering data, they can be used as a tracking device. A cookie generally cannot read data to find out your identity or your home address. However, if you provide such information to a site, it could be saved to a cookie. As more information is gathered, it is associated with the value kept in your cookie. In general, cookies allow faster access to websites of interest to a specific user.

CRC   Acronym for cyclic redundancy check. Error-checking technique in which the frame recipient calculates a remainder by dividing frame contents by a prime binary divisor and compares the calculated remainder to a value stored in the frame by the sending node.

cryptanalysis   An analysis of the strength of the cryptography used to secure information. Cryptanalysts continually evaluate the manner in which codes are broken to produce even more sophisticated ciphertext, which is often eventually broken, thereby fueling rounds of "cat and mouse." In the end, however, true data security is established not by the sole use of a highly sophisticated encryption technique, but by maintaining a minimum level of security for the entire operation. Also referred to as *code breaking.*

CSMA/CD   Carrier Sense Multiple Access With Collision Detection (CSMA/CD), is an access methodology both for wired and wireless mediums in which a carrier sensing scheme is used. A carrier is the frequency of a transmitted signal that would be transmitted if it were not modulated. It is a later version of Carrier Sense Multiple Access (CSMA). Collision detection is used to improve transmission performance by terminating transmission as soon as a collision is detected. This minimized the probability of a second collision on retry of the transmission. A jamming signal from the primary radio (the *mother* radio if you will) within a group of radios, is typically sent which will cause all transmitters to back off by random intervals, reducing the probability of a collision when the first retry is attempted.

data encryption key   Used for the encryption of message text and for the computation of message integrity checks (signatures).

data-link layer   Layer 2 of the OSI reference model. Provides reliable transit of data across a physical link. The data-link layer is concerned with physical addressing, network topology, line discipline, error notification, ordered delivery of frames, and flow control. IEEE divides this layer into two sublayers: the MAC sublayer and the LLC sublayer. Sometimes this is simply called the *link layer*. It roughly corresponds to the data-link control layer of the SNA model.

dB   Abbreviation for decibel, a unit for expressing a ratio of power or voltage in terms of gain or loss. Units are expressed logarithmically and typically in watts. dB is not an absolute value, but rather is the measure of power loss or gain between two devices. Gain or loss is expressed with a plus (+) or minus (-) sign in front of the number. For example, -3dB indicates a 50 percent loss in power, and +3dB indicates a doubling of power. The rule of thumb to remember is that 10dB indicates an increase (or loss) by a factor of 10, 20dB indicates an increase (or loss) by a factor of 100, and 30dB indicates an increase (or loss) by a factor of 1000. Because antennas and other RF devices/systems commonly have power gains or losses of four orders of magnitude, dB is a more easily used expression.

dBi   Abbreviation for decibels of antenna gain referenced to the gain of an isotropic antenna (hence the *i*). An isotropic antenna is a theoretical antenna that radiates with perfect symmetry in all three dimensions. Real-world antennas have radiation patterns that are far from truly symmetric, but this effect is generally used to the advantage of the system designer to optimize coverage over a specific area.

dBm   Abbreviation for decibels of power referenced to a milliwatt; 0dBm is 1mW.

dBW   Abbreviation for decibels of power referenced to 1 watt.

DDR   Dial-On-Demand Routing (DDR) is a technique used by routers to automatically initiate and close sessions between end stations which help keep the session alive. DDR enables routing telephone lines using an ISDN modem.

demodulator   The part of a receiver that assembles signals from the radio into a format usable by the network or device attached to the radio. The corresponding device on the transmission side of a system is a *modulator.*

DES   Acronym for Data Encryption Standard. Standard cryptographic algorithm used by the U.S. National Bureau of Standards. In networking terms, DES also stands for destination end station.

DHCP   Acronym for Dynamic Host Configuration Protocol. Provides a mechanism for allocating IP addresses dynamically so that addresses can be reused when hosts no longer need them.

DNS   Acronym for Domain Name System (as well as Domain Name Service).

domain   A general grouping of LANs based on organization type or geography.

downtilt   The downward angle used on directional antennas, such as parabolas or yagis, which enhances coverage closer to the base of the antenna mast or tower. Typically, most antennas have zero to six degrees of downtilt, but this depends on the application and deployment scenario.

DS-0   Acronym for Digital Signal level 0, a framing specification used in transmitting digital signals over a single channel at 64 Kbps. Compare with DS-1 at 1.544 Mbps (commonly referred to as 1.5 Mbps), and DS-3 at 44.736 Mbps (commonly referred to as 45 Mbps).

DSSS   Acronym for direct sequence spread spectrum, a spreading technique in which various data, voice, and/or video signals are transmitted over a specific set of frequencies in a sequential manner from lowest to highest frequency or highest to lowest frequency. See also spread spectrum, FHSS.

E-1   Wide-area digital transmission scheme used predominantly in Europe that carries data at a rate of 2.048 Mbps. E-1 lines can be leased for private use from common carriers.

EAP   Acronym for Extensible Authentication Protocol. Ensures mutual authentication between a wireless client and a server that resides at the Network Operations Center (NOC). EAP by itself does not provide mutual authentication, as is evidenced by EAP-MD5. The server for an 802.1X authentication type does not have to reside at the NOC.

EAP-MD5   Acronym for Extensible Authentication Protocol-Message Digest 5. An IETF standard for carrying various authentication methods over any Point-to-Point Protocol (PPP) connection. EAP-MD5 is a username/password method that incorporates MD5 hashing for security.

EAP-SIM   EAP for use in GSM-type phones, which are used predominantly in Europe and Asia, though they are becoming more common in the United States. SIM refers to the SIM cards that can be manually embedded into phones and other devices and that contain user information and security elements. EAP-SIM is a protocol that would enable devices such as mobile phones to authenticate to 802.11 networks.

EAP-SIM6   Same definition as EAP-SIM, except that it refers to the emerging IPv6 network protocol.

EAP-TLS   Acronym for Extensible Authentication Protocol-Transport Level Security, a protocol that provides for mutual authentication, integrity-protected cipher negotiation, and key exchange between two endpoints.

EIRP   Acronym for effective isotropic radiated power. Expresses the performance of a transmitting system in a given direction. EIRP is the power required by a system with an isotropic antenna to send the same amount of power in a given direction that would be required by a system with a directional antenna. EIRP is usually expressed in watts or dBW. EIRP is the sum of the power at the antenna input plus antenna gain, expressed in dBi.

electromagnetic spectrum   The full range of electromagnetic (same as magnetic) frequencies, a subset of which is used in commercial RF systems.

EMC   Electromagnetic Compatibility. A set of regulatory requirements set forth in most industrialized counties to minimize electronic interference between electrical devices.

encapsulation   Wrapping of data in a particular protocol header. For example, Ethernet data is wrapped in a specific Ethernet header before network transit. Also, when bridging dissimilar networks, the entire frame from one network is simply placed in the header used by the data-link layer protocol of the other network.

encryption   Application of a specific algorithm to data to alter the appearance of the data, making it incomprehensible to those who are not authorized to see the information.

equalization   Technique used to compensate for communications channel distortions.

ESD   Electro-static discharge; is a discharge of electrical energy between two devices with unequal electrical build up. It is more often than not an unwelcome event, and for electronic devices can induce partial or catastrophic electronic component failures. The feeling of a small electrical jolt when one grabs a door handle after crossing a carpet is a common ESD event.

Ethernet   Baseband LAN specification invented by Xerox Corporation and developed jointly by Xerox, Intel, and Digital Equipment Corporation. Ethernet networks use CSMA/CD and run over a variety of cable types at 10 Mbps. Ethernet is similar to the IEEE 802.3 series of standards.

ETSI   Acronym for European Telecommunication Standards Institute, an organization created by the European PTTs and the EC to propose telecommunications standards for Europe.

Fast Ethernet   Any of a number of 100 Mbps Ethernet specifications. Fast Ethernet offers a speed increase ten times that of the 10BaseT Ethernet specification, while preserving such qualities as frame format, MAC mechanisms, and multiple tenant unit (MTU). Such similarities allow the use of existing 10BaseT applications and network management tools on Fast Ethernet networks. It is based on an extension to the IEEE 802.3 specification.

FCC   Acronym for Federal Communications Commission, a U.S. government agency that supervises, licenses, and controls electronic and electromagnetic transmission standards.

FDMA   Acronym for Frequency Division Multiple Access, the modulation scheme that divides the total available spectrum into subsets that are commonly used in parallel across one or more links.

FH   Acronym for frequency hopping, which occurs when a transmitter sends bits of information sequentially over a number of radio channels in what is called a pseudo-random order—that is, there are so many combinations of the radio channels that it appears to be random, but it is vital that both the transmitter and receiver know which channel to be on and for how long at any given point in time.

FHSS   Acronym for frequency hopping spread spectrum. A spreading technique in which various data, voice, and/or video signals are transmitted over a specific set of frequencies in a pseudo-random order, rather than in a sequential manner from lowest to highest frequency, or highest to lowest frequency, as with DSSS. See also DSSS, spread spectrum.

file virus   The most common kind of virus, which typically goes after a file with a certain extension, such as .doc or .exe. File viruses attack by overwriting parts of the file so that the file becomes unusable or highly unstable, which then crashes the PC, server, or router. File viruses, as with sector viruses, can often reside in the RAM portion of the PC, server, or router, so care needs to be taken in rooting them out during the repair phase.

FIPS   Acronym for Federal Information Processing Standards. FIPS refers primarily to standards with regard to information security. More than a dozen various types of FIPS standards exist, and a good summary can be found here: www.csrc.nist.gov/publications/PubsFIPS.html.

firewall   A router or access server, or several routers or access servers, designated as a buffer between any connected public networks and a private network. A firewall router uses access lists and other methods to ensure the security of the private network.

fixed wireless   The type of wireless in which both the transmitter and receiver are nonmobile. Today's wireless systems are typically capable of data rates in excess of 1.5 Mbps, though the links can be throttled to data rates below that, but typically not less than 256 Kbps downstream and 128 Kbps upstream.

flow control   Technique for ensuring that a transmitting entity, such as a modem, does not overwhelm a receiving entity with data. When the buffers on the receiving device are full, a message is sent to the sending device to suspend the transmission until the data in the buffers has been processed.

footprint   The geographical area covered by a transmitter.

Fourier transform   Technique used to evaluate the importance of various frequency cycles in a time series pattern.

fragmentation   Process of breaking a packet into smaller units when transmitting over a network medium that cannot support the original size of the packet.

frame   Logical grouping of information sent as a data-link layer unit over a transmission medium. Often refers to the header and trailer, used for synchronization and error control, that surround the user data contained in the unit. The terms *cell*, *datagram*, *message*, *packet*, and *segment* are also used to describe logical information groupings at various layers of the OSI reference model and in various technology circles.

frequency   Number of cycles, measured in hertz (one cycle per second), of an alternating current signal per unit of time. For example, a 1 MHz frequency would have a full cycle (a complete sine wave) pass a given point in space at the rate of 1 million cycles per second. A 1 GHz frequency would have sine waves pass a given point in space at the rate of 1 billion times per second, and so forth.

frequency reuse   One of the fundamental concepts on which commercial wireless systems are based, which involves the partitioning of an RF radiating area (cell) into different frequencies. The design theory calls for a cell, or area, to be covered in one frequency, and the cells adjacent to it in other frequencies. The prevailing idea for adjacent cell frequency is to prevent interference problems.

   Frequency reuse in mobile cellular systems means that each cell has a frequency that is far enough away from the frequency in the bordering cell to prevent interference problems. Identical frequencies are ideally at least two cells apart from one another. This practice enables cellular providers to have many more customers for a given site license. For 802.11 or other unlicensed users, the idea is to use frequencies in the most efficient manner that allows for reliable, high-speed wireless connectivity across the required number of users.

Fresnel zones   Theoretically, ellipsoid-shaped volumes that reside in the space between a transmitting and receiving antenna. The industry rule of thumb for line-of-sight links is to leave 60 percent of the centermost part of the first Fresnel zone free from physical obstruction. There are many Fresnel zones within an RF link, and they are often referred to as the First Fresnel Zone, Second Fresnel Zone, and so on, as the area referred to is farther from the center of the beam path.

FTP   Acronym for File Transfer Protocol, an application protocol that is part of the TCP/IP protocol stack and used for transferring files between network nodes.

full duplex   Capability for simultaneous data transmission between a sending station and a receiving station. Half duplex occurs when only one side of a link can transmit at a time; simplex occurs when only one transmitter and one receiver are included in a link.

gain   Most commonly understood and used today with regard to antennas. For an antenna, the ratio of its directivity in a given direction is compared to a reference antenna that is typically theoretical. The higher the gain, the more directional the antenna pattern.

Gb   Abbreviation for gigabit. Approximately 1 billion bits.

Gbps   Abbreviation for gigabits per second.

GHz   Abbreviation for 1 billion cycles per second.

goodput   The net amount of data transmitted minus the overhead traffic to manage the link or connection. Sometimes referred to as *throughput*. This term is generally used more for outdoor than indoor wireless systems, and is arguably a somewhat dated term.

GRE   Acronym for generic routing encapsulation, a protocol that allows an arbitrary network protocol to be transmitted over any other network protocol. This is accomplished by encapsulating the packets of the source network within GRE packets, which are carried by the receiving, or transit, network.

headend   Main point, or hub, of a licensed outdoor wireless network. All clients units connect to the headend; the headend then transmits toward a number of client devices.

header   Control information placed before data when encapsulating that data for network transmission.

H-REAP   An acronym for Hybrid Remote Edge Access Point, a protocol used to configure and control multiple access points in a branch or remote office from a remote location.

HSRP   Acronym for Hot Standby Routing Protocol. HSRP allows for redundant paths for information on a "hot standby" basis. If the primary route goes down, the packets will be sent over a secondary path with no apparent delay or disruption to the network users.

HTTP   Acronym for Hypertext Transfer Protocol, a low overhead protocol that allows for text and images to be carried over a wide array of information systems. It is a generic object-oriented protocol that can be used for many similar tasks, such as name servers and distributed object-oriented systems, by extending the commands, or methods, used.

IAPP   Acronym for Inter Access Point Protocol, a protocol proposed by the largest providers of 802.11 equipment, with the intent of having a high degree of interoperability with regard to security, mobility, handover, and other higher functions that are not generally addressed by the Wi-Fi certification provided by the Wireless Ethernet Compatibility Alliance. It is an extension of the IEEE802.11 implemented on top of IP and uses UDP/IP and SNAP as the transfer protocol.

IEEE   Acronym for Institute of Electrical and Electronics Engineers.

interference   Unwanted communication noise that decreases the performance of a link or prevents a link from occurring. Interference can also come from physical objects placed temporarily or permanently within the radiating path between two radios. The general difference between electronic interference and physical object interference is that the former adds energy to one or both ends of a radio link, and the latter attenuates, or reduces, the energy received by at one or both ends of a radio link.

IOS   Acronym for internetwork operating system.

IPSec   Short for Internet Protocol Security.

ISDN   Integrated Services Digital Network; is a set of communications standards enabling telephone lines to carry other services such as video in addition to voice.

ISM Bands   It is generally, but not always agreed that the Industrial Scientific and Medical bands are 902 to 928 MHz, 2.4 to 2.485 GHz, 5.15 to 5.35 GHz, and 5.725 to 5.825 GHz.

isochronous transmission   Asynchronous transmission over a synchronous data link. Isochronous signals require a constant bit rate for reliable transport. Compare with asynchronous transmission.

ISP   Acronym for Internet service provider.

ITU   Acronym for International Telecommunication Union. International body that develops worldwide standards for telecommunications technologies.

IV   Acronym for initialization vector, an external value needed to start off cipher operations; in other words, a mathematical value upon which the ciphertext depends for encrypting. An IV often can be seen as a form of message key. Generally, an IV must accompany the ciphertext, and so must always expand the ciphertext by the size of the IV. In 802.11 networks, it is recommended that a unique IV be deployed on a per-packet basis to eliminate a predetermined sequence that hackers can exploit. In particular, this makes it difficult for hackers to write or use attacks that use mathematical tables that simply cycle the number of key combinations until one or more are discovered that work.

IXC   Acronym for inter-exchange carrier, a common carrier providing long-distance connectivity between Local Access and Transport Areas (LATAs). The three major IXCs as of this writing are AT&T and Sprint, but several hundred or more IXCs offer long-distance service in the United States.

jitter   Analog communication line distortion caused by a signal that is sent in random time occurrences or excessive variances in signal timing. Jitter can cause data loss, particularly at high speeds.

Kb   Abbreviation for kilobit. Approximately 1000 bits.

Kbps   Abbreviation for kilobits per second.

key   Similar to lock and key, this is used to "unlock" ciphertext. A single key can generate a large number of different versions of ciphertext from the same plaintext. Different kinds of keys can be used, such as the running key, which encrypts the sequence of a number of bits, and a message key, which is different for each and every message. In the use of keys such as message keys, both the transmission source and receiving source must know the order and specific key that is used on each transmission.

LAN   Acronym for local area network, a high-speed, low-error data network covering a relatively small geographic area (typically up to a few thousand meters). LANs connect workstations, peripherals, terminals, and other devices in a single building or other geographically limited area. LAN standards specify cabling and signaling at the physical and data-link layers of the OSI model. Ethernet, FDDI, and Token Ring are widely used LAN technologies. Compare with MAN and WAN.

latency Referred to as a delay between the times a device requests access to a network and the time it is granted permission to transmit. Another definition is that of a delay between the time a device receives a frame and the time that frame is forwarded out the destination port. Excessive latency is not generally a problem with e-mail, but it can readily become a problem with latency-sensitive applications such as voice and video.

LEAP Acronym for Lightweight Extensible Authentication Protocol. A version of EAP (Extensible Authentication Protocol) and should be viewed as a shorthand name for EAP-Cisco Wireless, an 802.1X authentication type developed by Cisco and licensed to a restricted set of vendors, including some Cisco competitors. About five variants of EAP exist as of this writing, including LEAP, EAP-SIM, EAP-PEAP, EAP-TTLS, and EAP-TLS. See also EAP.

license The purchased right to transmit RF waves over a given BTA on certain frequencies for a certain period of time. The license tightly governs the design parameters of an RF system and its use. Licenses are usually granted in a way that ensures a greatly reduced probability of interference from other users of the same spectrum. Depending on the licensed service and the country in which the license is issued, the license may be issued as the result of an auction or as the result of a "beauty contest" in which the regulator evaluates the merits of proposals to use the spectrum. The theory behind auctions is that they use free-market forces so that spectrum is put to its best use.

LMDS Acronym for Local Multipoint Distribution Service, a relatively low-power license for transmitting voice, video, and data. In the United States, two licenses are typically granted in three frequencies, each to separate entities within a BTA. These licenses are known as Block A or Block B licenses. In the United States, Block A licenses are from 27.5 to 28.35 GHz, 29.10 to 29.25 GHz, and 31.075 to 31.225 GHz for a total of 1.159 GHz of bandwidth. Block B licenses operate from 31.00 to 31.075 GHz and 31.225 to 31.300 GHz for a total of 150 MHz of bandwidth. LMDS systems have a typical maximum transmission range of approximately 3 miles, as opposed to the transmission range of an MMDS system, which is typically 25 miles. This difference in range is primarily a function of absorption due to precipitation and other physical phenomena, as well as FCC-allocated output power limits.

load balancing In routing, the ability of a router to distribute traffic over all of its network ports that are the same distance from the destination address. Good load-balancing algorithms use both line speed and reliability information. Load balancing increases the use of network segments, thus increasing effective network bandwidth.

logic bomb A virus, similar to a physical bomb planted by an individual, that lies in wait until triggered by an event such as a specific date, the number of times a program is executed, or even the deletion of a file. These viruses can be very destructive and are often difficult to locate prior to being executed.

LOS Acronym for line of sight. Refers to the fact that a clear, unobstructed path between the transmitters and receivers is an optimal condition in which wireless links can operate. This is essential for millimeter wave products such as LMDS and most microwave products lacking modulation and other schemes specifically designed to overcome the effects of a partially occluded (blocked) beam path. Having an LOS path enhances general performance in every RF deployment, as opposed to partially obstructed data paths. The opposite of LOS is NLOS, or non-line of sight (also referred to as near line of sight). Most WLANs include a significant amount of NLOS and yet perform surprisingly well, at times because the WLAN energy can penetrate certain kinds of lightweight walls and doors, and at other times because the energy "leaks" around corners of physical objects.

LWAPP Light Weight Access Point Protocol, which defines how multiple APs can be managed, configured, and controlled from a central device called a controller.

MAC Acronym for Media Access Control. The lower of the two sublayers of the data-link layer defined by the IEEE. The MAC sublayer handles access to shared media, such as whether token passing or contention will be used.

MAC address Standardized data-link layer address that is required for every port or device that connects to a LAN. Other devices in the network use MAC addresses to locate specific ports in the network and to create and update routing tables and data structures. MAC addresses are 6 bytes long and are controlled by the IEEE. Also known as a hardware address, MAC layer address, and physical address.

MAN Metropolitan Area Network.

macro virus Resides within the application and is executed when loaded onto a hard drive. Macro viruses are not as well known as other virus types and most commonly reside in Microsoft Office applications such as Word, Excel, PowerPoint, and Access.

Mb Abbreviation for megabit. Approximately 1 million bits.

Mbps Abbreviation for megabits per second.

MD5 A protocol that takes a message of arbitrary length and produces as output a 128-bit fingerprint or message digest of the input. MD5 was developed by Ron Rivest of MIT (who also helped develop RSA). MD5 ensures that no two messages will produce the same message digest or produce any message having a given prespecified target message digest. MD5 is intended for use where a large file must be digested in a secure manner before being encrypted with a private (secret) key under a public-key cryptosystem such as RSA. MD5 is considered a more reliable way to verify data integrity, as opposed to the more simple checksum and other commonly used methods.

MDU Acronym for multiple dwelling unit. Condominium or apartment building.

MIC Acronym for message integrity check.

MKK The Japanese version of the U.S. FCC.

MMDS Acronym for Multichannel Multipoint Distribution Service, a licensed frequency in the United States. The FCC has allocated two bands of frequencies to this service, which are 2.15 to 2.161 GHz and 2.5 to 2.686 GHz. Licenses have been assigned by BTA.

mobile wireless   The type of wireless used in mobile phones, smartphones such as Blackberries and iPhones, PDAs, pagers, and other small, portable, battery-powered devices that can transmit and/or receive information by radio.

modulation   Process by which the characteristics of electrical signals are transformed to represent information.

MTU   Acronym for multiple tenant unit. Building with multiple business tenants.

MxU   Acronym for multiple tenant unit or multiple dwelling unit.

NAT   Acronym for Network Address Translation, a mechanism for reducing the need for globally unique IP addresses. NAT allows an organization with addresses that are not globally unique to connect to the Internet by translating those addresses into globally routable address spaces. Also known as Network Address Translator.

NEBS   Acronym for Network Equipment Building Systems. Covers spatial, hardware, craftsperson interface, thermal, fire resistance, handling and transportation, earthquake and vibration, airborne contaminants, grounding, acoustical noise, illumination, EMC, and ESD requirements.

network elements   Network elements are commonly referred to as "boxes" or, more specifically, "electronic boxes." This typically includes any powered network device such as a router, switch, access point, and so forth.

network layer   Layer 3 of the OSI reference model. Provides connectivity and path selection between two end systems. The network layer is where routing occurs. Other associated terms include *application layer*, *data-link layer*, *physical layer*, *presentation layer*, *session layer*, and *transport layer*.

network management   Generic term used to describe systems or actions that help maintain, characterize, or troubleshoot a network.

NIAP   Acronym for National Information Assurance Partnership. Serves as the joint NSA/NIST program that serves U.S. industry to help define criteria for security measures and algorithms.

NIST   Acronym for National Institute of Standards and Technology, a U.S. federal technology agency that develops and promotes standards in security and other standards for measurement, standards, and technology.

NLOS   Acronym for Near Line Of Sight; also commonly referred to as Non Line Of Sight. Refers to physical obstructions located between transmitting and receiving antennas. See also Fresnel zones, LOS.

NOC   Acronym for Network Operation Center, an organization with equipment responsible for maintaining a network, generally on a remote basis.

NSA   National Security Agency; involved in NIST security protocol efforts and standards.

OFDM Acronym for Orthogonal Frequency Division Multiplexing, an FDM modulation technique for transmitting signals by splitting the radio signal into various frequencies that are then transmitted simultaneously. One of the key differences between OFDM and DHSS or FHSS is that the signals in OFDM are sent simultaneously as opposed to sequentially over time.

omni-directional antenna An omni-directional antenna radiates more or less equally in all directions around a 360-degree axis. All antennas radiate in all directions simultaneously, though not equally, because magnetic fields must operate on a three-dimensional basis.

open authentication A type of authentication in which an access point will grant authentication to any client, regardless of whether or not it is native to the network of that particular access point. Arguably it is more common with simple data devices, such as bar code scanners, that have little processing power.

OSI Short for the Open System Interconnection reference model, and sometimes referred to as the OSI reference stack. Network architectural model developed by ISO and ITU-T. The model consists of seven layers, each of which specifies particular network functions such as addressing, flow control, error control, encapsulation, and reliable message transfer. The lowest layer (the physical layer) is closest to the media technology. The lower two layers are implemented in hardware and software, while the upper five layers are implemented only in software. The highest layer (the application layer) is closest to the user. The OSI reference model is used universally as a method for teaching and understanding network functionality. It is similar in some respects to SNA. Other associated terms include *application layer*, *data-link layer*, *network layer*, *physical layer*, *presentation layer*, *session layer*, and *transport layer*.

Here are the seven layers of the OSI stack:

- Physical
- Data
- Network
- Transmission
- Session
- Presentation
- Application

In simple terms, electronic traffic is managed by these seven network layers to assure reliable and orderly transmissions of information on a large scale.

Two popular mnemonic devices for remembering the seven layers are "please do not throw sausage pizza away" and "all people seem to need data processing."

OSS Acronym for operations support system. Network management system supporting a specific management function, such as alarm surveillance and provisioning, in a carrier network. Many OSSs are large centralized systems running on mainframes or minicomputers. Common OSSs used within an RBOC include NMA, OPS/INE, and TIRKS.

out-of-band signaling   Transmission using frequencies or channels outside the frequencies or channels normally used for information transfer. It is often used for error reporting in situations in which in-band signaling can be affected by whatever problems the network might be experiencing. Contrast with in-band signaling.

oversubscription   The method of having more users on a network than the network can accommodate if all the users were to use the network simultaneously. What makes this work is the premise that rarely, if ever, do all users actually use the network at the same time. Oversubscription is mission-critical to the financial models used by Internet service providers (ISPs) and other entities, and in many cases, oversubscription is what keeps an entity solvent. Oversubscription rates can be anywhere from a factor of 6 to a factor of 50 or more, depending on the class of service the subscriber has agreed to and other factors, including how much bandwidth the subscribers use.

packet   Logical grouping of information that includes a header containing control information and (usually) user data. Packets are most often used to refer to network-layer units of data. The terms *datagram, frame, message,* and *segment* are also used to describe logical information groupings at various layers of the OSI reference model and in various technology circles.

parabolic antenna   A dish-like antenna that sends and receives radio waves in a highly focused manner, most commonly in outdoor RF systems. Such antennas provide very large antenna gains and are highly efficient. They are typical of most point-to-point RF systems, but are not the only design available or appropriate for a given RF link. The primary task of an antenna is to provide gain (signal boost) and to radiate in particular directions in accordance with the network's intended use—for example, point-to-multipoint, or point-to-point, or to cover a prescribed geographic area.

passband   The frequencies that a radio allows to pass from its input to its output. If a receiver or transmitter uses filters with narrow passbands, then only the desired frequency and nearby frequencies are of concern to the system designer. If a receiver or transmitter uses filters with wide passbands, then many more frequencies in the vicinity of the desired frequency are of concern to the system designer. In a frequency division multiplexing (FDM) system, the transmit and receive passbands will be different. In a time division multiplexing (TDM) system, the transmit and receive passbands are the same.

PAT   Acronym for Port Address Translation, a function provided by routers that allows hosts on a LAN to communicate with another LAN without revealing their own IP address. All outbound packets have their IP address translated to the LAN edge router's external IP address. Replies come back to the router, which then translates them back into the internal IP address of the original host within the LAN. It is used to enhance security measures.

patch antenna   A patch antenna is a small, rectangular antenna that affords directional transmission and reception of RF signals. A patch antenna is a type of antenna used both indoors and outdoors that allows fairly high amounts of gain that typically improve signal quality and reduce interference at one or both ends of an RF link.

path loss   The power loss that occurs when RF waves are transmitted through the air. This loss occurs because RF waves expand as they travel through the air, and the receiver antenna captures only a small portion of the total radiated energy. In addition, a significant amount of energy may be absorbed by molecules in the atmosphere or by precipitation when the carrier frequencies are above 10 GHz. The amount of absorption due to precipitation depends on the amount of precipitation and is usually a factor only for systems that operate at frequencies above 10 GHz.

The amount of atmospheric absorption depends greatly on the particular frequency used. At 12 GHz, water vapor absorbs a great deal of energy, and at 60 GHz, oxygen molecules absorb even more energy. Systems that operate at those frequencies have very limited ranges.

PDU   Acronym for protocol data unit. OSI term for packet.

PEAP   Acronym for Protected Extensible Authentication Protocol, which provides mutual authentication and key generation in a manner such that the user authentication phase is protected—for example, the user identity can be kept secret. This protocol is particularly useful for quick reauthentication when a user roams between devices such as access points.

physical layer   Layer 1 of the OSI reference model, which defines the electrical, mechanical, procedural, and functional specifications for activating, maintaining, and deactivating the physical link between end systems. It corresponds with the physical control layer in the SNA model. Other associated terms are *application layer*, *data-link layer*, *network layer*, *presentation layer*, *session layer*, and *transport layer*.

plaintext   The readable information transmitted or received. It is usually a set of alphanumeric characters but can also be other forms of data, such as values or mathematical symbols.

POP   Acronym for point of presence, a term commonly used to describe a centralized facility that subscribers use to access the Internet.

POP-2   Acronym for Post Office Protocol-2. POP is an Internet e-mail server protocol that provides an incoming message storage capability. It works in conjunction with the SMTP (Simple Mail Transfer Protocol) to enable the movement of e-mail from one system to another. The current version is called POP-3, as defined in RFC 1939 (Post Office Protocol-Version 3, May 1996).

presentation layer   Layer 6 of the OSI reference model. It ensures that information sent by the application layer of one system will be readable by the application layer of another. The presentation layer is also concerned with the data structures used by programs and therefore negotiates data transfer syntax for the application layer. It corresponds roughly with the presentation services layer of the SNA model. Other associated terms include *application layer*, *data-link layer*, *network layer*, *physical layer*, *session layer*, and *transport layer*.

propagation delay   Time required for data to travel over a network, from its source to its ultimate destination.

protocol   Formal description of a set of rules and conventions that governs how devices on a network exchange information.

protocol stack   Set of related communications protocols that operate together and, as a group, address communication at some or all of the seven layers of the OSI reference model. Not every protocol stack covers each layer of the model, and often a single protocol in the stack will address a number of layers at once. TCP/IP is a typical protocol stack.

PSTN   Acronym for Public Switched Telephone Network, a general term referring to the variety of telephone networks and services in place worldwide.

PTM   Acronym for point-to-multipoint. Common variants include pt-mpt and P2MP. However, all versions denote the same concept, which is a communication between a group of sites that interfaces a single hub site. PTM is commonly set up in three or four segments to enable frequency reuse, but it can be designed for as many as a dozen or more segments within a single cell.

PTP   Acronym for point-to-point; a common variant is pt-pt. However, both versions denote the same concept, which is to provide communication between two endpoints. In the United States, PTP systems are typically found in the ISM, U-NII, and LMDS bands.

PTT   Acronym for Post, Telephone, and Telegraph, generally used outside the U.S. government agency that provides telephone services. PTTs exist in most areas outside North America and provide both local and long-distance telephone services.

QAM   Acronym for Quadrature Amplitude Modulation, a method of modulating digital signals onto a radio-frequency carrier signal involving both amplitude and phase coding. Numbers indicate the number of code points per symbol. The QAM rate or the number of points in the QAM constellation can be computed by 2 raised to the power of the number of bits/symbol.

QoS   Acronym for Quality of Service, a feature of certain networking protocols that treats different types of network traffic differently to ensure required levels of reliability and latency according to the type of traffic. Certain kinds of traffic, such as voice and video, are more sensitive to transmission delays and are therefore given priority over data that is less sensitive to delay.

As an example, some systems traditionally have four levels of QoS, but some systems have as many as thirteen levels of QoS, depending on how many bits are used to prioritize the traffic. Most systems use either three or four levels of QoS, which are commonly referred to as Unsolicited Grant Service (USG), Committed Bit Rate (CBR; sometimes referred to as CIR or Committed Information Rate), and Best Effort Rate (BER). USG has priority over CIR/CBR, which has priority over BER. QoS levels are set in Layer 2 (data-link layer) of the OSI reference stack.

QPSK   Acronym for Quadrature Phase Shift Keying, a method of modulating digital signals onto a radio-frequency carrier signal using four phase states to code 2 digital bits.

RBOC   Regional Bell Operating Company. A regional telephone company.

RC4   A security algorithm used by WEP. Openly considered a defeated algorithm, RC4 was developed in 1987 by Ron Rivest for RSA Data Security, and was a propriety algorithm until 1994, when the code was posted to the Internet and thus to the rest of the world.

repeater   A device that regenerates and propagates radio or electrical signals between two network segments.

RF   Acronym for radio frequency. Generally refers to wireless communications with frequencies below 300 GHz. The term RF is commonly used too broadly to cover all types of wireless.

RFC   Acronym for Request for Comments, a document series used as the primary means for communicating information about the Internet. Probably the best-known RFC versions are from the IEEE. Some RFCs are designated as Internet standards. Most RFCs document protocol specifications such as Telnet and FTP, but some are humorous or historical. RFCs are available online from numerous sources.

RJ connector   Short for Registered Jack connector, a standard connector originally used to connect telephone lines. RJ connectors are now used for telephone connections and for 10BaseT and other types of network connections. RJ-11, RJ-12, and RJ-45 are popular types of RJ connectors.

round   A term of art relative to security that refers to a set of encryption operations performed on a block of information. For example, 64 DES uses 16 rounds of operations to produce the final version of the ciphertext, which can then be transmitted over an open BBFW link or other unsecured method of transmission.

router   A router, in IT parlance, is a network element that typically operates at Layer 3 of the OSI stack, and it essentially performs the task for which it is named—the routing of information. A router is used to connect two or more personal computers, and is therefore quite common to home-based networks. It typically also interfaces a small office or home office network and the Internet at large; in other words, it can also be a gateway device between a network and other networks.

Home office and smaller enterprise networks often have 802.11 wireless capabilities built into the router; this allows wireless access by the local network elements such as smartphones and desktop and laptop computers, and provides connectivity to the outside world.

RSA   A public-key cryptographic system that may be used for encryption and authentication. Named for the inventors of the RSA security technique: Rivest, Shamir, and Adelman.

RTS   Acronym for Request to Send. EIA/TIA-232 control signal that requests a data transmission on a communications line. Compare to CTS, Clear to Send.

sector virus   Sector viruses modify the data that resides within sectors. These viruses are usually far larger than the 512 bytes available in a sector and therefore usually reside within the RAM portion of a PC, server, or router and then go on to affect the data in sectors. Because this type of virus can take up residence within RAM, even if the disc is repaired, it can recontaminate the disc immediately after being repaired.

session layer   Layer 5 of the OSI reference model establishes, manages, and terminates sessions between applications and manages data exchange between presentation-layer entities. Corresponds to the data flow control layer of the SNA model. Other associated terms are *application layer*, *data-link layer*, *network layer*, *physical layer*, *presentation layer*, and *transport layer*.

SID   Acronym for Service ID, a number that defines (at the MAC sublayer) a particular mapping between two network devices. The term is used in cable standards such as DOCSIS. The SID is used for the purpose of upstream bandwidth allocation and class-of-service management.

SKA   Acronym for shared key authentication. SKA requires an AP to demand a WEP key from a client.

SMPT   Acronym for Simple Mail Transfer Protocol.

SNA   Acronym for Systems Network Architecture, a large, complex, feature-rich network architecture developed in the 1970s by IBM. It is similar in some respects to the OSI reference model, but with a number of differences. SNA essentially comprises seven layers: data flow control layer, data-link control layer, path control layer, physical control layer, presentation services layer, transaction services layer, and transmission control layer.

SNMP   Acronym for Simple Network Management Protocol, the network management protocol used almost exclusively in TCP/IP networks. SNMP provides a means to monitor and control network devices and to manage configurations, statistics collection, performance, and security.

SOHO   Acronym for small office/home office.

spoofing   A scheme used by routers to cause a host to treat an interface as though it were up and supporting a session. The router spoofs replies to keep-alive messages from the host to convince that host that the session still exists. Spoofing is useful in routing environments such as DDR, in which a circuit-switched link is taken down when there is no traffic to be sent across it to save toll charges. See also DDR.

Spoofing also refers to the input of a malicious hacker who illegitimately claims to be sending e-mail from a real address when in fact it is not the actual sending address. Spoofing is designed to foil network security mechanisms such as filters and access lists.

spread spectrum   A spreading technique in which data, video, or voice signals are distributed over a wide range of frequencies; signals are then collected and collated at the receiver.

SQL   Acronym for Structured Query Language, a data manipulation language for searching within relational databases.

SSID   Acronym for service set identifier, an ID that allows logical separation of WLANs. A client such as a PCMCIA card has an SSID that allows the upstream devices, such as the AP, authentication servers, and so on, to allow the client to become part of the WLAN. Clients are often commonly segregated by SSIDs in a virtual LAN (though there are other ways of segregating VLAN participants).

SSL   Acronym for Secure Sockets Layer, a protocol for establishing mutual authentications and encrypted sessions between web servers and web clients. SSL starts with a handshake from either client, which establishes a TCP/IP connection. Next, the server is authenticated to the client by verifying its public key. Once authenticated, the server selects the strongest cryptographic algorithm supported by both clients, and then a shared secret key is generated to encrypt all data flowing between the client and server. Finally, an encrypted SSL connection is established.

station authentication   The event of authenticating an 802.11 device, such as a bridge or access point, as opposed to authenticating a client, such as a PCMCIA card.

stooge   A security term of art; a network used by a hacker to attack other networks.

switch   Like a network hub, except a switch has more intelligence and can inspect data packets as they are received. A hub is generally "dumb" device that simply provides a physical junction from one to many connections. Switches classically operate at Layer 2 of the OSI stack.

system sector virus   A system sector virus affects not just data, but hard drive sectors. Sectors are not files but are areas on a PC disc, server, or router that are read in chunks. For example, DOS sectors are 512 bytes in length. Sectors are invisible to your applications but are vital to the operation of a PC, server, or router because they contain the basic information for applications and data. When the sectors are disrupted, the results are terminal for the performance of the PC, server, or router.

T1   Telecommunications service line that transmits DS-1-formatted data at 1.544 Mbps through the telephone-switching network.

T3   Telecommunications service line that transmits DS-3-formatted data at 44.736 Mbps through the telephone-switching network.

TCP   Acronym for Transmission Control Protocol, a connection-oriented, transport-layer protocol that provides reliable full-duplex data transmission. It is part of the TCP/IP protocol stack.

TCP/IP Acronym for Transmission Control Protocol/Internet Protocol. Common name for the suite of protocols developed by the U.S. Department of Defense (DoD) in the 1970s to support the construction of worldwide internetworks. TCP and IP are the two best-known protocols in the suite.

TDMA Acronym for Time Division Multiple Access, a technique for splitting transmissions on a common frequency into time slots, which enables a greater number of users to access a given frequency. This technique is commonly used as opposed to CDMA and Frequency Division Multiplexing Access (FDMA).

Telnet Standard terminal emulation protocol in the TCP/IP protocol stack. Telnet is used for remote terminal connection, enabling users to log in to remote systems and use resources as if they were connected to a local system.

TFTP Acronym for Trivial File Transfer Protocol, a simplified version of FTP that allows files to be transferred from one computer to another over a network.

throughput The net amount of data transmitted minus the overhead traffic to manage the link or connection. The more common specification for wireless links includes overhead traffic and does not therefore clearly indicate link performance. As a general rule of thumb, overhead represents an additional 30 to 50 percent of bandwidth over throughput.

TKIP Acronym for Temporal Key Integrity Protocol. TKIP, like WEP, is based on RC4 encryption but is enhanced over WEP for reasons that include the generation of new encryption keys for every 10KB of data transmitted.

topology A group or design of network elements that may be organized or referred to in a logical, physical, or virtual sense. Topologies are commonly considered part of an engineering design discussion or review.

traffic shaping Use of queues to limit surges that can congest a network. Data is buffered and then sent into the network in regulated amounts to ensure that the traffic will fit within the promised traffic envelope for the particular connection. Traffic shaping is used in ATM, Frame Relay, and other types of networks. Also known as *metering, shaping,* and *smoothing.*

transport layer Layer 4 of the OSI reference model is responsible for reliable network communication between end nodes. The transport layer provides mechanisms for the establishment, maintenance, and termination of virtual circuits; transport fault detection and recovery; and information flow control. Corresponds to the transmission control layer of the SNA model. Other associated terms include *application layer, data-link layer, network layer, physical layer, presentation layer,* and *session layer.*

Trojan horse Named after the wooden Trojan horse that was delivered as a gift to the city of Troy but that secretly contained Greek soldiers, this type of Trojan horse is a seemingly harmless computer program that delivers destructive code, such as a logic bomb, and therefore is a carrier, not a virus. This type of attack appears as a useful piece of software until it's executed.

truck roll   The concept of "rolling" trucks to the installation site to install, repair, or upgrade equipment.

UDP   Acronym for User Datagram Protocol.

U-NII   Acronym for Unlicensed National Information Infrastructure, which is primarily a U.S. frequency band. The wireless products for U-NII are in the 5.725 to 5.825 GHz range frequency for outdoor use. Two other U-NII bands are 5.15 to 5.25 GHz and 5.25 to 5.35 GHz. The 5.15 GHz band is for indoor use only in the United States, while the 5.25 to 5.35 GHz band can be used either indoors or outdoors in the U.S. Both of the lower two sets of U-NII frequencies are transmitted at lower power levels than the 5.725 to 5.825 GHz band.

These frequencies do not require the use or purchase of a site license, but the gear does require certification by the FCC and strict compliance to FCC regulations. U-NII was a term coined by federal regulators to describe access to an information network by citizens and businesses. Equivalent to the term *information superhighway*, it does not describe system architecture, protocol, or topology.

Unix   Operating system developed in 1969 at Bell Laboratories. Unix has gone through several iterations since its inception.

VDSL   Acronym for Very-High-Speed Digital Subscriber Line, one of many DSL technologies. VDSL delivers 13 to 52 Mbps downstream and 1.5 to 2.3 Mbps upstream over a single twisted copper pair. The operating range of VDSL is limited to 1000 to 4500 feet (304.8 to 1372 meters).

virus   Potentially destructive software that spreads itself from program to program, from computer to computer, and from LAN to LAN, most commonly by e-mail attachments.

VLAN   Acronym for Virtual Local Area Network, a group of clients that are situated at different physical locations but that communicate with each other as if they were all on the same physical LAN segment.

VoIP   Acronym for Voice over IP. Enables a router to carry voice traffic (such as telephone calls and faxes) over an IP network. In VoIP, the DSP segments the voice signal into frames, which are then coupled in groups of two and stored in voice packets. These voice packets are transported using IP in compliance with ITU-T specification H.323.

VPN   Acronym for virtual private network, a private link that resides between two parties but travels across public networks.

WAN   Acronym for wide area network, a data communications network that serves users across a broad geographic area and often uses transmission devices provided by common carriers.

WAP Acronym for Wireless Access Protocol, a language used for writing web pages that uses far less overhead compared to HTML and XML, which makes it preferable for low-bandwidth wireless access to the Internet from devices such as PDAs and cell phones that also have small viewing screens. WAP's corresponding operating system (OS) is the OS created by 3Com in its Palm Pilot. Nokia has recently adopted the Palm OS for its web-capable cell phone. WAP is based on the Extensible Markup Language (XML), which dictates *how* data is shown, whereas HTML dictates *where* data is located within a browser page.

WEP Acronym for Wired Equivalent Privacy, a security protocol used primarily in 802.11 radios to secure wireless communications from eavesdropping and theft of data, and to prevent unauthorized access to a wireless network. This standard was superseded by WPA and then WPA2.

Wi-Fi Alliance Acronym for Wireless Fidelity Alliance. Of interest, it's not broadly known that the term "Wi-Fi" is actually owned by the Wi-Fi Alliance, a global, non-profit association of approximately 300 wireless industry professionals. Its charter is to promote the 802.11 and other standards that help develop WLANs. This alliance provides certifications to entities that provide 802.11 devices to the network industry and end customers, and to date it has completed more than 4000 such certifications.

wireline The use of copper phone, cable lines, or fiber. Wireline advantages include high reliability, high tolerance to interference, and generally easier troubleshooting. In the case of fiber, wireline also has exceptionally high bandwidth. Wireline is the technological opposite of wireless.

WLAN Acronym for wireless local area network. It generally, but not always, refers to a collision domain of 802.11 devices—that is, a series of devices that contend for shared connectivity.

worm Software that makes copies of itself and then distributes those copies, which create more copies, and so on. The typical objective of a worm is to generate an enormous amount of e-mail so quickly that a system can't handle it and shuts down.

WPA and WPA2 Acronym for Wi-Fi Protected Access, a protocol established by the Wi-Fi Alliance to provide a second generation of security beyond the original security known as WEP (Wired Equivalent Privacy). WPA2 is the generation of WPA intended for use with the 802.11i standard, which refers to how 802.11 networks are secured.

xDSL Group term used to refer to ADSL, HDSL, SDSL, and VDSL. All are emerging digital technologies using the existing copper infrastructure provided by the telephone companies. xDSL is a high-speed alternative to ISDN.

APPENDIX B | Relevant Mobility Standards

You'll find it helpful to have a list of some of the standards enacted by the most broadly accepted and used standards group, the Institute of Electrical and Electronics Engineers (IEEE, pronounced "eye-triple-ee"). Here's a summary of the most important and relevant standards in use today, or those that are likely to become useful and broadly adopted in the near future. Not all of the 802.11 standards are indicated here; instead, this list pertains to the standards you are more likely to hear about in WLAN planning and maintenance discussions.

IEEE Overview

The IEEE non-profit organization is not to be confused with the IEE, the Institution of Electrical Engineers, which is an international organization comprising engineers, scientists, and students with more than 365,000 members in 150 countries—making it one of the largest, if not the single largest, technical professional organization in the world today.

The IEEE is headquartered in New York City on the 17th floor of 3 Park Avenue, and its current formation is largely based on the merging of the Institute of Radio Engineers (founded in 1912) and the American Institute of Electrical Engineers (founded in 1884).

The primary work of this body is to establish technical standards in wired, wireless, light, and power systems. The history and indeed light intrigue involved in the creation of standards is worthy of a book in and of itself, but suffice it to say that society and commerce greatly benefit from companies of all sizes agreeing to common standards in an immense array of electrical and electronic devices.

802.11

802.11 is a set of standards carrying out wireless local area network (WLAN) computer communication in the 2.4, 3.6, and 5 GHz frequency bands. They are created and maintained by the IEEE LAN/MAN Standards Committee (IEEE 802).

The 802.11 group of standards is essentially based on a common set of over-the-air modulation techniques. The first and most popular of the 802.11 standards are those defined by the 802.11b and 802.11g protocols and are amendments to the original standard. The 802.11 standards were not ratified in alphabetic but in chronological order; hence 802.12b became a ratified standard before 802.11a. The alpha designation suffix is intended to refer to the workgroup that established the standard rather than the order in which the standard is released to the world engineering community at large.

802.11-1997 was the first wireless networking standard, but 802.11b was the first widely accepted one, followed by 802.11g and then 802.11n. Security was originally purposely weak in the initial releases of this standard due to export requirements of some governments and was later enhanced via the 802.11i amendment after governmental and legislative changes allowed more enhanced encryption techniques to be exported. 802.11n is a new multistreaming modulation technique. Other standards in the family (c–f, h, j) are service amendments and extensions or corrections to previous specifications.

802.11b and 802.11g use the 2.4 GHz band, operating in the United States under Part 15 of the U.S. Federal Communications Commission (FCC) Rules and Regulations. Because of this choice of frequency band, 802.11b and 802.11g equipment may occasionally suffer performance degradation from microwave ovens, cordless telephones, and Bluetooth devices.

Both 802.11 and Bluetooth largely control their interference and susceptibility to interference by using spread spectrum modulation, although proximity to potentially interfering devices can be an even better method for managing and reducing interference. Bluetooth uses a frequency hopping spread spectrum (FHSS) signaling method, while 802.11b and 802.11g use the direct sequence spread spectrum (DSSS) signaling and orthogonal frequency division multiplexing (OFDM) methodologies, respectively.

802.11a

802.11a is a standard that specifies operation in the 5 GHz band using orthogonal frequency division multiplexing (OFDM), which is a high-performance modulation method. 802.11a supports data rates ranging from 6 to 54 Mbps. Products from this standard began appearing in the market in late 2001.

The 5 GHz U-NII frequency band offers eight non-overlapping channels rather than the three non-overlapping channels offered in the 2.4 GHz ISM frequency band. While it is popularly believed that performance is essentially reliant on frequency selection, real-world implications for performance go well beyond that to include a pantheon of contributing elements such as engineering design, environmental stability and selection, antenna selection, and configuration of access points and the controllers that manage them.

Initially, operation in the 11a band afforded less interference from other sources and virtually complete interference from 802.11 and 802.11b devices as well as other devices such as certain cordless phones and microwave ovens. However, with the immense popularity of this standard, densities of 11a are now more or less as common as those found in the 802.11 or 11b/g standards.

With high data rates and often less interference, 802.11a is considered excellent for voice and video transport use.

802.11b

The primary objective of the 802.11b standard was to increase data rates from 1 Mbps to as much as 11 Mbps. This standard became ratified in late 1999. To provide the higher data rates, 802.11b uses CCK (Complementary Code Keying) modulation, which is a more efficient variant of the modulation used in 802.11.

802.11c

802.11c is a standard that ensures bridge operations and is much better known and understood by product developers than end users and marketing personnel, because it resides well inside devices such as access points.

802.11d

This standard is often referred to as the "Global Harmonization" standard. Initially, only a handful of regulatory domains such as the United States, Europe, and Japan had federal rules in place for the operation of 802.11 WLANs. Used in both the 2.4 GHz and 5 GHz spectrums, this standard helps products operate more compatibly across different countries, a boon for those with laptops purchased in the United States who use them on business trips in Europe or Japan. As with 802.11c, this standard is more relevant to product developers than end users and consumers.

802.11e

With the 802.11 standard now very much the norm for network connectivity in most industrialized nations, it became imperative that the wireless interface between devices such as access points, laptops, and smartphones have a Quality of Service (QoS) capability on par with wired networking elements. The existing version of the 802.11 standard enables the transmission and reception of voice and video. WLAN products using this standard generally became available in mid-2003.

802.11f

11f, as this standard is generally known, specifies how clients such as laptops, smartphones, and so forth roam between access points. Restated, if a user carries their client from one physical area to another, such as between the floors of a building or down long hallways, or from one room to another, this standard allows the laptop to remain connected to the network while the RF link between the client and the access point is weakening as the user walks away from the access point, and the signal strength is increasing between the user's laptop and the access point to which they are approaching. The 11f standard specifies how the laptop "roams" from one access point to the other.

Like many other IEEE standards, most technology providers build substantial capabilities to enhance the fundamental framework of standards such as 11f. Some argue that most WLAN capabilities reside in the extra, and vital, additional development work provided by the equipment vendors. The IEEE standards ensure *minimum* compatibility; the real work of compatibility, which primarily resides between access points and clients, is additional work performed and assured by the technology vendors such as Cisco, Aruba, HP, and so forth.

802.11g

The objective of the 802.11g task group was to develop speeds greater than those transmitted in the 802.11b standard. The speed increase is primarily due to the higher performance levels of RF modulation, in this case orthogonal frequency division multiplexing (OFDM) from direct sequence spread spectrum (DSSS). This jump in speed was considerable given that 11b was at 11 Mbps and the 11g standard is 54 Mbps; both 11b and 11g operate in the 2.4 GHz band. Backward compatibility allows 11b and 11g devices to interoperate, though this is generally considered only with most or all security measures removed or reduced.

802.11h

802.11h is specifically for use by devices sold or used in Europe. The 11h standard allows dynamic channel selection (DCS) and transmit power control (TPC) for devices used in the 5 GHz spectrum (802.11a). This standard largely came about for the European theater because of the potential for interference between 802.11 WLANs operating in the 5 GHz spectrum and European satellite communications, which have primary use designations for that spectrum.

802.11i

802.11i was established as a standard by the IEEE to help augment security standards to counter security issues related to the wired equivalent privacy (WEP) standard, which was an intentionally weak encryption methodology. WEP has been quite easy to hack into with free tools broadly available over the Internet. This standard came online in 2003 and is a precursor to the much more sophisticated AES-based encryption now commonly in use.

802.11k-2008

This standard refers to the management of RF energy radiated from an access point or client device, with particular regards to client roaming requests, RF measurements, and data involving channel selection and optimizing RF performance as well as balancing traffic loads between a single client and multiple access points. This work initiated in 2002 and was completed in 2005.

802.11r-2008

This standard involves the hand-off of wireless voice calls and video from handheld clients such as 802.11 and smartphones that have incorporated Wi-Fi. This standard is particularly important because it allows the user to roam between access points without manually reauthenticating for security purposes.

802.11n

This is arguably one of the most passionately argued and debated standards work ever undertaken within the 802.11 task forces. Initial discussions began on this standard in 2002, yet the standard was not ratified by the IEEE until 2009. 11n features much higher speeds than 11g, upwards of 600 Mbps in some devices, as provided by the technology vendors.

802.11y-2008

802.11y-2008 is an amendment to the IEEE 802.11-2007 standard that enables high-powered Wi-Fi equipment to operate on a co-primary basis in the 3650 to 3700 MHz band in the United States, except when near a grandfathered satellite Earth station. It was approved for publication by the IEEE on September 26, 2008.

802.16

802.16 is a series of outdoor wireless protocol. The current version of the standard is known more properly as 802.16j-2009, though it is most commonly is referred to as WiMax.

This standard is one of the longest standing 802 WLAN workgroups, having been established by the IEEE Standards Board in 1999. The primary deliverable of this workgroup is to develop standards for the global deployment of high-speed wireless systems across metropolitan areas.

The most popular implementation of the 802.16 standard is the 802.16e-2005 amendment now in deployment in more than 140 countries and operated by more than 475 entities. Some argue this standard is much more broadly utilized outside the United States and in semi-industrialized nations more than highly industrialized nations, though as the author of this appendix, I have seen only anecdotal data supporting that point.

802.20

Often referred to as "Mobile-Fi," this standard was initiated in early 2006, operates in the 3.5 GHz frequency, and features speeds of just over 1 Mbps. It's similar in intent to the 802.16 standard.

iBurst

Also known as High Capacity Spatial Division Multiple Access (HC-SDMA), iBurst is a standard for high-performance licensed mobile handsets. It has not been not broadly adopted by the industry.

LTE

LTE stands for Long Term Evolution and is also known as "4G" to represent fourth generation in mobile phone technology. Most major mobile carriers in the United States and worldwide have begun adopting this standard, which features speeds of 150 Mbps, though this is not likely to occur routinely once adoption rates move upward as carriers convert to this standard.

Also noteworthy, public safety agencies in the United States have also endorsed LTE as the preferred technology for the new 700 MHz public-safety radio band.

Allocated Frequencies

The following table is from http://en. Wikipedia.org/wiki/Comparison_of_wireless_ data_standards#cite_note-2 and http://en.wikipedia.org/wiki/ISM_band:

Allocated Frequencies

Standard	Frequencies	Spectrum Type
UMTS over W-CDMA	850 MHz; 1.9, 1.9/2.1, and 1.7/2.1 GHz	Licensed (Cellular/PCS/3G/AWS)
UMTS-TDD	450, 850 MHz, 1.9, 2, 2.5, and 3.5 GHz; 2 GHz	Licensed (Cellular, 3G TDD, BRS/ IMT-ext, FWA)
CDMA2000 (inc. EV-DO, 1xRTT)	450, 850, 900 MHz; 1.7, 1.8, 1.9, and 2.1 GHz	Licensed (Cellular/PCS/3G/AWS)
EDGE/GPRS	850 MHz, 900 MHz, 1.8 GHz, 1.9 GHz	Licensed (Cellular/PCS/PCN)
iBurst	1.8, 1.9, and 2.1 GHz	Licensed
Flash-OFDM	450 and 870 MHz	Licensed
802.16e	2.3, 2.5, 3.5, 3.7, and 5.8 GHz	Licensed
802.11a	5.25, 5.6, and 5.8 GHz	Unlicensed 802.11a and ISM
802.11b/g/n	2.4 GHz	Unlicensed ISM
Bluetooth	2.4 GHz	Unlicensed ISM
Wibree	2.4 GHz	Unlicensed ISM
ZigBee	868 MHz, 915 MHz, 2.4 GHz	Unlicensed ISM
Wireless USB, UWB	3.1 to 10.6 GHz	Unlicensed Ultrawideband
EnOcean	868.3 MHz	Unlicensed ISM

Comparative Speeds and Ranges

The following table is from Cisco Systems.

Standard	Throughput (Mbit/s)		Range	Typical Downlink
	Max Downlink	Max Uplink		
CDMA RTT 1X	0.3072	0.1536	~18 mi	0.125
CDMA EV-DO Rev 0	2.4580	0.1536	~18 mi	0.75
CDMA EV-DO Rev A	3.1000	1.8000	~18 mi	
CDMA EV-DO Rev B	4.9000	1.8000	~18 mi	
GSM GPRS Class 10	0.0856	0.0428	~16 mi	0.014
GSM EDGE type 2	0.4736	0.4736	~16 mi	0.034
GSM EDGE Evolution	1.8944	0.9472	~16 mi	
UMTS W-CDMA R99	0.3840	0.3840	~18 mi	0.195
UMTS W-CDMA HSDPA	14.400	0.3840	up to 124mi[1]	4.1 (Tre 2007)
UMTS W-CDMA HSUPA	14.400	5.7600	up to 124mi[1]	
UMTS W-CDMA HSPA+	42.000	22.000	up to 124mi[1]	
UMTS-TDD	16.000	16.000		
LTE	326.4	86.4		
iBurst	24	8	~7.5 mi	>2
FLASH-OFDM	5.3	1.8	~18 mi	avg 2.5
WiMax 802.16e	70.000	70.000	~4 mi	>10
WiFi: 802.11	54.000	54.000		
WiFi: 802.11b	11.000	11.000	~30 meters	2
WiFi: 802.11g	54.000	54.000	~30 meters	10
WiFi: 802.11n	200.00	200.00	~50 meters	40

APPENDIX C | Key Mobility Groups and Information

Aruba Networks   www.arubanetworks.com/

Borderless Networks at Cisco   www.cisco.com/en/US/partner/solutions/ns340/ns414/ns742/ns982/landing_sBus_archit.html#

Certified Wireless Network Professional   www.cwnp.com

Cisco Mobility Channel programs   www.cisco.com/web/partners/sell/promotions/index.html

Cisco Mobility Demo Solutions   www.cisco.com/en/US/products/ps7320/products_white_paper09186a008096d82a.shtml

Cisco Mobility Partner Community   www.cisco.com/go/partnercommunity/mobility

Network Assessment Programs–Cisco Partner Central   www.cisco.com/web/partners/pr11/incentive/core.html

Smartphone Comparison   http://reviews.cnet.com/smartphone-reviews/

IEEE Standards Site   http://ieee.org/portal/site

Motorola Wireless Networks   www.motorola.com/business/

HP WLANs   www.hp.com/united-states/wireless/

Wi-Fi Alliance   www.Wi-Fi.org

Index

W

Y

Z